הסטוריה

ArtScroll History Series®

Rabbi Nosson Scherman / Rabbi Meir Zlotowitz
General Editors

LIEUTENANT

Published by

Mesorah Publications, ltd

ב"ה

To

READ & ENJOY

WITH TORAH TRUE

GREETINGS

SINCERELY

Meyer

BIRNBAUM

A SOLDIER'S STORY

GROWING UP JEWISH IN AMERICA, LIBERATING THE D.P. CAMPS, AND A NEW HOME IN JERUSALEM

by Meyer Birnbaum
with Yonason Rosenblum

FIRST EDITION
Five Impressions: December 1993 . . . March 2000

Published and Distributed by
MESORAH PUBLICATIONS, Ltd.
4401 Second Avenue
Brooklyn, New York 11232

Distributed in Europe by	*Distributed in Israel by*
J. LEHMANN HEBREW BOOKSELLERS	**SIFRIATI / A. GITLER – BOOKS**
20 Cambridge Terrace	10 Hashomer Street
Gateshead, Tyne and Wear	Bnei Brak 51361
Distributed in Australia & New Zealand by	*Distributed in South Africa by*
GOLD'S BOOK & GIFT CO.	**KOLLEL BOOKSHOP**
36 William Street	Shop 8A Norwood Hypermarket
Balaclava 3183, Vic., Australia	Norwood 2196, Johannesburg, South Africa

ARTSCROLL HISTORY SERIES ®
LIEUTENANT BIRNBAUM: A SOLDIER'S STORY

© Copyright 1993, by MESORAH PUBLICATIONS, Ltd.
4401 Second Avenue / Brooklyn, N.Y. 11232 / (718) 921-9000 / www.artscroll.com

Birnbaum, Meyer, 1918-
    Lieutenant Birnbaum : a soldier's story : growing up Jewish in America, liberating the D.P. camps, and a
new home in Jerusalem / by Meyer Birnbaum with Yonason Rosenblum. — 1st ed.
    p.   cm. — (ArtScroll history series)
    ISBN 0-89906-462-0 — ISBN 0-89906-463-g (pbk.)
    1. Birnbaum, Meyer, 1918- . 2. Jews—New York (N.Y.)-
-Biography. 3. World War, 1939-1945—Personal narratives, Jewish.
(N.Y.) 6. Jews, American—Israel—Biography.   I. Rosenblum,
Yonason. II. Title. III. Series.
F128.9.J5B525   1993
973'.04924'0092—dc20
[B]   94-2536
                                                                                      CIP

Typography by Compuscribe at ArtScroll Studios, Ltd.

Printed in the United States of America by Noble Book Press Corp.
Bound by Sefercraft, Quality Bookbinders, Ltd. Brooklyn, N.Y.

❧ Table of Contents

PART II: OUT OF UNIFORM

❧ Publisher's Foreword

OVER THE PAST TWELVE YEARS, WE HAVE BEEN Reb Meyer Birnbaum's frequent guests on his daily drive to the *vasikin minyan* at the *Kosel*. In addition to the thrill of a sunrise *davening* at the *Kosel*, joining Reb Meyer has provided an opportunity to listen to stories of his experiences as an Orthodox Jewish soldier in World War II and of the six months he spent living in the Displaced Persons' camps among those who escaped with their lives from the jaws of the Nazi Death Machine.

Hearing these stories, we recognized that Reb Meyer was privy to a unique perspective on the overwhelming tragedy that befell our people in this century. For years we urged him to commit his memories to writing, but his response was always the same: Who am I to write about my life? After years of fruitless pleading, we finally hit upon the idea of presenting him with a tape recorder, ten ninety-minute tapes, and a simple request: "Talk!" And talk he did.

When it came time to transform those tapes into a book, one more obstacle still had to be overcome. Though Reb Meyer's tapes were naturally in the first person, he balked at the idea of an autobiography. The idea of writing about himself was repugnant to him. We pointed out, however, that a first person account removes the spotlight from the subject and places it on the people he has met and the events he has witnessed, whereas a third person biography suggests that the subject's own life is of such intrinsic importance as to justify a full-length biography. Reb Meyer would be the last person in the world to claim such importance for himself. In fact, the choice of the autobiographical form forced us to omit many precious stories involving Reb Meyer, who has been accurately described as a "human tornado of *chesed*," because of his aversion to talking about himself.

Though *Lieutenant Birnbaum* touches on all periods of Reb Meyer's eventful life, the book focuses on Jewish life in New York in the '20s and '30s and Reb Meyer's four years as an Orthodox officer in the United States Army. Whatever has been included from the rest of Reb Meyer's life has been chosen for its historical interest, the importance of the people mentioned, or as a reflection of the heightened sense of Hashem's *Hashgachah Pratis* (Divine Providence), with which he was left by his wartime experiences.

We are not alone in having been enthralled by Reb Meyer's reminiscences. More than a decade ago, Rebbetzin Beruriah David — Dean of Bais Yaakov Seminary of Jerusalem and the daughter of Reb Meyer's *rebbe*, Rabbi Yitzchak Hutner — first asked him to speak to her students about what he had witnessed during World War II and in the Displaced Persons' camps. Since then he has been a regular speaker at a wide variety of seminaries and yeshivos in Jerusalem. These presentations last anywhere from four-and-a-half to six hours without a break, punctuated only by the stifled sobbing of his listeners. When he is done, the first question is invariably: Why isn't there a book of these stories so that we can share them with our families and friends?

ArtScroll\Mesorah takes great pride in the fact that now there is.

❧ Prologue

I WILL NEVER FORGET THE HAUNTED LOOK ON the face of that sixteen-year-old boy.

It was my first taste of the concentration camps. Piled at the entrance to Ohrdruff, an annex to Buchenwald, were the dead bodies left by the retreating Germans. Many of the bodies were warm, the blood still flowing from machine-gun holes. I began searching for any Jews who had escaped the final spasm of hatred of the defeated Nazis, and found two in the typhus ward.

I entered the ward. Lying on bare wood slats were a Polish Jew, between thirty and thirty-five, and a sixteen-year-old Hungarian boy. The boy had nothing on from the waist down, and I gave him a blanket to cover his grotesquely protruding hipbones. They were barely able to move, though the older man was in better shape than his younger companion. They had been far too sick to respond to the order to gather in the courtyard, and had thus been spared the fate of their fellow prisoners.

Their first request was for a plain piece of bread. It was a request I would hear over and over again for the next year. We soon learned that we had to be very careful about what food we gave the survivors. Too many who survived years of living hell in the camps had their stomachs burst as they hastily gulped down the first food offered to them by their well-intentioned liberators.

In the camps there was no point talking to fellow prisoners about loved ones lost — everyone had their own horror tales. But the sight of a Jew who had been spared such losses gave the two survivors an opportunity to share their pain. As they recalled their murdered families, they both broke into heaving sobs. Only their eyes remained dry. It was a phenomenon I would notice frequently over the next months. These Jews had cried so much that the wellsprings of their tears had actually run dry.

After about fifteen minutes of bitter sobbing, the sixteen-year-old suddenly looked at me and asked whether I could teach him how to do *teshuvah*. I was taken aback by his question and tried to comfort him.

"After the stretch in hell you've been through, you don't have to worry about doing *teshuvah*. Your slate is clean. You're alive, and you have to get hold of yourself and stop worrying about doing *teshuvah*," I told him.

But my words had no effect. I could not convince him. He kept insisting: "*Ich vill tuhn teshuvah* — I want to do *teshuvah*. *Ich muz tuhn teshuvah* — I must do *teshuvah*."

Finally, I asked him, "Why must you do *teshuvah*?" in the hope that talking would enable him to let go of some of the pain I saw in his eyes. He pointed out the window and asked me if I saw the gallows. Satisfied that I did, he began his story, which the Polish Jew subsequently confirmed in every detail.

Two months ago one of the prisoners escaped. No one even knew whether he was a Jew or a goy. We were so caught up in our own survival that we didn't even bother to find out the name of the person on the next bunk, much less anything else about him.

The guards realized at roll call that one of the prisoners was missing but had no way of knowing who he was, since roll call was by number, not by name. The camp commandant was furious about the escape and demanded to know the identity of the escaped prisoner. No one could provide him with the information he was seeking.

At this point in the boy's narrative, his companion interjected that sometimes the prisoners knew the first name of the worker next to them, but most of the time they just concentrated on conserving their strength and speaking as little as possible. Even the effort required to say a few words could leave one exhausted. I tried to imagine being so tired that even speaking would be beyond my physical capacity.

In his fury, the commandant decided to play a sadistic game with us. He demanded that any pairs of brothers, or fathers and sons, step forward. We were terrified of what he might do if we did not comply. My father and I stepped forward.

They placed my father on a stool under those gallows and tied a noose around his neck. Once the noose was around my father's neck, the commandant cocked his luger, placed it at my temple, and hissed, "If you or your father doesn't tell me who escaped, you are going to kick that stool out from under your father."

I looked at my father and told him, "Zorgst sich nit — Don't worry, Tatte, I won't do it." But my father answered me, "My son, you have to do it. He's got a gun to your head and he's going to kill you if you don't, and then he'll kick the chair out from under me and we'll both be gone. This way at least there's a chance you'll survive. But if you don't, we'll both be killed."

"Tatte, nein, ich vell dos nit tuhn — I will not do it. Ich hab nit fargessen kibbud av — I didn't forget kibbud av (honoring one's father)."

Instead of being comforted by my words, my father suddenly screamed at me: "You talk about kibbud av. I'm ordering you to kick that stool. That is your father's command."

"Nein, Tatte, nein — No, Father, I won't."

But my father only got angrier, knowing that if I didn't obey he would see his son murdered in front of him. "You

talk about kibbud av v'eim," he shouted. "This is your father's
last order to you. Listen to me! Kick the chair!"

I was so frightened and confused hearing my father scream-
ing at me that I kicked the chair and watched as my father's
neck snapped in the noose.

His story over, the boy looked at me, his eyes still dry, even
as my own tears flowed freely, and asked, "Now, you tell me. Do
I have to do *teshuvah*?"

❈ ❈ ❈

Such stories were my daily fare for the half year beginning
with the liberation of Ohrdruff and Buchenwald. One cannot live
with these memories pent up inside, and I haven't. For the last
eleven years, I have been sharing with seminary and yeshiva students in Jerusalem my experiences while serving as an Orthodox
officer in the United States Army and living among the survivors of the death camps.

Above all, I have tried to convey to my young listeners my
own strong belief that the real heroes of the war were not on the
front lines. The real heroes were those who went through the
death camps and somehow managed to emerge with their faith
intact. The strength required to watch one's wife and children,
mother and father, sisters and brothers slaughtered, often in front
of one's own eyes, and to nevertheless start again — remarry,
raise other Jewish children — is itself one of Hashem's unfath-
omable miracles.

When the Satmar Rebbe was preparing to leave *Eretz Yisrael*
for America, he was asked by Reb Asher Zelig Margolis, "Now
that you're leaving, who can I go to for a *berachah* (blessing)?"
The Rebbe told him, "Go into any *shtiebl* and ask the first Jew
you see wrapping *tefillin* over the concentration camp numbers
on his arm."

Most of those to whom I lecture have, of course, read and thought
a great deal about the destruction of European Jewry. Some of them
are the children or grandchildren of my heroes. Yet the knowledge
that an entire nation — in many ways the most civilized, cultured,

and scientifically advanced — could have set as its highest purpose the extermination of the entire Jewish people, and actually succeeded in murdering six million Jews while the world remained largely indifferent, remains beyond the capacity of the human mind to comprehend. There must always remain something surreal about the cold-blooded murderous fury of the Nazis for all who did not experience it in their own flesh.

I, too, was spared that fury, but for six months I lived among those who were not spared, as they first began to awaken from a real-life nightmare more terrible than any mind could imagine. As they lay at night in the camps, wrapped in their private pain, each would start crying over his lost loved ones, until they formed a symphony of sobbing in unison.

When we first entered Ohrdruff and Buchenwald, and witnessed the horror all around us, it did not occur to us that fifty years later there would be those who would deny that this had ever taken place. That is yet another reason to preserve these memories.

Over the years that I have been lecturing in Jerusalem, my stories have had a powerful and sometimes totally unpredicable effect on my listeners. After one lecture, an eighteen-year-old girl asked if she could come to my home for Shabbos. That Shabbos she shocked my younger children by revealing that she had a father even older than their own. Her father had lost his first wife and children in the War, and he had not remarried until well past sixty. His daughter had never understood why she had such an old father until she heard me discuss the courage that it took for the survivors to rebuild their lives, and what it meant for her father to bring children once more into the world. Her respect for her father, she told us, had grown immeasurably as a consequence of what I had said.

During another lecture, I noticed one of the girls pacing furiously around the hall. The story that stirred her was of a survivor who had spit on me and reviled my facile faith — a faith untested by what he had endured. I restrained both my personal anger at being spit on and my righteous indignation over his blasphemy by reminding myself that I could not be confident that my own faith would have survived what he had been through. It turned out that this girl was a recent *baalas teshuvah*, who had cut off all contact with her non-religious parents. She heard my words as a call to reopen the lines of communication with her parents.

Though I have no idea precisely what effect these stories will have on readers — and I imagine that those effects will be as varied as the number of readers — I offer them in the hope that they will bring each reader to a deeper faith in *Hashem Yisbarach*, for that is the effect that these experiences have had on me.

> **To**
> **My Wife Goldie**
> **and**
> **All My Children**

PART I —

A
SOLDIER'S
LIFE

CHAPTER ONE

An American Kid

LIKE MOST PEOPLE, MY STORY BEGINS WITH MY mother. But in my case the connection is even stronger than usual.

My Mother My mother was my first and greatest teacher. Though she had no formal education, she was my *Shulchan Aruch* and instilled in me the *emunah p'shutah* that is the greatest gift any Jewish parent can give his or her child.

She was small in stature, but had an iron will. Without any Jewish learning beyond what she picked up as a girl in her father's house, she nevertheless had an unshakeable faith in Hashem's beneficence and a determination that her children grow up to be good Jews.

My mother was the youngest of eleven children born to Meyer and Tova Roth in the tiny Polish *shtetl* of Pishemesh. Photographs of my grandparents show a chassidic man with a long beard and *peyos* and a woman whose hair-covering came down to just above her eyes. When my mother was still a young girl, her mother passed away. Her father remarried, and my mother's relationship with her stepmother was strained. As a consequence, her father suggested that she follow her older siblings to America.

She arrived at Ellis Island in 1898, a young girl of thirteen. I heard the story of her welcome many times. The first thing her brothers told her was that her name was no longer Sarah but Sadie. "In America, we don't use the name Sarah; it's not nice, it sounds too religious," her brothers said. (She always hated the name Sadie and was delighted later in life when she no longer had to use it.) Next she was told: "You're thirteen years old; you're a big girl. You have to go to work and make a living. Everybody works here."

The last news was the worst: "Shabbos does not exist in this country. Expect to work on Shabbos if you want to live, because you have to earn a living to buy bread." The introduction to America complete, her older brothers told her that they would help her find a job.

Though she found herself in an alien land totally dependent on her older siblings, for she knew not a word of English, still she refused to believe that there was no more Shabbos in America. She turned down job after job. Finally, she went to visit a chassidic *Rebbe* on the Lower East Side by the name of Halberstam. (When I was a young child, my mother used to bring me to him for blessings.) He advised her to take a job as a waitress. Even though she would still have to work on Shabbos, she didn't have to take tips and could avoid any *melachah d'oraisa*.

In the end, my mother took a job in a non-kosher restaurant owned by the husband of one of her older sisters. She wouldn't drink more than a glass of cold water there. On Shabbos, she lit candles at home and walked to work. She took only as many orders as she could remember at one time so that she wouldn't have to write. Her refusal to write or touch the tips that were left for her earned her the nickname, "Sadie the *meshugeneh*." Customers would tell her, "Look, I'm leaving you a tip. Last week you didn't take it. Here it is." And she would smile, as if to say, "Thank you," but the money remained where it had been placed.

MY MOTHER WAS DETERMINED TO MARRY SOMEONE religious like herself, preferably from her own chassidic background. The problem was that there were few such potential

My Parents' Marriage spouses to be found. Most of the young men her own age had cast off *Yiddishkeit* due to the pressures of earning a living and the lures of American society. The fact that my mother had no religious relatives who could help her make a *shidduch* also lessened her chances of finding the kind of husband she wanted. The result was that despite being a very beautiful woman she was still unmarried at thirty.

My father was five or six years younger than my mother. At the time they met, he was an amateur boxer and worked delivering bread for a bakery. One of the bakery's customers was my uncle's restaurant, and so my father would come in several times a week. He took a shine to my mother, but she, of course, had no interest in him because he was too American and had virtually no religious education.

If my mother was proof that with sufficient determination and *emunah* it was possible to remain *frum* in the most difficult circumstances, my father was a good example of what could happen to children from even the most religious families in America. He came to America with his parents in 1891 when he was still an infant. They came from the area around Kamenitz in Poland. My *zeide* was a shoemaker. He used to make shoes from start to finish himself, and it would take him about a day to finish each pair. I can still remember his store, which was about fifteen feet by ten feet. He had a number of cutting machines in that area, though he did all the sewing by hand.

My father's formal education ended with third grade. From then on he was self-taught. The area of the Lower East Side in which he lived was predominantly Jewish, but there was an Irish neighborhood nearby. The Irish boys used to come down my father's street taunting the Jewish boys and calling them "kikes" and the like. Fights were frequent. My father was proud of being Jewish and not one to back away from a fight, and he soon became the leader of the Jewish boys in these fights. That was how he discovered that he had a natural talent for boxing. (As a boxer my father always remained faithful to his roots. Even after he turned pro, he would never fight another Jew.)

Despite his lack of religious education, I am sure that one of the things that attracted him to my mother was that she was religious. Why else would a strong, handsome, young fellow have been interested in someone so much older than he was?

My parents together with Blimie, my son Akiva Yosef's wife, at Akiva's wedding

One day my father asked my mother to come with him to meet his parents. His parents were very religious — I remember my *zeide*'s nice red beard — and my father hoped that my mother would be more favorably disposed to him if she met his parents. He was right.

As I said, my mother was then thirty years old, and the fear of remaining unmarried her whole life preyed upon her. Still, before she would go ahead with the marriage, she made my father promise that there would be no compromising on *kashrus*, family purity, and Shabbos — and that she would have a free hand to raise the children in a religious manner. My father agreed, and my mother decided to take a chance. She told me once that she thought to herself, "I'll just have to take the gamble and hope that I do not lose." And she didn't. My parents were happily married for sixty years.

Actually, as strange as it sounds to today's generation, marriages between people with widely varying degrees of religious commitment were not so uncommon in those days. Most of them, however, did not work out as well as my parents' marriage. To make such a marriage work requires a tremendous amount of respect and love on the part of the less religious spouse for the more religious one. It is easy to make promises at the time of marriage, but to stick to those promises and never ask your more religious spouse to make some compromises takes remarkable restraint.

There was never any question of my father's love for my mother, and he had tremendous respect for her determination to raise us as religious Jews. He never did anything to give us mixed messages concerning the religious education my mother gave us with her every word. I have no doubt that he regretted not being more like his parents and wanted his children to be *frum* Jews. In that respect, taking my mother to meet his parents was not false advertising; he was close to his parents and had a warm spot in his heart for their religious practices.

Only once did my mother ever complain about anything my father did with respect to us kids. When I was about nine years old, he took me with him to some amateur fights. In the course of the afternoon, a friend of his bought me a non-kosher sandwich when my father wasn't paying attention. I asked the man if the sandwich was kosher, and he lied to me and told me that it was. (In those days, many people assumed they were doing a kid a favor if they could wean him from his old world superstitions.) As soon as I got home, I vomited, and my mother immediately saw that I had eaten some meat. She screamed at my father, "You'll never take Meyer out again. I can't trust you. Look, he ate *treif*, and his stomach can't take *treif*."

The *Gemara* makes clear that a woman exerts a much more powerful influence over her husband's spiritual growth than he does over hers. My mother certainly had that kind of effect on my father. Over the years, he became a real *baal teshuvah*.

We used to *daven* together in the Young Israel of New Lots, and I can still remember how he was always the first to answer every appeal. He would say loudly, "What's the matter with these guys? Are they sleeping? Of course we've got to give. It's a very worthy cause. You heard what the rabbi said." I'd have to calm him down by telling him, "Dad, please take it easy. They'll all give eventually. They're just figuring out how much."

He had the softest heart in the world. I contracted pneumonia as a child and had to be hospitalized. My mother remained stoic, but my father could not keep from crying as he carried me downstairs to be taken to the hospital. Even when we had no money ourselves, he never turned down a beggar on the street. "If he's got his hand out, he must need," was his motto. And when beggars came to the door, he invariably gave far in excess of his means. If anything riled my father's sense of justice, watch out. I was once with him on the subway when the fare collector got into a dispute with a pregnant woman and threw her down. My father rushed over and with one punch knocked the guy out cold. He was arrested for his chivalry.

My parents were married in 1916, and my father was drafted soon afterwards. My mother ran from one chassidic *Rebbe* to another asking them to pray that my father not be sent overseas, and if he were sent, that he not come to any harm. While still in basic training, my father worked himself up to become the army champion in his weight class. The championship fight was just before he was supposed to ship out overseas. After my father won, he tried to vault out of the ring to celebrate. Somehow his shoelaces got caught and he ended up breaking his leg instead. As a consequence, he did not ship out with the infantry unit with which he had been training. The ship carrying that unit was torpedoed and sank, so it seems as if my mother's prayers did indeed save my father's life.

Certainly my mother needed no proof of the efficacy of prayer. The son of Rabbi Chaim Krueger, who was an *av beis din* on the Lower East Side, recently told me that he remembers my mother coming to his father shortly after I was inducted into the army and giving him some money to *daven* for me every day for the duration of the war. I am sure Rabbi Krueger was not the only rabbi of whom she made the same request.

After the war, my father turned professional. Boxing has always been a sport for the very poor, and in those days Jews were very poor. The fight game was filled with Jews, even Orthodox ones. Boxing was one of the few ways for someone with no education, like my father, to make a decent living.

My father was a very good boxer, and eventually fought Gene Tunney for the right to meet the Manassa Mauler, Jack Dempsey, who was then heavyweight champion of the world. Tunney and my father were good friends from their days in the service. They were both in the same weight class and Tunney had been the Navy champion while my father was the Army champion. In any event, Tunney really clobbered my father. After the eighth round, in which he knocked my father down, he went up to the referee and told him, "I will not hit Bobby [my father fought under the name Bobby Dawson] anymore. Either you stop this fight right now or I'll quit." The referee took another look at my father and followed Tunney's advice.

My father and Tunney remained friends all their lives. Tunney was one of the few fighters to stop while he still had his brains intact. After beating Dempsey in the famous "long-count" fight, he retired as undefeated heavyweight champion. For the rest of his life, he always sent my father a card on Rosh

Before my first haircut — wearing a pair of shoes made by my zeide

Hashanah, and during the Depression, when we really struggled, he would send us furniture and other things.

After the Tunney fight, my father retired, though he remained involved in boxing for many years as a trainer and later as a judge. He trained a number of world champions.

I WAS BORN IN 1918, AND THREE OTHER SIBLINGS followed in the next six years — two sisters and a brother.

Growing Up Poor
Any way you look at it, we were poor. During the Great Depression, of course, we were far from the only ones struggling for every penny, and that made being poor somewhat easier to take. Still, you have to put food on the table and clothes on your back.

My father worked for the Works Progress Administration and brought home eighteen dollars a week. My mother did not work, and when I was about eight years old, she lost her sight in one eye. That only made our situation worse since even the housework became much more difficult for her. From the time I was ten or eleven, I used to skip Friday afternoon classes in the winter months so that I could help my mother clean the house and prepare for Shabbos. Even though I was only an average student, my principal was sympathetic and gave me permission to leave at lunchtime. This continued through my first two years in high school.

We were so poor that we couldn't afford to pay the electric bills and we lit the house with gas lanterns. Even toilet paper was beyond our means. I used to go to fruit stores and take the tissue paper in which the fruits were packed. All our clothing was handed down from our cousins. One of my uncles bought me my bar mitzvah suit. It was the first new clothing I had ever worn. A new pair of shoes was a major financial crisis. My mother would buy shoes that were several sizes too large for us and stuff them with newspaper. As our feet grew, we would remove the newspaper from the toes. Every two or three months, I would go to Woolworth's and buy new rubber soles for my shoes and for those of my younger siblings. Then I would scrape the soles, put on a special glue and replace the worn-out ones.

My first two years in high school were spent in an annex of Thomas Jefferson High School, which was several miles from my home. It was a long walk, especially in the winter, when the snowdrifts piled up and the wind was blowing. The better-off kids took the subway, but I couldn't afford the fare.

My aunt and uncle, who lived downstairs from us, owned a wholesale fruit business. Once a week, there would be a package of fruits and vegetables left at the bottom of the steps. Potatoes were the staple of our diet. My mother could make anything with potatoes.

My friends and I hit upon a stratagem for supplementing our supply of potatoes. There was a railroad siding that divided Brownsville from East New York. Railroad cars carrying produce for the Brooklyn Terminal Market were brought there. The cars were guarded to make sure that no one tried to steal the produce. We would go down to the rail yard and throw pebbles against the cars. When the guards heard the ping of stones hitting the cars, they would start throwing potatoes and onions, or sometimes coal, back at us. They couldn't chase us because they were afraid to leave the cars unguarded. When we had enticed them into throwing enough to fill the scrub pails we brought with us, we would gather up whatever was lying around and scurry home. While today I'm not proud of this story, it gives you an idea of the poverty of the times.

My bar mitzvah celebration was fully commensurate with our economic status. I had an *aliyah* on Monday morning at the Malta Street *shul* down the block from us. After *davening,* a *minyan* of men from the *shul* came back to our house, where my mother served them egg *kichlech,* herring, and coffee. Not a single friend of mine was present. Such quiet, unostentatious bar mitzvahs were not at all uncommon in those days. Most of my friends celebrated their bar mitzvahs in exactly the same way.

On one thing, however, there was no scrimping: my *tefillin.* I can still remember my mother taking me to a *sofer* on Riverdale Avenue in East New York to purchase them. They cost between twenty and twenty-five dollars which, my mother told me later, almost bankrupted us, but they were truly kosher. My mother asked the *sofer,* a chassidic man with a long beard, to give me a *berachah,* something she did whenever we met an older religious Jew.

LIKE MOST KIDS, I WANTED A LITTLE SPENDING MONEY, which I obviously wasn't going to get from my parents. I got my

Odd Jobs

first job when I was eight years old. My mother told me that she couldn't give me a penny for some candy, and I decided to go out and earn the money myself. Across the street from us there was a soda manufacturer by the name of Chester Club. When I walked in and asked for a job, the owner took one look at me and started laughing. But in the end he gave me a job as a bottle washer. In three or four hours after school, I could make fifty to seventy-five cents plus a soft drink, which I would save for Shabbos.

My other job at that age was the traditional one of shining shoes. As people came off the IRT on Pennsylvania Avenue, I'd shout, "Shoe shine, shoe shine, five cents, five-cent shoe shine."

It took fifteen minutes for that nickel shine, and if we were lucky, the customer would add a nickel tip.

I hated shining shoes. I found kneeling down on my hands and knees in front of someone degrading. Even with a kneepad, my knees used to bleed after a while. I vowed that when I grew up, I would never let anyone shine my shoes for me.

One of those whose shoes I shined was the infamous Louis Lepke, the head of Murder, Incorporated. He was raised in Brownsville and used to return to the area to visit his family. He came from a traditional Orthodox family; his brother, a sweet man, was a pharmacist in the neighborhood. The paradox of a gangster growing up in a traditional home and still maintaining ties to the old neighborhood was typical of those days — strange as it may seem today. Lepke was nice to us kids. He never tipped me less than a dime, and near the holidays he sometimes threw me a dollar. When I got that type of tip, you can be sure that my workday was done.

During the long summer vacation, I used to sell Big Bear ice creams at Coney Island. We would pick up wooden boxes filled with dry ice from the Big Bear plant on Blake Avenue in Brownsville and from there take a forty-five-minute ride out to Coney Island, where we walked along the beach selling our ice cream pops to the bathers. We'd pay three cents apiece for the pops and sell them for five cents. Sometimes at the end of the day, I would give my mother as much as two or three dollars — which was not bad for a ten-year-old — and she would praise me, "*A gutter. Er is azoi gut* — A good person. He's so good."

One of the occupational hazards of this job was that it was illegal. There were concession stands along the boardwalk, and moving vendors were prohibited. When the owners of the concession stands caught sight of us, they would call the police. The bathers, of course, sided with the cute little kids against the cops, and they would warn us of the cops' approach and sometimes even run interference for us. When we saw the policemen coming, we would run out into the water. The cops would not wade out after us, but would stand on the beach threatening us. After a while they usually wandered away and the people on the beach who had been jeering at them would call out, "It's okay, kid; the coast is clear."

I was once collared from behind by a policeman in the midst of a big sale and hauled off in a paddy wagon to the police station on West 8th Street in Coney Island. The ice cream boys whom the police had caught that day were all placed together in the police station garage, which is also where they took the bodies of drowning victims. We sat there trembling at the thought of the bodies covered with newspaper. We made a deal that whichever boy's parents arrived first would take out the other kids as well.

Another of my summer jobs made me the envy of all my friends. An older cousin managed a roller coaster called the Cyclone. Each seat held two people. Whenever there was a lone rider, especially if it was a young child, I would ride next to him to make sure he did not lean forward and hit his head on the bar in front of him. Actually the ride quickly became boring, despite the delirious screaming of the riders, but the five dollars my brother and I picked up in a day seemed like a fortune to us.

Some of the jobs really built me up physically. One of these was as a "puller" in a commercial laundry. I had to lean over a large bin of wet laundry and separate the large from the small pieces as I pulled them out. Sopping wet laundry can get pretty heavy, and this job strained me to the utmost until my body adjusted.

But the hardest job of all was cleaning windows. By my last two years of high school, I had become a pretty serious student. In order to have time to study at night, I took a job cleaning windows early in the morning. Getting up long before sunrise was just one of the job's hardships. In the wintertime, I had to work very quickly — first getting the water off the sponge so that it did not freeze and render the sponge useless, and then removing the water from the windows before it froze. We used to put alcohol in the water to prevent it from freezing. By the time I finished my hands were ice, and the rest of me was not much warmer.

After graduating high school, I found a job working for Robert G. Horowitz, a wholesale clothing firm. For working ten hours a day, six days a week, I earned eight dollars, but at least the work was steady. Three nights a week, I would gulp down a sandwich around six p.m. and hurry over to the local branch of City College for classes in accounting and commercial law. Two nights a week, I learned in Mesivta Chaim Berlin.

Working at Horowitz's

The manager at Horowitz's was a *frum* fellow named Aaron Papellowitz. Aaron had a peculiar sense of humor. One day he sent me into the stockroom to get a 38-regular blue serge suit and told me to pick out an extra pair of pants. He then sent me to O'Brien's Funeral Parlor carrying the suit and the extra pants. It was my first trip to a gentile funeral parlor. Some of the bodies — "stiffs" they called them — were sitting up in their coffins and others were lying down. They were all made up in such a way that you would never know they were dead. Somber organ music played in the background. I made my delivery, and the owner took one look at it and started laughing uproariously. "Tell me," he asked, "what is one of these stiffs going to do with an extra pair of pants?" He called over the other workers and they all stood around guffawing. When I got back to work, Aaron Papellowitz and the other workers had a good laugh at my expense.

CHAPTER TWO

Religious Education

DESPITE MY MOTHER'S DETERMINATION TO RAISE us as *frum* Jews, I had little formal Jewish education as a child and teenager. Perhaps because my mother was raised in an environment so permeated with *Yiddishkeit* and her own faith was so firm, she did not realize how important yeshiva training was for an American boy. In addition, the East New York section of Brooklyn in which we lived had no yeshivos in those days. To get to the Lower East Side, where most of the yeshivos were, would have involved taking two trolley cars and several trains, something beyond the capacity of most young kids.

An Afternoon Rebbe

In any event, I was a regular public school kid all the way. All my friends were non-religious. In the afternoons, I would play ball with them wearing my homemade *yarmulke*. They would laugh at me when the *yarmulke* fell off as I was running the bases, but I got used to it. I learned early in life not to be fazed by being laughed at, and that ability served me well during my years in the army.

What little formal Jewish education I had consisted of an hour a day after school with a private *rebbe*. Six or seven other boys and I would recite *aleph-beis* (or in later years *Chumash*), while the *rebbe* sat there paying more attention to the onions or potatoes he was peeling to help his overburdened wife than to us. It was very discouraging. By my bar mitzvah, I told my mother that she was wasting her money and that I should go to yeshiva instead.

My only real teacher as a young boy was my mother. Every day she would come down to where I was playing ball and escort me to *shul* for *Minchah-Maariv* services. I was always the only young kid there and someone would invariably ask, "Do you have to say *Kaddish*?" In the worst winter weather, my mother would open up the window and call out for me to go to *shul*. She would watch me from the window the entire way to make sure I went. Whenever I looked back, I would see my mother in the window — watching.

What is interesting is that I do not remember ever resenting my mother's close supervision. Her authority was unchallenged. I never told her, "Oh Ma, leave me alone." I didn't try to fool my mother or forget *cheder* or *davening* whenever the ballgame got too exciting, as other boys did.

Not one of my mother's ten older brothers and sisters remained religious. I don't have even one religious cousin. One of my uncles used to take off my *yarmulke* and tell me that I would go bald from wearing such an old-fashioned thing on my head. My mother would grab it back, put it on my head, and lead me to a corner where she would console me. Eventually we stopped visiting that uncle.

When I was sixteen or seventeen, a rich uncle offered me twenty-five dollars to work six nights a week, including Shabbos, at his stand in the Washington Square Market in Manhattan, which was then the largest wholesale fruit and vegetable market in the United States. Twenty-five dollars a week was a fortune to us — my father was then bringing home only eighteen dollars a week for full-time work. My mother's response was blunt: "There is not enough money in the world to buy Shabbos. We'll starve to death before Meyer works on Shabbos."

In those days, there were many who came from religious homes who were eager not only to give up religious observance themselves but also to lure others away. They must have felt guilty about having been unable to withstand the temptations of America, and the sight of others who had been able to resist was a constant reproach to them.

As a youngster, I was always asked at family celebrations to make *hamotzi* over the *challah*. No one else in the family could even make a blessing. When I got older, I refused. I sensed that my relatives were treating the blessing as some sort of joke. At family gatherings, my mother would stress to my siblings and me that we could not eat anything without her explicit permission.

Most important of all, my mother instilled in me a love of doing *chesed* (good deeds). If she looked out the window and saw someone carrying a number of packages or bags of groceries, she would send me outside to help. When I returned from these little missions, she would praise me so warmly that I could hardly wait for the next opportunity to help someone. She herself was a model of *chesed*. When people came door-to-door for donations, she always gave them a nickel and invited them in for coffee and cake or some pickled herring. Never did she just give someone money.

When I was younger, my mother was also a member of the *Chevrah Kadishah*, which prepares bodies for burial. Those who worked with her in this *chesed shel emes* (true *chesed* — i.e., one undertaken without any possibility of being reciprocated) told me years later how she was always the first one there for every *taharah* (purification of the body prior to burial). Though my mother was a small, slight woman, and the process of doing the *taharah* can be physically strenuous, she nevertheless had the strength for this great *mitzvah*.

My mother was a bastion of strength for every Jew in the neighborhood who needed encouragement to remain firm in his or her religious observance. It was not easy to be *frum* in those days. Besides the economic pressure to work on Shabbos, religious Jews were subjected to continual ridicule for holding on to their old-country ways. Whenever my mother felt people were in danger of succumbing to either the economic or social pressures, she would visit them and encourage them. Jews who felt their religious resolve weakening often came to see her. Her own faith was so rock hard that it inevitably strengthened those who were wavering.

From the time I was a little boy, I was always attracted to *Yiddishkeit*. By ten, I was a regular *kiruv* professional. On Shabbos afternoon, I would stand outside the movie theater. As boys came out I would speak to them and try to convince them to come to the Young Israel and experience some taste of *Yiddishkeit*. I was pretty good at this, and was even given a prize for bringing the most kids to the Young Israel. Some of my best friends to this day are those whom I picked up outside the Biltmore theater.

The Young Israel of New Lots

AS A YOUNG BOY, I USED TO *DAVEN* IN THE MALTA STREET *shul* near my house. I was the only kid there. Almost everyone else seemed like an old man to me. I remember that there was a spittoon in the *shul* and the members made liberal use of it. All in all, it wasn't the place for an eight-year-old boy, and I told my mother that I was going to look for some other place to *daven*.

One Shabbos shortly thereafter, I was walking past a *shul* named Congregation New Lots Talmud Torah, and I noticed some young people *davening*. This was my introduction to the Young Israel of New Lots, which soon became a second home for me and remained so for nearly three decades. There I would absorb most of the *Yiddishkeit* that I picked up outside of the home.

Young Israel met downstairs in Congregation New Lots Talmud Torah. Each member paid only a nickel a week in dues so the *shul* must have been giving us the use of the downstairs pretty much for free. We conducted all the Shabbos *davening*, through *Maariv* of *Motzaei Shabbos*. Every Shabbos afternoon, there was a *Minchah minyan*, followed by an older boy telling stories, and a *shalosh seudos* of herring. On *Motzaei Shabbos*, there was another meeting to keep the kids occupied.

Essentially, Young Israel was a youth organization. Our mentors were teenagers only a few years older than ourselves. Dovid Hershowitz was the leader of the group when I arrived. Dovid's father died when he was eleven, and he had to go to work at fourteen. As a teenager, he somehow came into contact with a number of the *gedolei Torah* already in America — — Rabbi Moshe Rosen, *zt"l*, Rabbi Nisson Telushkin, *zt"l*, and later Rabbi Yitzchak Hutner, *zt"l* — and was inspired by them. When some of the older boys began to sprout beards, Dovid went out and bought

Rabbi Nisson Telushkin

them all electric shavers so that they would not be tempted to shave with a straight-edge razor. They paid him back in small weekly installments.

Just like Elisha who, upon seeing Eliyahu for the first time, put down his plow, kissed his parents goodbye, and followed him (*Melachim* I 19:19-23), Dovid was so impressed when he met Rabbi Elchonon Wasserman, *Hy"d*, in 1938 that he dropped everything and followed Reb Elchonon back to Baronowich, where he remained for a year and a half, until the Nazi invasion of Poland. He returned filled with stories of yeshiva life in Europe and the great people he had met, including Rabbi Chaim Ozer Grodzinski, *zt"l*, with whom he spent a Shabbos in Vilna just prior to leaving Europe. It was *Reb* Dovid who pushed many of the boys from the Young Israel of New Lots into yeshiva and the girls into Bais Yaakov. For nearly thirty years *Reb* Dovid has led a *kollel* in Bnei Brak.

In addition to our own leaders, some older fellows from the Young Israel of East New York used to teach us on Shabbos afternoon and *Motzaei Shabbos*. One of them, Harry Hisiger, didn't marry until he was close to forty, and he was like a father to me when I was growing up. Another of our teachers from the Young Israel of East New York was Yosef Schechter, the father of Rabbi Aharon Schechter, Rosh Yeshiva of Mesivta Chaim Berlin. He was a wonderful speaker, who held us entranced with his gems of Torah. When I was in high school, the *baal kriah*, Yerachmiel Yitzchak Lasker, would learn *mishnayos* early in the morning with my friend Moshe Swerdloff and me. That may have been where I developed my lifelong habit of getting up very early in the morning.

Everyone in our group went to public school, and many did not come from religious homes. The level of ignorance was unbelievable. On Yom Kippur, we had to supply slippers for all those who came to *shul* wearing their regular shoes. During the *Kol Nidrei* appeal one year, someone pledged thirty-three dollars — twenty-three for the *shul* and ten for the slippers, which he apparently thought were some sort of door prize. My friend Moshe Swerdloff once took a group of younger boys to a basketball game at Madison Square Garden. He had to use all his persuasive powers, and the promise of an after-game treat of lox and bagels on the Lower East Side, to keep them from purchasing the non-kosher hot dogs.

But if the level of knowledge was low, the transformations that the kids experienced in Young Israel were remarkable. The boy in Moshe's group who had the hardest time understanding why he should not eat the non-kosher franks is today a yeshiva *rebbe*. By the early '40s, *bachurim* in Chaim Berlin looking for a wife who would cover her hair after marriage knew that the place to begin their search was the Young Israel of New Lots. Of my close friends in the organization, I would guess that ninety-five percent have children and grandchildren today who are *bnei Torah*, many of them *maggidei shiur* or prominent members of the Orthodox community. If not for the Young Israel of New Lots, it is unlikely that many of those friends would even have remained religious.

These are just a few of the outstanding members of our New Lots branch: Willie Auslander, Ina May Beer, Joe Blaustein, Basya Sabolsky Borenstein, Seymour Borenstein, Eli Brodsky, Isaac Candiotti, Molly Aptner Feinstone, Dovid Fisher, Shloma Fisher, Alvin Fontek, Chunie Fontek, Gloria Green Friedman, Lillian Tuller German, Lenny Gewirtzman, Pearl Erden Gewirtzman, Aidel Green, Moishe Green, Pinkey Green, Rafael Green, Rivie

*Rabbi Hutner at a Young Israel dinner with many East New Yorkers whom
he inspired. From right to left. Yitzchak Lasker, Irving Hunger, a"h,
Rabbi Hutner, zt"l, Rabbi Dr. Samson Raphael Weiss, zt"l,
Yosef Schechter, Alan Schreiber, and myself.*

Green, Heshy Kalmus, Avraham Kamelhar, Max Lasker, Benny
Lasker, Zina Hirsh Lazar, Marvin Lieberman, Leo Reich, Joe Reich,
Adel Beckerman Rubinfeld, George Rushfield, Sammy Scheier,
Yudel Schreiber, Julius Shidlovsky, Gitel Shulman Resnick, Heshy
Sidlofsky, Esther Levy Swerdloff, and Lillian Lederman Ziskind.

One of the crucial factors behind the success of our organization
was Rabbi Yitzchak Hutner's move to Brownsville in the late 1930s. He
inspired us all, and even some of those from non-religious homes entered the high school of Mesivta Chaim Berlin. Unfortunately for me, I
was already too old by the time the high school opened.

Rabbi Hutner used to give a Friday night *Chumash-Rashi* class
in his home on Pennsylvania Avenue. For many of us, that class
was our first real exposure to Torah learning. I remember that
one of those who attended did not even know that there is a
prohibition against carrying on Shabbos. He would come every
week toting his *Chumash* with him. Rabbi Hutner forbade us to
say anything to him for fear that he would be embarrassed and
stop coming altogether. That young man went on to become both
a prominent public official and the lay head of one of America's
largest Orthodox organizations. In the latter capacity, he played
a crucial role in lifting the religious standards of the organization.

Rabbi Freifeld

The incomparable Rabbi Shlomo Freifeld, *zt"'l*, was also first inspired in the Young Israel of New Lots. He eventually became one of Rabbi Hutner's closest disciples. I doubt whether anyone else possessed his ability to help an individual discover previously undreamt-of inner resources. He was a unique personality and a giant of the spirit. Interestingly, he later became the *rav* of the Young Israel of New Lots before founding Yeshiva Sh'or Yoshuv in Far Rockaway, where he was the mentor of hundreds of young men and their families. No doubt much of his inspiration lay in his own experience of developing religiously in our organization. Another of our products was Rabbi Ephraim Sturm, who became the National Director of the National Council of Young Israel.

Many of my friends from Young Israel of New Lots have remained lifelong friends. Some of those include: Moshe Berl, *a"h*, Harry Brisman, Pesach Feldman, Irving Hunger, *a"h*, Pincus Iseson, *a"h,* Sam Litman, Lenny Maline, Yosef Nayowitz, Alan Rubenfeld, Michel Rubenfeld, Jack Rubowsky, George Rushfield, Moshe Stern, Moshe Swerdloff, Max Zakon, and Sidney Zahner. My good friend Alan Schreiber and his wife Esther were moving forces in the Young Israel, and Esther's father Mr. Greenberg, *a"h*, was a father figure and inspiration to each of us.

When Rabbi Elchonon Wasserman visited America in 1938, he spoke in our Young Israel. In order to reach American teenagers, he made an exception to his general practice and allowed a simultaneous English translation of his speech. But it was clear that he was far from comfortable with having a translator; several times he asked the translator to repeat to him in Yiddish what he had just told us in English. Though few of us were capable of fully understanding Reb Elchonon's words, just the sight of a *gadol* of his stature had a profound impact. I remember that he compared Torah to the bell that a shepherd places around a cow's neck so that it can be found if it strays from the path. Similarly, the Torah ensures that a Jew does not leave the path of truth despite being beset on all sides by the temptations of the *yetzer hara*.

Reb Elchonon

After the War, Rabbi Leib Malin, *zt"l*, arrived in New York from Shanghai, together with a group of survivors of the Mirrer Yeshiva. Rabbi Malin was already renowned throughout the pre-War European Torah world, and those who came with him — Rabbi Shmuel Charkover, *zt"l*, Rabbi Leizer Hordjesky, *zt"l*, Rabbi Chaim Wysokier, *zt"l*, and *ylch"a*, Rabbi Shalom Menashe Gottlieb and Rabbi Yisroel Perkowski — were some of the greatest of the *alte Mirrers*. This group established Yeshiva Beis HaTalmud in New Lots, with Reb Leib as Rosh Yeshiva.

Though few, if any, of us had the learning background to fully appreciate their greatness, still the fact that there was a group of young American men filled with reverence for *talmidei chachamim* was a source of encouragement to these remnants of a world that had been totally destroyed.

The exposure to *gedolim* of such stature had a profound effect on many of us in the Young Israel of New Lots. Some — in particular Moshe Swerdloff — became very involved in Beis HaTalmud. Rabbi Yisroel Perkowski of Beis HaTalmud eventually became the *rav* of the Young Israel of New Lots. At the time he was selected, there was opposition from those who feared that

בית התלמוד
מרכז לתורה ויראה

Beth Hatalmud

INSTITUTE FOR TALMUDIC RESEARCH

579 PENNSYLVANIA AVENUE • BROOKLYN 7, NEW YORK
TELEPHONE EVergreen 5-2823

ESTABLISHED BY THE UNION OF ORTHODOX R
OF THE UNITED STATES AND CANADA

June 11th, 1961
Sivan 27, 5721

Mr. & Mrs. Meyer Birnbaum
753 New Jersey Avenue
Brooklyn 7, New York

Dear Friends:

As one of the most ardent and staunch friends of the Beth Hatalmud throughout the years, and especially of the Yeshiva Ketana which has with the will of the Almighty, in its relatively short existence succeeded in developing such fine fruits, the dearest and most precious which we have - our children; - we have the honor and privilege in expressing to you our sincere appreciation for being the guest of honor at the Banquet which was tendered in benefit of the Yeshiva Ketana.

Especially do we want to express to you our deep feelings of gratitude for all the genuine effort, energy and toil you have invested and given of yourself so that this affair be a success. And as you know, indeed it was a success. The entire program was performed with tact, poise, due order and with magnificent ornateness. And last but not least, also the appeal was a great success.

In general it was felt by everyone that this affair was a true "Kovod Hatorah", an affair befitting the Holy cause and the great Institution for which it was made. You and your dear wife may take pride that through your endeavors this rescue project was conducted to bring the necessary aid we so badly needed at this time.

Through the high regard and esteem, as well as the warm enthusiastic ovation you received by your honored guests, we have seen that although you always try to shun and side track the honors due you, yet it seemed to catch up with you this

Please make checks payable to Beth Hatalmud

A letter of appreciation from Rabbi Leib Malin on the occasion of my being the guest of honor at the first annual Beis HaTalmud dinner

we were turning the *shul* into a yeshiva. But the most vociferous op-
ponent of Reb Yisroel's selection
became, with the passage of time,
his staunchest supporter. He ended
up sending all his children to
yeshivos, partly due to Reb
Yisroel's influence, and every one
of his sons is today a *maggid shiur.*

Another great *talmid chacham*
with whom we had frequent contact was Rabbi Avrohom Pam, Rosh
Yeshiva of Torah Vodaath, who
davened regularly in the Young Israel of New Lots in the late 1940s.
Though he steadfastly refused any
official position or title, he was our
unofficial *rav* for a number of years.

HaRav Pam

In general, the effect the many European-trained *talmidei
chachamim* who arrived in America after the War had on the
development of American Orthodoxy is a fascinating subject.
There were many English-speaking young men like myself, with
limited yeshiva background, who found something we had been
looking for in the newly-arrived European scholars. Their
example and *ehrlichkeit* were unquestionably responsible for the
fact that many of my contemporaries, with little advanced Jewish
learning of their own, have produced sons who are leading *bnei
Torah.*

Rabbi Yaakov Moshe Shurkin, *zt"l,* who had been a *talmid*
of the Chofetz Chaim in Radin and, after coming to America,
was a *maggid shiur* in Chaim Berlin for close to thirty years,
used to give a twice weekly *Gemara shiur* in the Young Israel
of New Lots. We once asked him why in all his examples to
illustrate cases of the *Gemara,* the wrongdoer was invariably
named Jake. He explained that if he used one of the more com-
monly employed names — like Reuven or Shimon — there
might be someone in the *shiur* by that name who would be
offended. Therefore he always gave the bad guy his name,

Yaakov, so that there could be no suspicion he was trying to insult anyone.

I was once with Rabbi Shurkin when a *shul* rabbi tried to persuade him to take over his *shiur* in *Kitzur Shulchan Aruch* while he was on vacation. Rabbi Shurkin refused on the grounds that he would have to spend too much time preparing. This excuse seemed preposterous to me. Only years later did I learn from one of his sons that the real reason was that he feared that the *baalebatim* would prefer his *shiur* to their rabbi's, and he did not want to undermine the rabbi's position in any way. Being around someone of this degree of sensitivity, and others like him, gave us American-born young men a taste of what the great yeshivos of Europe had been like.

A Stink Bomb in Shul

IN MANY WAYS YOUNG ISRAEL WAS THE FIRST AMERICAN *baal teshuvah* movement. It was Young Israel, for instance, which built the first modern *mikvaos*, and worked to increase the observance of *taharas hamishpachah* in America. The English announcements and the melodies that were introduced into the *davening* were meant to attract American-born, English-speaking youth put off by the rapid-fire, undecorous *davening* in their parents' *shuls*. This younger generation was often striving for higher religious standards than those prevalent in the congregations of their European-born parents. In our group, we had many instances of parents who became religious due to the influence of their children.

The paradox of American-born youth more religious than their European-born parents is nicely illustrated by the incident that led to our eviction from Congregation New Lots Talmud Torah. It was not uncommon in those days for prominent actors from the Yiddish stage to perform in *shuls* on *Motzaei Shabbos*. Often tickets to these performances were sold in barbershops on Shabbos itself. Among the most prominent Yiddish actor-singers was Moshe Oysher. Despite the fact that we once saw him eating on Yom Kippur, he was a frequent *chazzan* in various New York *shuls.* When he *davened,* his back was to the *Aron Kadosh* and towards the audience, as if it were an opera recital.

In any event, Congregation New Lots Talmud Torah decided to sponsor a *Motzaei Shabbos* concert featuring Moshe Oysher and a women's chorus from the Roland Yiddish Theater. My friends and I were scandalized at the thought of a synagogue sponsoring a concert with a women's chorus singing and dancing. We went to Rabbi Hutner, who had only recently come to America, to ask him what we should do. Our plan was to take an old rubber inner tube and set it on fire at the start of the concert, hoping that the stench would force its cancellation. Rabbi Hutner indicated neither approval nor disapproval, which we interpreted as a form of tacit approval.

The night of the concert, we climbed up into the attic and cut up an inner tube and placed the pieces inside metal cans. Then we set the rubber alight. The smoke and putrid smell made it impossible to get inside the *shul.* The fire department was called and went crazy trying to locate the source of the fumes because there was no actual fire. We had been careful to set the stink bomb going in such a way that it would not ignite. Needless to say, our group was summarily evicted from Congregation New Lots Talmud Torah, but we had the satisfaction of knowing that other *shuls* had to think twice before scheduling such concerts.

News of that stink bomb reached all the way to California, where a Jewish paper described what had happened in an article entitled "Revolution in Shul."

> *Can you conceive of young people leaving a shul because their elders are not Orthodox enough for them? Well, just this happened recently in Brooklyn at Congregation New Lots Talmud Torah. . . . The old-timers love to hear juicy davening, so they hired Yiddish actor-singers to be cantors. This scandalized the boys and girls who are undergoing a religious revival. Now they have a shul of their own and it is called Young Israel. It's strictly traditional and English speaking. . . .*

ONE PERSON WHO HAD A MAJOR IMPACT ON ME AS I was growing up was Elimelech "Mike" Tress. I first met Mike

Mike Tress when I was about fourteen or fifteen years old. I had made a number of friends in Williamsburg by that time, and I met Mike there through the Williamsburg branch of Zeirei Agudath Israel. That branch eventually developed into the national headquarters of ZAI and ultimately Agudath Israel of America.

Mike knew that I was a public school kid, as he himself had been, and he showed a great deal of interest in me. He mentioned that he had heard a great deal about the Young Israel of New Lots and would like to visit. An invitation to speak at an upcoming *Melaveh Malkah* was immediately extended.

I don't remember much of what Mike spoke about that night, but I do remember the effect on me. Mike didn't speak with his mouth; he spoke with his heart. The words may have come out of his mouth but they were directly from the heart. I am not embarrassed to say that I fell in love with this man. His warmth was like that of a fire on a cold winter's day — you simply wanted to cuddle closer to him. Just standing near him inspired you.

Mike visited our Young Israel chapter a number of times, and some of my friends and I became more involved with the Williamsburg ZAI chapter at 616 Bedford Ave. At one *Melaveh Malkah*, Mike welcomed all the various Zeirei branches that were represented, and when he finished, he said, "And now let me welcome the most active and finest Zeirei branch by far — the Young Israel of New Lots." My friends and I were in seventh heaven.

Actually Mike's description of the Young Israel of New Lots as a ZAI branch was to prove not altogether fanciful. After the founding of the State of Israel a motion was introduced that the National Council of Young Israel should affiliate with one of the political parties in Israel. A national convention was held and all the branches were polled as to what party they were in favor of affiliating with. Every single branch, except for the Young Israel of New Lots, voted to affiliate with Mizrachi. We shocked the convention by announcing our intention to affiliate with Zeirei Agudath Israel, which was not even a political party. That lone dissent was sufficient to prevent

Young Israel from affiliating at all. After we announced our intention of supporting ZAI, Irving Bunim stood up and made an impassioned plea that Young Israel remain apolitical as it always had been, and his motion carried.

I personally continued to pay my ZAI dues as a kind of tribute to Mike Tress until I made *aliyah* at the age of sixty-two. By that time I was surely the oldest member of Agudath Israel's young people's division, and they made a dinner in my honor for my nearly fifty years as a member. Rabbi Avraham Pam, the Rosh Yeshiva of Torah Vodaath spoke, and I, of course, had no intention of speaking after him. But Rabbi Pam insisted. I got carried away and spoke for about an hour, which must have bored just about everyone there to death. But it was worth it. When I was finished, my father came over to me and said, "Meyer, thanks for introducing yourself to me. I knew nothing about your years in the army or how you thought. We should be talking to each other more." I was thrilled that my father wanted to get closer to me even at that late date — he was eighty-eight at the time and died later that year.

The summer after the *Melaveh Malkah* at which he had spoken so effusively of the Young Israel of New Lots, Mike asked me what I was doing for the summer. I told him that I would be trying to earn some money as I did every summer. "How would you like to come up with me for a Shabbos to Camp Mesivta?" he asked.

"That's for yeshiva guys," I replied.

"Well, I'm not a yeshiva guy and I'm going."

"Yeah, but you have to sleep there, and I haven't got money to pay for the camp."

"Don't worry about that, I'll get you in."

Mike brought me up for several Shabbosim that summer. I used to babysit for the children of Rabbi Sender Linchner, the camp's director. One Shabbos Mike and I were sharing a room and had a chance to talk. I remember that one of the things we talked about was our common name.

"Mike, you know my name is also Mike?" I began.

"Sure I know."

"I was thinking that now that I'm getting older I'd like to

Yosef Nayowitz (far left) and Meyer Birnbaum (far right) at Camp Mesivta

change my name. Mike doesn't seem like the most appropriate Jewish name, and I was thinking of changing it to Meyer, which is the name I was given at my *bris.*"

In those days almost everybody had an Americanized name. Mike did not advise me against changing my name, but he did suggest that the decision was not perhaps as crucial as I was making it out to be. "It's not the name they call you but what you represent," he told me.

"Well, I know you didn't change your name."

"There's no reason to change my name. I try to do the best I can with the name I have."

Probably as a consequence of that discussion I didn't start using the name Meyer until I was drafted.

One of the biggest shocks of my life was the week Mike was married. I wasn't invited, and I couldn't understand how he could have forgotten to invite his best friend. I mentioned this over-sight to a few of my friends, and in each case the reaction was the same: "What do you mean you're his closest friend? I'm his closest friend." None of us, unfortunately, could bring any definite proof — we had all been left off the guest list. Mike's magnetism was such that whenever you were near him he made you feel that you were the most important person in the world to him.

One of the few people I went to visit prior to my induction into the army was Mike. He told me that a number of Zeirei boys had already been drafted and many more were sure to be drafted soon. He

Mike Tress, in the uniform of a UNRAA officer, in Europe following the liberation

gave me a *berachah* that I should return safe and sound and told me to keep in touch. I wrote him often concerning some of the difficulties I had to face as a religious soldier, and even though he was working around the clock trying to get Jews out of Europe, he would write back with advice as to how I should conduct myself.

In the course of a lifetime, one meets two or three outstanding individuals who tower above everyone else. Mike Tress was one such person. One of the honors that meant most to me in my life was being permitted to lower one side of his *aron* into the ground at his funeral.

CHAPTER THREE
You're in the Army Now

DECEMBER 7, 1941 WILL ALWAYS BE REMEMBERED
as the day that "will live in infamy." However, for the yeshiva
Drafted   world of New York it was a black day long before
we had heard of the Japanese attack on Pearl
Harbor. I left the house early that morning for the funeral of Rabbi
Dovid Leibowitz, one of the first of the European giants to try to
transplant the Torah of Europe to America's often unreceptive
soil. He was Rosh Yeshiva in Mesivta Torah Vodaath, and later
founded Yeshivas Yisroel Meir HaKohen (popularly known as
Yeshivas Chofetz Chaim). There he tried to recreate a spiritual
elite along the lines of the Slabodka Kollel, of which he had been
among the most prominent members.

As we were walking with the *aron* along Williamsburg's
Bedford Avenue, someone ran over to me and asked if I had heard
of Pearl Harbor. "I don't know her," I told him, not realizing Pearl
Harbor was a naval base not a girl.

About half an hour later, someone else told us that Pearl
Harbor had been bombed and much of the United States Navy's

Pacific fleet destroyed. The news still didn't make much of an impression on me, but as soon as the funeral was over, we all ran home to listen to the radio and find out what was going on. Only then did we realize that war with Japan was inevitable. Those of us with low draft numbers, like myself, knew that we would soon be receiving a letter from our local draft board.

A few days later, the dreaded letter arrived. My mother immediately sensed that it didn't contain glad tidings and asked me what it was about. When I told her that it was an induction notice from the draft board, she comforted me by saying that they would never take anyone as skinny as me. I then weighed 129 pounds, which was stretched pretty thin over my six-foot-three-inch frame.

I remember that I went for my draft physical somewhere in Canarsie. My mother hovered around me when I returned home, eager to know the results of my physical. I didn't know, but a few days later I received another letter informing me that I had been declared 1-A, which meant that I would be drafted very soon.

I was no hero chafing at the bit to see action, and I rushed to my Rosh Yeshiva Rabbi Hutner to ask him whether he could help me obtain a 4-D exemption for divinity students.

Rabbi Hutner was sympathetic, but told me that he could not help me obtain a 4-D exemption because I was not a full-time student. He taught me a valuable lesson that would remain with me throughout the next five years in the army and beyond: A *frum* Jew must always consider whether his actions will be a *kiddush Hashem* or a *chillul Hashem*. He explained that if it were discovered that the yeshiva had improperly aided boys in obtaining draft exemptions a tremendous *chillul Hashem* would result. Later I realized how right he was, when there started to be mutterings about the "Jew War" foisted upon Roosevelt by Jewish bankers. The anti-Semites would have had a field day claiming that American boys were dying on behalf of the Jews of Europe while American Jews were sitting on the sidelines.

Rabbi Hutner gave me his *berachah* and told me to recite *Tehillim* 91, *Yosheiv Beseiser,* as many times as I could each day. That *kappitel* (chapter of) *Tehillim*, which speaks of "a thousand fall[ing] at your left side and ten thousand at your right side," remains my favorite to this day.

MY NEXT STEP WAS TO MAKE AN APPOINTMENT WITH
Rabbi Shmuel Schecter, who had been my *rebbe* at Chaim

Preparing for the Army

Berlin. Rabbi Schecter was a Canadian by birth, who had been learning in the Mirrer Yeshiva in Europe when the War broke out. Upon returning from Mir in 1938, he became a *rebbe* in Chaim Berlin. Later he joined the first *kollel* in America, Beth Medrash Govoha, which was comprised almost entirely of American young men who had learned in Europe. At that time, the *kollel* was located in White Plains, New York. Subsequently, of course, that *kollel* evolved into Lakewood Yeshiva under the leadership of Rabbi Aharon Kotler, *zt"l*.

I went to see Rabbi Schecter in White Plains, and the first thing he did was hand me a *sefer* and told me to memorize it. That *sefer* was *Machaneh Yisrael*, written by the Chofetz Chaim as a guide for Jewish boys serving in the Russian army. The work is a virtual *Shulchan Aruch* for a Jewish soldier serving in a gentile army: what can be skipped when there is only a brief time for *davening*, how to eat bread, what is the earliest time one can *daven* in the morning, etc. Rabbi Schecter and I spent the next week learning through the *sefer*.

We finished learning *Machaneh Yisrael* the day before I was to be inducted. When we were done, Rabbi Schecter gave me a final pep talk; this would be our last time together before my induction.

"Meyer," he began, "I know that your time in the army is not going to be a pleasant one. But before you go I want you to have some understanding of why you were drafted." Since he knew that I was an avid baseball fan, he made his point with a long *mashal* (parable) about baseball:

> *Imagine that you are the lowliest substitute on your team. All year long, the only time that you ever get into the game is either when your team has an insurmountable lead or when the game is hopelessly lost.*
>
> *Your team has made it into the World Series. The first six games are split three-three, and in the decisive seventh*

game your team falls three runs behind. It's the bottom of the ninth, and with two out, your team manages to load the bases and the pitcher is due up.

The manager looks up and down the bench for a pinch-hitter. All of a sudden, he points at you. You stare at him in disbelief and pantomime to make sure that he really means you. He nods his head yes. You grab for your bat, but you can barely hold it because your hands are shaking so badly.

As you walk towards the plate, you wonder if your knees are knocking together and if you look as scared as you feel. All the while you're trying to figure out what the manager could be thinking of.

Now, Meyer, you're right to be scared. But you have to know that the manager chose you for his reasons. As you stand at the plate, who do you see in the first base coach's box? Avraham Avinu. Behind second base is Yitzchak Avinu [Rabbi Schecter didn't know too much about baseball and apparently got the umpires and coaches confused], and over in the third base coach's box is Yaakov Avinu. You look up in the grandstand, and who do you see there? The Dor HaMidbar (Generation of the Desert). They're on their feet cheering for you. You look into the box seats down the first and third base lines, and you see the Tannaim and Amoraim. And in the bleachers are the Rishonim and Acharonim.

Millions of eyes are watching you; all their hopes are pinned on you. You know that you can't disappoint such a cheering squad; you've got to hit a home run.

Meyer, you have to remember that the Ribbono Shel Olam does not give someone a test that he can't pass. Every test he gives a person is within his capacity to pass. Now the Ribbono Shel Olam is sending you into the army, and it is a tremendous test. But He knows you can pass it. Just remember who is cheering for you and depending on you to succeed — all the Tannaim, Amoraim, Rishonim, and Acharonim.

With that, he gave me a *berachah* that Hashem should watch over me, put his arms around me in a bear hug, and kissed me goodbye.

TWO DAYS LATER, I WAS ON A TRAIN FROM PENN STATION to Camp Upton on Long Island. Just before leaving, I was surprised to receive a letter from the chairman of the local draft board notifying me that I had been chosen to be in charge of all the men from the local draft board on the train ride to Camp Upton. I had no idea why I had been selected, but nevertheless it gave me the feeling that the *Ribbono Shel Olam* was watching over me from the start of my army career.

Right Foot Forward

I was placed in charge of approximately one hundred men from the local draft board. For much of the three-hour ride, everyone tried to figure out why I had been placed in charge, a subject about which I was as much in the dark as they were. One wanted to know whether I had served in the reserves, another whether I was an Eagle Scout, and yet a third whether I had a relative on the local draft board.

By the time we reached Camp Upton, it was late at night, and we had missed both lunch and dinner. We were starving and exhausted. When the train stopped, the group leaders were asked to come forward and state whether all the men in their charge were accounted for. Once that was done, our careers as group leaders were over.

There must have been three thousand young men on that train, and as we got off we were herded into a huge tent where the soldier's oath of allegiance was to be administered. A loud whistle blew, and then we heard an officer's voice over the loudspeaker telling us to repeat after him the soldier's oath: "I, Meyer Birnbaum, do solemnly swear to G-d and my country, to defend the Constitution of the United States, to defend its possessions."

Having taken the oath, the voice over the loudspeaker informed us, "Congratulations, you are now soldiers in the United States Army. From now on, we can give you orders, and you must obey them."

Our first order was also our first exposure to the army slang with which we would soon become familiar: "Double time it to the mess hall and have some chow."

Despite not having eaten since morning, I was not hungry. Instead of going to the mess hall, I went to get my barracks' assignment. Each barracks had thirty bunks on a side, with a private room at the end for the non-commissioned officer in charge. Altogether there were between a hundred and a hundred and twenty soldiers in each barracks. Names were taped to every bed, and after finding mine, I lay down to try to gather my racing thoughts.

I was already homesick. It seemed to me that every face I had seen since leaving home was a gentile one, not that I considered myself any great expert in telling Jews and gentiles apart. Certainly, there were no familiar faces from my East New York neighborhood or the Young Israel of New Lots.

My feeling of being terribly out of place was hardly lessened when my fellow recruits returned to the barracks from the mess hall. We introduced ourselves. I met this Billy, and that Johnny, and a fellow named Jimmy. I was asked how I had liked my first meal in the U.S. Army and had to confess that I hadn't eaten. I made up some excuse about having eaten earlier and not having an appetite. My barracks' mates commiserated with me and began to describe in graphic detail the fantastic meal I had missed: baked ham. The consensus seemed to be that if the first meal was any indication, life in the army wouldn't be so bad after all.

After taps, the lights went out, except for a dim bulb in the latrine at the back of the barracks. I lay awake in bed, my thoughts tumultuous. I wasn't the only one. The time after lights out was known in the army as "Tear Time," as the new recruits thought about how long it would be before they would see their families again. These were boys being called upon to do men's work.

The discussion of baked ham brought home to me how many situations I would be confronted with when I would have to make decisions on the spur of the moment. For now my quandary was how I was going to put on my *tefillin* in the morning without everyone seeing me. No solution presented itself immediately, and worrying about it kept me from falling asleep.

At last, I felt my eyes closing. I took out my pocket *siddur* and walked to the window where I could read *Krias Shema al Hamittah* by the light of a street lamp outside. Before I dozed off, a solution to the *tefillin* problem came to me. I remembered that it is permissible to *daven* even before sunrise when there is no alternative (*besha'as hadechak*). Back home, some of those who had to get to work very early in the morning had come to *shul* while it was still dark outside. Based on the halachic shortcuts I had learned from *Machaneh Yisrael*, I estimated that it would take me between five and ten minutes to *daven*, and I would be done before anyone else woke up.

I waited in the dark until around four o'clock in the morning. Then I got out of bed, took out my flashlight, and started putting on my *tefillin*. It was absolutely still in the bunk. Everyone was sound asleep. As I *davened*, I thought to myself happily, "What a beautiful idea. I'm going to get away with this."

After about five minutes, I heard someone stirring. He got up to use the latrine and must have noticed my flashlight in the pitch darkness. I felt him tiptoeing closer and closer to me. Next thing I knew he woke up another soldier, and then another. In no time, the entire barracks was awake and staring at Meyer Yaakov Birnbaum.

It didn't take long for the wisecracks to start flying. "Do you see what I see?" someone called out. "Take a look, this guy is taking his blood pressure."

"No, no," another opined, "he's not sick. He's bucking for a Section 8." (A Section 8 discharge is for those found not mentally fit to serve.) By this time, I no longer needed a flashlight. The glow on my face could have lit the room.

The tumult in the barracks awakened the corporal who was sleeping in the private room. He came running in and asked what was going on. One hundred and twenty hands pointed in my direction. I was no longer *davening*, but I still had my *siddur* in my hands and my *tefillin* on.

"Soldier, what are you doing?" he asked.

"Sir."

"Don't 'sir' me. I'm only a corporal."

"Well, sir, I'm praying to my G-d."

"You're praying to your G-d? And what have you got on your head?"

"It's called phylacteries."

"And on your hand?"

"The same name."

"That's how you pray to your G-d?"

"Yes."

"Well, in that case come into my room next door."

Corporal Wilkinson took me into his room and told me, "Soldier, you can pray here, every day, as long as you're here." I thought to myself, "The *Eibishter* (One Above) is really looking out for me. I can't believe I'm getting such fast responses."

After I finished *davening*, I lay down again

My first day in Camp Upton

until reveille, when we all ran outside for morning calisthenics. By this time, I had not eaten in a day. As we entered the mess hall, I was greeted by the smell of bacon for the first time in my life. The aroma was delicious, and my salivary glands began working overtime. I was so disgusted with the thought of eating *treife* that I kept taking out my handkerchief and spitting into it.

The only thing I could eat for breakfast was a new product I had never seen before — Cheerios. No sooner had I poured the milk over the Cheerios, than I realized that I had another one of those split-second decisions on my hands: How should I make a blessing before eating? Should I just pretend to be placing my hand over my head and make a hurried blessing or should I take out the *yarmulke* in my pocket? My buddies noticed that I wasn't eating and asked me what was wrong. I could hardly explain my dilemma to them.

One of the last things Rabbi Schecter had told me was: "In

the jargon of the army, be sure to start with your right foot forward. Remember, your first step is your most important." Those words flashed into my mind. I reached into my pocket for my *yarmulke*, made a blessing and started eating. For the second time in four hours, I felt myself turning bright red as hundreds of curious soldiers gaped at me. Judging by the comments, apparently no one in the mess hall had ever seen a *yarmulke* before. Someone at the table asked me whether I was trying to cover a bald spot.

I was sitting there eating with my *yarmulke* perched on my head for what was probably no more than five minutes, but which seemed like an eternity, when I heard someone calling, "Mike, Mike." I looked around and saw my friend Schmiel Karper from the East Side.

"How did you get up the nerve to put on that *yarmulke*?" he asked me.

"Don't ask me," I replied. "I don't know."

"Well, thanks a lot, anyway," he said, as he took a *yarmulke* out of his pocket. "From here on in, I'll eat with a *yarmulke* too."

Rabbi Hutner wrote a letter of encouragement to my friend Moshe Swerdloff at the beginning of his army career. He began with a *mashal* from the laws of *treifos* (animals rendered unfit for consumption by virtue of an injury or condition from which they are certain to die within a year). If an animal falls and breaks a limb it may thereby become a *treifah*. To determine whether the limb has healed properly, the animal is placed in a stream, and forced to swim upstream. Only if it can swim against the current is it clear that the limb has healed properly and that the animal is not just being carried along. So too, wrote Rabbi Hutner, would our *Yiddishkeit* be tested in the army where we would be removed from our protective environment and forced to swim upstream. When I put on my *yarmulke* that first morning, I proved to myself that I could swim against the current, and that knowledge made the next four years in the army much easier.

After breakfast, the testing began. We took an IQ test, a Rorschach inkblot test, and others, before being interviewed by the army psychologists and psychiatrists. At the end of the whole process, we were interviewed by the officers who would assign us.

For the next week or so, things went pretty smoothly. I *davened* every morning in Corporal Wilkinson's office and no longer felt so self-conscious wearing my *yarmulke* in the mess hall. Then one morning as I was *davening,* I felt Wilkinson slip something into my pocket. When I had finished, I took the paper out of my pocket and saw that he had given me a pamphlet of excerpts from the Christian Bible.

The next morning he asked me if I had read the pamphlet. I told him that I had but that I had not understood it. That did not deter him, and he offered to explain it to me. I soon realized that Wilkinson was an enthusiastic evangelical Christian, and that as an Orthodox Jewish boy I was the most prized catch imaginable for his missionary activities.

It was then Pesach, and Wilkinson asked me why I had to eat such dry, tasteless crackers. "Do you really think the Lord Above likes you better because you make yourself suffer trying to chew these dried-out crackers?" he challenged me. "Guaranteed, He doesn't love you more. He wants you to be comfortable in this world."

I had come into the army a typical liberal-minded American boy, who had difficulty understanding some of the things about *goyim* I occasionally heard as a boy from older Jews. But as Wilkinson's proselytizing continued, I thought to myself that the next time a *goy* does something for me, I should be more careful to try to figure out his angle and what he wants from me.

IN MY INITIAL INTERVIEW AT CAMP UPTON, I MENTIONED that I knew how to type about forty words per minute. As a **Basic** consequence, I was given a job interviewing new recruits and typing up their vital statistics. Many **Training** recruits were nearly illiterate, and anything they wrote down themselves was unintelligible. I did this for about three months before being replaced by WACs (Women's Army Corps).

As a reward for having helped out for three months, my supervising officer told me that I could go into any corps that I wanted. He started listing the various possibilities: infantry, armored, cavalry, artillery, and so on. When he finished, he told me, "Now take your choice. Where do you want to go?"

I was pretty friendly with this officer and replied, "I'd like to go home."

"The joke is over," he said. "You're in the army now. Just tell me where you want to go."

I told him that I would prefer some place as close to home as possible, and he asked me how Fort Monmouth in New Jersey sounded. I found out that Fort Monmouth was connected to the Signal Corps. When I asked what that was, my officer said, "Well, there's equipment like the teletype that requires typing, and it's a nice clean job. I definitely suggest that you go there." So Fort Monmouth and the Signal Corps it was.

After completing basic training at Fort Monmouth, I was sent to Camp Edison, about eight miles away, for further training. The High Holidays were drawing near, and the captain in charge of my group noticed on my records that I was a divinity student. Since there were no Jewish chaplains available, he asked me to lead the Rosh Hashanah *davening,* which I did. The captain also asked me to lead the *davening* for Yom Kippur, but this time I did not accept immediately. I was friendly with him and decided to do a little bargaining.

"What's in it for me?" I asked him.

"What do you want?" he replied.

I had gotten to know Rabbi Abba Zalka Gewirtz, who later became the vice-president of Telshe Yeshiva in Wickliffe, Ohio, and who at that time had a *shul* in Bradley Beach, and I requested permission to *daven Ne'ilah* at his *shul.*

My request was granted. I explained to the captain that I could not carry a pass out of the base and that he should inform the Military Police along the way that I was allowed to travel without a pass to Bradley Beach. At camp, I led practically the entire *Kol Nidrei, Maariv, Shacharis, Mussaf,* and *Minchah davening,* with some help from another soldier. After *Minchah,* I headed towards Bradley Beach. At the outpost, the guard greeted me and asked if I was Private Birnbaum. Informed that I was, he told me that they would be looking out for me until I got to Bradley Beach.

The walk to Bradley Beach was several miles. When I entered the *shul,* Rabbi Gewirtz motioned for me to join him up front.

That was the last thing I remember. When I awoke, I was being treated by a doctor in the rabbi's house, with his wife hovering anxiously nearby. The sudden contrast between the fresh air outside and the crowded, stuffy *shul*, especially after fasting all day, leading the *davening* and the long walk, was too much for me, and I had fainted as soon as I entered the *shul*.

CHAPTER FOUR

Second Lieutenant

WHEN I ARRIVED BACK AT CAMP EDISON, MY captain approached me and said, "You know, Private Birnbaum,

Officer Training School

your IQ is not too bad."

"So what is it?" I replied.

"That we can't tell you."

"Then why bring it up at all?"

"For the simple reason that you have a number of problems. Everyone knows that you have a problem praying in the morning. And you have a problem eating. You hardly eat anything. And I was just thinking, since you have the IQ, that I might recommend you for OCS."

"What's OCS?"

"Officer Candidate School. After three months, you come out as what they call a ninety-day wonder. That means you become a second lieutenant like any West Point graduate after four years. It's very intense, but you may be able to make it."

"So how do I apply?"

"Well, first we'll have to recommend you, then you'll be

interviewed by three officers. If they decide that you are potential officer material, you may be accepted."

Two weeks later, I received a notice that I was to report on October 20 to Officer Candidate School in Fort Monmouth. The course was unbelievably intense. Classes ran continuously from eight-thirty in the morning until six in the evening. One had to sign in for every meal because it was known that otherwise the candidates would skip meals in order to find a few extra minutes for cramming. From six until nine-thirty, one could study, and then it was lights out. There was not enough time in the day to absorb everything thrown at us. All night long, the guys rotated in forty-five-minute shifts studying by the light in the latrine. When one had finished, he woke up his buddy so that he could grab the extra time for studying. With my two years of nighttime accounting courses at the 23rd Street campus of City College of New York, I found myself thrown in with men who had college degrees, MAs and PhDs.

At the end of the first month, one-third of the group was eliminated. We were asked to list those in our group in the order of their ability to succeed as an officer in the Signal Corps. Those evaluations and the results from the various tests we took formed the basis of the first elimination. My luck held out through the first cut.

A month later, another third were weeded out. To my surprise, I was selected by my fellow candidates as the one most likely to succeed as an army officer and voted the class captain. That meant that the men had to salute me, even though I was still only a corporal.

THE COURSES BECAME EVEN MORE GRUELING AS THE third month progressed. Finally, I had only two weeks to go until I would receive my commission as a second **Court-martial** lieutenant. As I was eating in the mess one day, with my *yarmulke* on as always, a West Point graduate named Lieutenant Jones walked in. He had been at Pearl Harbor when the Japanese attacked and was left too shell-shocked for a combat unit. So he had been reassigned to teach tactics in OCS.

In any event, this Lieutenant Jones strode right up to me, stared at the *yarmulke* and then at my name tag on the left side of my jacket, and addressed me. "Corporal Birnbaum, are you familiar with an army regulation governing the entry into a building or other enclosed structure, such as a tent?"

"Yes, sir!"

"Corporal Birnbaum, can you tell me the number of that army regulation?"

" Yes, sir. That regulation is 270-1."

"Excellent, Corporal Birnbaum. Report to my office immediately after chow."

I finished eating and went to Lieutenant Jones' office. I saluted, and he returned the salute and told me to stand at ease. Then looking me straight in the eye, he told me, "You know, Corporal Birnbaum, I think you would make the world's worst officer, and I am bringing you up for a court-martial to have you dismissed immediately from OCS." I asked him why he felt I was not officer material, and he replied that someone who knew the regulation against head-coverings indoors and deliberately ignored it was not fit to lead others. "Within the next few hours," Lieutenant Jones continued, "someone from the Judge Advocate General's office will contact you to help you prepare a defense." I saluted him, made an about face, and went back to my barracks.

My mind was racing. For two and a half months, I had been torturing myself so that I could be an officer, studying far harder than I had ever studied before. And now, I thought to myself, I'm out just because of my *yarmulke*. I tried to console myself that it had been a good experience while it lasted and to remember that if I wasn't going to be an officer the *Ribbono Shel Olam* must have his reasons. But it was a bitter pill to swallow nevertheless.

As I lay in my bunk that evening, still stewing in my own thoughts, my defense counsel, a nice Jewish boy from the Bronx, walked in. He assured me that he had figured out any number of ways to beat the charges and that he would have me back in OCS by the end of the next day. I could not imagine what kind of defense there could be to the charge of knowingly violating an army regulation, but found myself buoyed by his confidence. As he explained his strategy, however, my hopes sagged again.

Basically, my attorney's plan consisted of my telling the court that I had not really known of a regulation concerning covering one's head inside and that I had only taken a wild guess when Lieutenant Jones asked me whether I was familiar with a regulation on the subject. "It's a white lie. You're not hurting anyone," he assured me.

"Tell me the difference between a white lie, a red one, and a black one," I challenged him. "Even if you don't hurt anyone, it's still a lie, isn't it?"

"Yeah, but you've finished two-and-a-half months. I looked through your record. You've got just two weeks to go and you'll be an officer. You can't afford to give that up."

"That all depends on the price. I'm not going to lie."

"*Oy*, I see I've got a tough customer. Well, tell them that you just took a wild guess at that number 270-1. Even Lieutenant Jones doesn't know it wasn't a wild guess."

"But I know it. Isn't that enough?"

"That's just the point. Only you know it. Just say it, and you'll be able to finish in two weeks."

I turned him down.

The next morning the court-martial convened. The presiding officer was a colonel, who was flanked by two captains. After Lieutenant Jones told his story, the colonel turned to my attorney and asked him whether he was prepared to present a defense. My lawyer answered sheepishly, "Not really." When the colonel asked him whether he had met with me, he told him that he had, but that I was not putting up a defense.

At that point, the presiding judge looked at me and urged me to get together with my attorney and to let him take care of me. "I've looked through your record in OCS, and it's a good one," he told me. "It would be a shame if you didn't defend yourself." Then he declared a ten-minute smoke break, and urged us again to think up some kind of defense.

During those ten minutes, I was completely occupied with the question: Why did Hashem put me through the grind of two-and-a-half months in OCS if He knew I wasn't going to be an officer? I didn't yet realize that the whole court-martial was a custom-made *nisayon* (test) for me.

When the court reconvened, the presiding colonel asked me whether I was ready to present a defense. I answered that I would like to say something, even though it was not directly related to my defense. The colonel looked surprised but granted my request. I began, still not quite sure where I was going:

"Nine months ago, upon my entry into the United States Army, I took the soldier's oath. At that time, I swore to 'G-d and my country, to defend the Constitution of the United States of America.' Our forefathers, who composed that oath, put G-d before country, not vice versa. When I put on a *yarmulke* to eat, I did the same thing."

My defense took the judges completely off guard. The colonel who was presiding looked to the two captains for confirmation that my description of the soldier's oath was indeed accurate. "How the devil does that oath go? Is this man quoting it accurately?" he asked. Told that I was, he looked at me and said, "I never heard of someone winning his case without a defense. But you just did, Corporal Birnbaum. Now get back to class."

Two weeks later, I graduated from OCS as a second lieutenant. My diploma listed twenty-three different areas we had covered and been tested on. From even a quick glance at the list of courses, you can see why I had been so miserable about being court-martialed with graduation only two weeks away and after having worked so hard.

MY FIRST ASSIGNMENT AS A SECOND LIEUTENANT WAS in Philadelphia, where I was to take a five-month course in the

More Training use of the sigabra machine for encoding our own messages and decoding those of the enemy. My schooling was being extended into the second year of my army career.

The sigabra machine was highly classified, and before I was chosen, the FBI did a thorough background investigation on me. I only found this out when neighbors of my parents told them that men were going around to the pool halls of East New York asking about me. In those days, the ball games were transmitted by ticker tape to the pool halls, and there was a fair amount of

EASTERN SIGNAL CORPS SCHOOLS
UNITED STATES ARMY
Fort Monmouth, Red Bank, N. J.

THIS IS TO CERTIFY THAT

MEYER J. BIRNBAUM

has satisfactorily completed the prescribed
OFFICER CANDIDATE COURSE
at Eastern Signal Corps Schools during the period
October 22, 1942, to January 19, 1943,
covering the following subjects:

International Morse Alphabet and Radio Procedure
Military Law
Military Sanitation and First Aid
Military Courtesy and Customs of the Service
Defense Against Chemical Attack
Weapons
Signal Supply
Administration
Mess Management
Map and Aerial Photograph Reading
Organization, Tactics, and Signal Communication of Larger Units
Identification of Aircraft and Vehicles
Motor Transport
Tactics and Technique of Signal Communication
Wire Communication
Radio Communication
Training Management
Interior Guard Duty
Safeguarding Military Information
Rules of Land Warfare
Elements of Electricity
Classification Procedure and Army Postal Service

W O Reeder

Colonel, Signal Corps,
Commandant.

January 19, 1943

My OCS citation listing all the courses I had taken

gambling conducted there. The FBI wanted to make sure that I was not someone who might run up large gambling debts, and thereby become susceptible to selling top secret information. When they had finished with the local pool halls, the FBI agents also queried many of the local rabbis about me.

I arrived in Philadelphia late on *erev Shabbos,* and asked the first cabby I could find to take me to the nearest synagogue. He dropped me at a synagogue in North Philadelphia. I inquired as to where the rabbi lived and was directed to the house next door. I ran in, introduced myself, and asked whether I could stay for Shabbos, all the while apologizing profusely for having arrived so late. The rabbi's wife welcomed me warmly.

When the rabbi walked in, I don't know what possessed me, but I asked him about the *kashrus* of the home. He replied that the synagogue was a Conservative one but that his home was kosher. Despite this assurance, the realization that he was a Conservative rabbi made me nervous and I asked whether there was any place where I could get *glatt* kosher meat. He candidly admitted that his was not the address and sent me to a Rabbi Potash who lived nearby. I left my bags at the first house and ran to the home of Rabbi Potash.

Rabbi Potash welcomed me with open arms. He himself was a *shochet* and put me at ease that everything in the home was *glatt* kosher. For the next five months, I lived with the Potash family. The rabbi treated me like a son that entire time and the rebbetzin filled me with delicious food that I can still picture to this day. When I left at the end of completing my course in encoding and decoding at the Signal Intelligence School, it was with a great deal of sadness.

While in Philadelphia, I often ate Shabbos meals with the Lipshitz and Weinberg families. Chaim Uri Lipshitz, who was slightly older than I, remains a friend to this day, as does Irwin Weinberg. The latter was drafted shortly after I was, and we met again in England in preparation for the Normandy invasion. Nearly fifty years later, I had the chance to repay his family's hospitality when his grandson became a *ben bayis* by us while studying in yeshiva in Jerusalem.

WITH THE COMPLETION OF THE COURSE, I WAS ASSIGNED to the outfit with which I would be going into combat, the 59th

Saturday Night Wallflower

Signal Battalion. The Signal Battalion consisted of close to nine hundred men and was capable of doing every aspect of the work of the Signal Corps, from telegraph to telephone to intelligence work. We were known as the eyes and ears of the army. Among our various duties were taking aerial reconnaissance pictures and interpreting them for the intelligence services. One of the reasons that I have so many pictures from my army years is that for a period of time I was with one of the picture-taking outfits.

I reported to Fort Jackson, South Carolina. My senior officer was Major (later Colonel) Mailman, a member of what used to be known as the Boston Brahmins, the Boston aristocracy that lived secure in the knowledge that their ancestors had come over on the Mayflower. In civilian life, he was a top executive in the Boston-area phone company.

At our first interview, Major Mailman mentioned to me that I would be the only Jewish officer in the outfit. "Oh, incidentally,"

Driving a jeep at Fort Jackson

he added at the end of the interview, "this Friday night you'll pull OD (officer on duty)." As I knew from my officer's training course, that meant I had to stay up all Friday night, with responsibility for the battalion until Major Mailman woke up in the morning.

I was uncomfortable starting my duties by requesting a special exemption, but nevertheless asked Major Mailman whether I could take OD another night. He asked why, and I explained that Friday night is the Jewish Sabbath. He thought quickly and asked whether I had any objection to Saturday-night duty. I told him that I didn't. Major Mailman then worked out one of those deals from which everyone benefits. I would take OD every Saturday night in return for which I would never have to work on Shabbos or Jewish holidays. Saturday night was the night that everyone was most eager to leave the base, and the major was delighted to have someone to take OD duty every Saturday night, especially since officers normally pulled OD only once every other week. It was not the last time that my fellow officers would find it convenient to have an Orthodox Jew as an officer in the battalion.

MY FIRST SATURDAY NIGHT I WAS SITTING IN THE MAJOR'S office filling out reports when a captain walked in and **A New Friend** introduced himself as Captain McVay. He was the only medical doctor for the entire battalion. Since McVay outranked me, I remained standing as long as he did. Eventually he sat down, and we began talking.

"The rumor around here is that you're pulling permanent OD every Saturday night. A young fellow like you — it doesn't make sense."

"Well, I have no reason to go out."

"Movies?"

"I don't go to movies."

"How about dates, dances? The Officers Club in Columbia, South Carolina is a beautiful place. They have dances there all night long on Saturday night."

"I realize that, but it's not my cup of tea." ("It's not my cup of tea"

Since I couldn't play an instrument, the men let me pretend I was conducting.
On the drums is Rojo, my right-hand man throughout the war.
He had played professionally with Xavier Cugat.

would become a constant refrain throughout my entire army career.)

"How come?"

"Well, I've got a few idiosyncrasies, and one of them is that I don't go out."

"Is it for religious reasons?"

"Yes."

"Oh, I admire you for it."

From that night on my friendship with Captain McVay grew steadily. He was the oldest man in the battalion and a good family man, so he had no more interest in going out on Saturday night than I did. Every Saturday night he kept me company. He taught me how to play bridge, and I taught him how to play chess. He served as a constant protector. No one could poke fun at me with him around. If anyone teased me in his presence, he became furious and put that person in his place.

One morning I sat down to breakfast in the Officers' Mess and found a dozen bananas and several dry cereals on my plate. McVay had gone around to the other officers telling them, "Look, Birnie doesn't eat anything else — no bacon or any other meat.

At least let him eat all the bananas and cereal he can."

The army has a rigid hierarchy and second lieutenants do not normally share quarters with captains. McVay, however, put in a request with Major Mailman that we share a little room, with just enough space for a bunk bed and two clothes lockers. He explained to me, "I see that whenever you put on those straps, guys are disturbing you, and you can't really pray properly. If you come into my room, no one will bother you. I guarantee that." And he was as good as his word. Whenever someone came to the room while I was *davening*, he would tell him, "Beat it. Birnie is praying to his G-d." I no longer had to rely on any shortcuts in my *davening*.

The Officers' Jew

THERE WAS AN OFFICERS' CLUB ON BASE WHERE THE officers would drink and play cards. The prices for a shot of whiskey or other alcoholic beverages were supposedly calculated so that there would be enough money in the kitty to constantly replenish the liquor supply. The problem was that there was never enough money left over, and it was suspected that some of the liquor was being siphoned off. Since I didn't drink, I was chosen to become the purchasing agent for the club, with responsibility for collecting payments from all the officers.

A short time later, hams started disappearing from the Officers' Mess. It was suspected that the officer in charge was giving them as presents to his girlfriend or selling them on the black market. Since there was no concrete evidence, they were unwilling to confront him directly. Instead they just called for a vote to choose a new officer to be in charge of the officers' mess. Again, I was the obvious choice. I had no interest in this job either, but my friend McVay pointed out that it would not be without its benefits. "You can have all the fruit you want," he told me. "No one is going to complain. And that favorite of yours — that fruit cocktail you're always eating — you can take as much as you want. If the bacon or the hams are missing, they'll complain about that. But we know we can trust you because you wouldn't touch it with a ten-foot pole."

Surrounded by the non-commissioned officers under my command

Actually the job of supervising the Officers' Mess did almost get me into trouble. Shortly after I took over the position, there was an outbreak of ptomaine poisoning in my outfit, and I was virtually the only one who did not get sick. The fact that I was one of the few to remain healthy and had access to the kitchen cast a great deal of suspicion on me, until the source of the poisoning was discovered: spoiled canned ham. At that point, my fellow officers told the MPs investigating the case that for religious reasons I did not eat anything except raw vegetables or those directly from the can and that was why I had been unaffected by the ham.

That fall we conducted maneuvers in Tennessee where there were large open spaces that allowed for simulated war games. For the first time, I had the experience of leading the men I had been training over the last several months in actual combat situations.

For Yom Kippur, I traveled to Nashville, where there was a large Orthodox synagogue. On arriving in Nashville, I went to

Myself with some of the other shomer Shabbos soldiers at Fort Jackson

the synagogue to make arrangements for sleeping. I was starved, after not having eaten all day, and very relieved when a Dr. Makovsky, who was originally from St. Louis and was then a major stationed in the army hospital in Nashville, invited me home for the large meal before the fast. I was surprised to see both my host and his sons wearing *yarmulkes* on the street, something that was very rare in those days outside of New York City. In *shul* I also met Isaac Candiotti, a friend of mine from East New York. When I was growing up, Isaac was one of the few Sephardi boys I knew, and he was an exceptionally sweet person. After the long Yom Kippur *davening*, Dr. Makovsky invited Isaac and me to his home to break the fast.

We spent two months on maneuvers before returning to Ft. Jackson. By that time, there were a number of Jewish boys on the

Velvel Sussman

base. There was Moish Gershbaum, a lawyer, Velvel Sussman from Williamsburg, my old friend Schmiel Karper from the East Side, and a fellow by the name of Tulli Gewirtz. Velvel's family had only been in the country a few years, but his father was already the best-known *sofer* in Williamsburg. Because Velvel still retained a heavy Yiddish accent, he was mercilessly teased by his fellow soldiers, and being among a group of *frum* Jews was a welcome respite for him. We ate every *Shalosh Seudos* together in my room. McVay seemed happy to see me together with friends and I was able to get whatever we needed — fruit cocktail, sardines — from the Officers' Mess. Eventually we had a whole *minyan* of *shomer Shabbos* guys who didn't go off the post on Shabbos. Occasionally, we would go for meals to Rabbi Kolitch in Charleston, which was not too far away.

THIS SEMI-IDYLLIC SITUATION DIDN'T LAST TOO LONG. In November of 1943 we received a red alert that we were not

McVay's Betrayal

allowed to leave the base at all. That night the men were confined to the barracks, and the officers were called together for an emergency meeting in the Officers' Club. Military Police surrounded the Officers' Club to ensure that nothing was overheard.

Major Mailman addressed us while standing on a table. "Gentlemen," he began, "the time has come to pay back the United States government for what it has cost them up until now to turn you guys into officers. At this point I'm not sure whether we'll be going to the Pacific or the Atlantic. Nevertheless, the alert is on. The men can no longer send any sealed mail. All mail that is sealed will be destroyed. Officers must read all letters and censor anything they feel is improper."

While Major Mailman was speaking, the men were all drinking, except McVay and me. But as the major continued, McVay too reached out for a drink. Within ten minutes, he swallowed three shot glasses of whiskey, and not being used to drinking, he immediately began acting up and tugging at the major's pants leg and asking for permission to speak. Major Mailman warned him, "Mac, you better behave," but he just kept pulling at the major's pants leg and wouldn't let him speak. Finally, someone suggested that we hear what he had to say so that the major could get on with his presentation. So Major Mailman turned to McVay and said, "Okay, Mac, tell us what you want to say. What's so important?"

Speaking like he had marbles in his mouth, McVay blurted out, "Why the devil do we have to fight this Jew war? Let them fight their own war!" Major Mailman tried to shut him up, telling him, "What's wrong with you? Birnie's right next to you." But McVay only responded, "I know Birnie. I know he's Jewish, but he's different from all the others."

I felt like I had been slugged hard in the stomach. I remembered being told once that when someone tells you, "You're different," then you know you are in the presence of a true anti-Semite. Major Mailman said to me, "Birnie, you know he's drunk. Take him back to the barracks and put him to sleep."

Still in a state of shock, I grabbed McVay under the arm and started walking him back to the barracks. He was swaying to and fro like any drunkard, and it was no easy matter keeping him upright. Then I thought to myself, "Why am I bothering to hold up this anti-Semite? That isn't my job." I just straightened out my arm and he fell to the ground like a sack of potatoes. That night McVay slept on the ground where I dropped him.

Until the moment that McVay started spewing forth his hatred of Jews, I had been a typical American kid, with limited exposure to blatant anti-Semitism. As a young man, I had cringed whenever I heard older Jews speak of non-Jews as anti-Semites and of atrocities that had been perpetrated against the Jews. Suddenly I found my whole attitude changing.

Looking back now, I realize that there was something terribly naive about my assumption that anti-Semitism was virtually non-

Target practice at Fort Jackson

existent in America. On the other hand, my reaction to the anti-Semitic McVay was also perhaps a little simplistic. There is no question that the man had befriended and protected me. He had no reason to stay in every Saturday night keeping me company or to go to the lengths he did to make sure I had as much to eat as possible. The funniest thing of all, I realize now, is that he really did respect me for being a religious Jew and sticking to my principles. But that more nuanced view of McVay would not come for many years. At the time, all I felt was an overwhelming sense of betrayal — that I had been deceived by someone whom I thought I could trust.

The next morning at breakfast, we learned that a special courier had arrived during the night to inform Major Mailman that we would be shipping out overseas very soon and should complete all preparations. That meant that we had to go through a whole series of inoculations for every possible type of disease. My immunization card at the time showed fourteen shots for different types of diseases to which we might be exposed. They didn't call us human pin cushions for nothing.

Before we began the inoculations, I went to Major Mailman and asked for permission to take my shots with another outfit so I wouldn't have to receive them from McVay. He tried to convince me that McVay hadn't meant one word he said when he was drunk, but when I persisted, he granted my request.

Three days later, I found myself on a train going north to Fort Dix, New Jersey, which would be our embarkation point for England. From Fort Dix, we would be sailing in a heavily guarded convoy to England, where we would prepare for the invasion of France.

CHAPTER FIVE
Preparing for War

England SHIPPED OUT FOR ENGLAND ON A TROOP carrier by the name of The Aquitannia. We were part of a well protected, seventy-eight-ship convoy. On all sides were destroyers and even a battleship or two.

The entire journey took two weeks, in large part because of the route we took to lessen the threat from German U-boats. We first headed north hugging the Canadian coastline, before sailing across the Atlantic through the iceberg region. There the U-boats were much less inclined to harass convoys for fear of running into icebergs. Most of an iceberg is submerged under water, and thus the U-boats could not operate freely.

The seas in November were very choppy, and to make matters worse, we followed a zig-zag route because of the icebergs and in order to make it more difficult for the U-boats to track us. As a consequence, I was seasick the entire journey and unable to hold down any food.

After landing in Scotland, near Edinburgh, we took a train down to Kittyminster, England, where I was able to call Moshe

*Left to right: Moreinu Reb Yaakov Rosenheim (President of World Agudah),
Rabbi Moshe Blau (head of Agudath Israel in Eretz Yisrael), and Harry Goodman
(head of Agudath Israel of England)*

Swerdloff, my closest friend from East New York. Moshe was a top sergeant, then working for Lend Lease as an accountant. He had already been in England for some time and was familiar with the religious community. He gave me a quick run-down of every place that one could go for a kosher meal. By that time, a good meal was just about the most important thing on my mind.

Looking at a map, Moshe told me that the closest major Jewish community was in Birmingham, and that the address there was 16 Constance Road, the home of Rabbi Reuven Rabinowitz. "In Manchester, which is a little further away than Birmingham," Moshe continued, "you can go to Gadol Halperin or to Yankel or Gedaliah Rabinowitz, Rabbi Reuven Rabinowitz's brothers. And in London the address is Mr. Harry Goodman. His house is wide open at any hour. Even if Mrs. Goodman is not in, the maid will take care of you."

Harry Goodman was, together with *Moreinu Reb* Yaakov Rosenheim — who was then in America — and Rabbi Moshe Blau in Israel, one of the three pillars of World Agudath Israel. (In those days there was not yet an indigenous Agudath Israel movement in America other than Zeirei Agudath Israel under Mike Tress.) In addition to his duties as Treasurer of World Agudah, Harry Goodman singlehandedly wrote most of the weekly Agudah newspaper in England. He was a wealthy suit manufacturer, who supplied uniforms for the British army during the war.

The *hachnassas orchim* in the Goodman house was extraordinary. His wife Miriam was an aristocratic woman, who ran an immaculate house. Her home was the first place where I ate with a cloth napkin. In East New York all we ever had were paper napkins. Mrs. Goodman did not just feed the visiting soldiers, she served them gourmet meals. With every meal there was soup, one or two side dishes, the main course, dessert, and tea. Tea, I soon learned, went with everything in England, and until this day tea and milk remains my favorite drink.

Through the Goodmans, I also met Reb Gedaliah Schwartz. Reb Gedaliah was a one-man charitable foundation. I think he was the *gabbai tzedakah* for Harry Goodman, but if so, that was only a part of his charitable activities. People from all over England used to give him money for his various projects. He was a refugee from Czechoslovakia, who did not speak a word of English.

Reb Gedaliah was an extremely warm person. When he greeted someone, he didn't just shake hands, but would engulf him in a bear hug. You had to be careful when he did that. Even though he looked rather corpulent in his huge *kapote*, that appearance was mostly the result of the veritable grocery store of rationed items, including whole chickens, he carried around with him. When he grabbed you, you were in constant danger of cracking the raw eggs that he kept in various pockets. Every time he saw me, Reb Gedaliah would pull an egg out of his pocket and give it to me. When he gave you an egg, he had the look — and rightly so — of someone doing you the greatest imaginable favor.

I became something of a regular at Reb Gedaliah's house during my trips to London. One day he cornered me and started speaking to me in rapid Yiddish about the upcoming invasion of

France. "I'm sure the *Eibishter* will bless you with *hatzlachah* (success). If you should happen to get to Czechoslovakia, please keep your eyes open for my dearest childhood friend Yechiel Roth, the Sulka *Rav*. Tell him that I escaped and am alive and well in London. Perhaps you'll even be able to bring us together."

The name Roth was easy to remember since it was my mother's maiden name, but I thought it a bit peculiar that he was asking me to look up a friend in Czechoslovakia, as if I were going on vacation and not into battle. Nevertheless, I humored Reb Gedaliah and told him, "Okay, if I come across him." Little did I dream at the time that I would one day be the means of reuniting the two childhood friends.

MY FAVORITE HOME FROM DECEMBER 1943 TO MAY 1944, when the intensive preparations for the D-day landing at

A Home Away From Home

Normandy began, was the Rabinowitzs' in Birmingham. The warmth that radiated in that house is beyond my power to describe. I know that I speak for many other Orthodox servicemen when I say that we were treated like members of the family and that the Rabinowitz children — Lorna, Avraham Hirsh and Elya David — were like younger siblings to us.

Rebbetzin Sarah Rabinowitz seemed to take my skinny build as a personal affront and did everything she could to fatten me up. Both eggs and milk were rationed items, usually available only for children under a certain age, but she would give me some of the younger children's eggs.

At night, the Rebbetzin would warm a large stone in the fireplace, wrap it in a towel and place it at our feet to keep us warm. There was no central heating in England in those days, and it could get good and cold in Birmingham.

The Rebbetzin was the daughter of the Sunderlander Rav, Rabbi Moshe Eliezer Rabinowitz, her husband's oldest brother. He had been a *chavrusa* of Reb Elchonon Wasserman, *Hy'd*, and was considered one of England's greatest scholars. Through my friendship with his daughter and brother's family, I had the privilege of visiting him several times in Sunderland, England.

Rabbi Reuven Rabinowitz

His face shone, and I will never forget the almost angelic purity I saw in him.

Rabbi Reuven Rabinowitz was an extremely distinguished-looking tall man, with a short, neatly trimmed beard. Though his bearing and appearance were aristocratic, he was very down-to-earth. It was easy to talk to him; he made you feel like he was your buddy.

The house was always full of soldiers, especially on Sundays when there was invariably a large contingent for lunch. One of those I met there was Captain Moshe Sandhaus, a *musmach* of Mesivta Torah Vodaath. He always came with a dentist whose name I can't recall. Jack Genauer from Seattle and Captain Moshe Gibber from Kiamesha Lake, New York, were other regulars. While he was in England, Moshe's mother passed away. I remember being very impressed by the efforts he made to round up a *minyan* so that he could say *Kaddish,* even though he had brothers in America who were also saying *Kaddish.* East New York was represented by Max Brand and my buddy Moshe Swerdloff, in addition to myself.

Rebbetzin Rabinowitz had a younger, single brother named Ruby. Ruby was an excellent chess player. For entertainment, we used to watch him beat the pants off Max Brand. Max fancied himself a good chess player — and in fact he could beat all the rest of us — but he never won a game with Ruby.

I spent Pesach of 1944 with the Rabinowitzs. I was able to get a little time off before the festival to help with the preparations. The way the family *kashered* the silverware for Pesach fascinated me. They would take a long string and tie it individually around thirty-five pieces of silverware, each one separated from the pieces on either side of it. The string was then lowered piece by piece into a large boiling pot and then rinsed off in cold water. I still employ this method today.

ONE SPRING DAY IN 1944, THE PHONE RANG IN THE
Rabinowitz home. The house was, as usual, full of American

Miracle in Air
servicemen. Suddenly we heard Rabbi
Rabinowitz repeating over and over, "Yes,
sir. Yes, sir. Yes, sir!" After another fifteen "yes, sirs," he hung up
the phone looking completely bewildered.

"You must have been drafted, Rabbi, judging from all the
'sirring' you've been doing for the last fifteen minutes," we teased
him. "Who were you 'sirring'?"

Rabbi Rabinowitz told us that his caller had been no less than
a general in the Royal Canadian Air Force. Fifteen minutes later,
the general walked in, together with a nineteen-year-old Jewish
boy, who looked like he had barely begun to shave. The boy was
no more than 5'4" tall, which contributed further to his air of
extreme youth. (I later learned that he had volunteered at
seventeen for the Royal Canadian Air Force because he was so
eager to fight against Hitler. He had originally wanted to be a
pilot, but was too short to comfortably reach the floor pedals,
with which planes were largely controlled in those days.)

We all stood there, our mouths agape, wondering what could
have brought the general and his young charge to Rabbi
Rabinowitz's house. We did not have to wait long to find out.

At that time, all bombing raids against German targets in
France were being carried out by Canadian Halifax-2 bombers
and American bombers. Virtually all British bombers had been
destroyed in the Battle of Britain in 1941. The Canadian planes
handled all the night missions, which they flew without lights
so as not to attract the attention of German Messerschmidts
patrolling the skies over France. The Halifax had a maximum
speed of no more that 150 to 175 miles per hour, less than half
that of the Messerschmidts.

The boy was a rear gunner, which meant that he sat in the
rear of the plane surrounded by glass. His job was twofold: to
direct the pilot which way to turn to evade any Messerschmidts
that were spotted, and to handle one of the three guns in case of
dogfights. The rear gunner was always the first target in any
skirmish because he was the eyes of the plane. The rear window
could be opened manually, and on their bombing runs the boy

used to drop out Yiddish newspapers sent to him from Toronto so that the Germans would know it was a Jew up there taking revenge.

Two nights earlier, on one of their bombing runs over France, they had encountered a large number of Messerschmidts. As a consequence, their plane was nearly out of gas by the time they approached their home base near Birmingham. Unfortunately for them, being low on gas gave them only a fourth priority to land behind more serious problems like an engine on fire.

After some time circling the airfield, the pilot realized that they were completely out of gas and tried to bring the plane down, but he erred in reading his altimeter, and ended up crash-landing fifteen miles from base. The plane hit the ground, rolled between two houses, narrowly averting both, and ended up in a nearby marsh. The plane was split completely in half by the impact — the landing wheels were never recovered — and many of the crew knocked unconscious or left with broken limbs.

The rear gunner, however, had escaped with no broken bones. He set out on foot in the pitch dark to call for help from the base, with only his sense of direction to guide him. Nearly three hours later, close to daybreak, he arrived at the base. Those on duty reacted as if they had seen a ghost. German Messerschmidts often followed bombers back across the channel, and when their plane had lost radio contact it was assumed that it had been shot down.

After describing the location of the plane, the exhausted boy was given a sedative and put to sleep. He did not awaken for another twenty-four hours. When he did, his first request was to be taken to Rabbi Rabinowitz. Since he was the hero of the hour, his request was granted, and he was even escorted there by a general. When he walked in, his first request was that Rabbi Rabinowitz teach him *Tehillim*.

The story of how he had come to ask for Rabbi Rabinowitz is itself an interesting one. Just a few weeks earlier, after flying three or four missions, he had been given some time for rest and relaxation. Suddenly he had been filled with some sort of premonition, and decided that he wanted to go to *shul*. Though he had been raised by Orthodox grandparents, and had some sort of religious education up until his bar mitzvah, since joining the air force his religious involvement had grown increasingly less intense, to the point that when he arrived in *shul* that day he was surprised to learn that it was the first day of Pesach. In *shul,* he was invited home for a holiday meal by Ben Winter, a son-in-law of the Sunderlander Rav and Rabbi Rabinowitz's brother-in-law. Out of that invitation to the Winter home came a visit to the Sunderlander Rav. The Rav spent four hours talking to the boy, much of the time devoted to the importance of the *mitzvah* of *tefillin.*

From the time his plane crashed, the boy was completely transformed. He was filled with an unquenchable thirst for learning and became fully *shomer mitzvos.* He ended his military career as a captain, after having flown the maximum thirty-four combat missions and winning the Distinguished Flying Cross for his heroism after the crash. After being discharged, he decided to stay on in England for another six months. During that time, he worked with Reb Gedaliah Schwartz, who had organized a group of women who prepared food parcels for survivors in the DP camps. Those parcels were sent to me in Buchenwald and later Feldafing thirty at a time through the U.S. Army mail.

Today every one of that boy's children is a *ben Torah* or married to a *ben Torah,* and in addition to helping them, he supports several other families of *bnei Torah.* He himself forgoes every luxury — and many things the rest of us consider necessities — in order to continually purchase additional pieces of the World-to-Come. I guess that comes from realizing that every moment of your life for the last fifty years is only by virtue of a miracle that Hashem did for you when you were nineteen.

UNTIL THE FIRST WEEK OF MAY 1944, WE WENT THROUGH our exercises without any idea of when the invasion would take

Preparation for D-Day

place. All we knew was that a great deal would depend on the weather. Only General Eisenhower and a few other members of the Allied High Command had any inkling of the projected time of the invasion.

Our first clue that something might be up came the second

week of May when we were confined to base and informed that we could no longer write letters home. Then on May 30, all the officers who would be taking part in the invasion were ordered to Southhampton to be addressed by the top brass for the first and only time before the invasion.

There was a large open field in the middle of which a makeshift stage about the size of a boxing ring had been placed. When we had all gathered, someone yelled, "Attention," and all the generals who would be leading the

General Charles de Gaulle

invasion walked in: General Eisenhower, the Supreme Allied Commander; General Montgomery, commander of the British forces; General de Gaulle, who would be leading the small contingent of the Free French forces; General Omar Bradley, who would be directing the actual operation from offshore, and General George Patton, commander of the Third Army.

General Eisenhower spoke first. He talked about all that had been invested so far in preparing us for the invasion and the sacred mission for which we had been chosen: to rid the world of a demonic madman. At the very end of his speech, he grew solemn, as he said, " I know, as I look at you, that some of you will not make it to the beach. Some of you will make it to the beach, but won't get any further. And others will fall on the soil of France. That is what war is all about. We can't expect miracles. But I want to wish you G-dspeed."

General Montgomery spoke next and basically echoed "Ike's" sentiments. DeGaulle referred to the small French force with which he had fled from Dunkirk to England and which would now be fighting to recapture its homeland.

General Bradley was introduced next. "I'm sure we all listened to what General Eisenhower said," he began, "but I want you to know one thing. I'll try to keep casualties as low as possible."

The last to speak was "Blood and Guts" Patton. Perhaps he sensed that the officers might have been demoralized by Eisenhower's dwelling on casualties. Whatever the reason, he began, "I don't know what in hell Ike was talking about. Something about casualties — is that something to look forward to? Hell no." He then proceeded to give a leering account of what the men could look forward to on the march to Berlin. He spoke as if we were a Viking raiding party, not an army

British General Bernard Montgomery (left), commander of all Allied ground forces in France, and Lieut. General Omar Bradley, U.S. First Army commander

fighting to preserve freedom and democracy and to destroy, once and for all, the greatest fiend in history. A couple of the chaplains sitting up front walked out during his speech, as did some of the nurses.

At least as disturbing as the speech itself was the reaction among my fellow officers, many of whom lustily cheered his picture of the rewards to be had in the forthcoming campaign. When he finished, there was much laughter and even some applause.

I went back to the barracks racked by doubts. I could not see myself being led into battle by a man like that and for the purpose of satisfying animal desires. This was not the war I had believed in.

Suddenly, I came up with what seemed like a great idea at the time: I would go AWOL. Even though it was forbidden to leave the premises, I slipped out and headed for Birmingham to see Rabbi Rabinowitz, who was like a father to me. When he saw me, he tried to keep things light. "If you're still here, I guess the invasion hasn't yet taken place," he began. But seeing my serious mien and knowing that I was almost never without a smile on my face, Rabbi Rabinowitz gave up the attempt at light-hearted banter and waited for me to tell him the purpose of my surprise visit.

I told Rabbi Rabinowitz that as I saw it we were as good as dead before we started if Patton's goals were ours. I reminded him that those chosen to fight Israel's wars had always been those free of sin, and that in *parashas Mattos* we learn that for every soldier in the front lines of the battle against Midian there was another one whose task it was to pray for those at the front. From this we see that prayer and the spiritual state of those fighting determine the outcome of the battle because victory is in the hands of Hashem. Led by someone like Patton, I saw myself marching to a certain death, and I begged Rabbi Rabinowitz to hide me until the end of the war.

When I had finished crying my heart out, Rabbi Rabinowitz told me that I was talking like a foolish child. He told me that he envied me because I was being given an opportunity to fulfill a *mitzvah* of the Torah that he would never get the chance to fulfill: the *mitzvah* of wiping out the memory of Amalek. Even the killing of one Amalekite was a fulfillment of this *mitzvah*. He told me that the Vilna Gaon knew how to read the signs in a person's face to determine if he was a descendant of Amalek. If he had seen such a person, he would have been obligated to kill him. But, on the other hand, living in Vilna he could not do such a thing because of the *chillul Hashem* involved. In order not to refrain from fulfilling the *mitzvah,* the Gaon had avoided looking at non-Jews. But now in the war against Germany, Rabbi Rabinowitz said, I would be fighting to wipe out Amalek with full sanction.

Rabbi Rabinowitz kissed me goodbye and gave me a small *Tanach,* which he said I should take with me. Then he hugged and kissed me again and started crying. "The next time I'll be hearing from you, you'll be somewhere in France," he said. "Now get back, and I have no doubt you'll come through with flying colors."

❁   ❁   ❁

Even before I went AWOL, thoughts of death were never far from my mind. A few years ago, Rabbi Hutner's daughter,

I Pvt. Meyer Jacob Birnbaum, being of sound mind and body, do entrust to Rabbi Isaac Hutner of 460 E. 9 2 St. Bklyn, N. Y. my entire bank account in deposite at the "Bank of Athens located at 33 St and 7ᵗʰ Ave. N. Y. C., in case of my death, with which to use same to the best of his discretion.

                    Meyer Jacob Birnbaum

Witnessed by: Pvt. Julian Audley Blumberg
Witnessed by: Pvt. Samuel R. Hurwitz

My wartime will

Rebbetzin Beruriah David, brought my wife the will I wrote in the army bequeathing all my worldly possessions to Rabbi Hutner and making him the beneficiary of my $10,000 army insurance if I was killed in service. The will is written on U.S.O. stationery. *Baruch Hashem*, Rabbi Hutner reaped no monetary benefit from that will, but he did profit in another way from my army service. Initially we received $21.00 a month in spending money. This later jumped to $50.00. I had absolutely no need for the money — the candy available at the army canteen wasn't kosher and we had no trouble hitching rides wherever we wanted to go. So my friend Moshe Swerdloff and I decided to send most of our monthly pay to Rabbi Hutner. This money went to pay for the tuition of two high school-age boys whose parents were unable to pay for their yeshiva education. We have had the great privilege over the years of not only watching these two boys grow into fine *bnei Torah* themselves but also seeing them raise families of *bnei Torah*.

Lenny Maline (right) and George Rushfield (left), the two boys Moshe Swerdloff and I supported in Chaim

CHAPTER SIX
Normandy

Seeing G-d's Hand

THE INVASION OF FRANCE WAS ORIGINALLY scheduled for June 5, 1944, but had to be put off until the next day due to the gale-force winds which made it impossible to land men from the ships offshore. Seven hundred and forty-five troop carriers in thirty-eight convoys transported the troops from England to the French coast in preparation for the largest invasion in history. In the first three days of fighting, over 4,000 landing craft carried 185,000 troops, 20,000 vehicles and 347 minesweepers to shore. Another 18,000 paratroopers were dropped in by air. The Allies had more than 13,000 support aircraft at their disposal.

Within a month, over a million Allied troops and two hundred thousand vehicles were ashore and ready for the drive through France to Germany. Most of the American troops were unseasoned recruits, except for the 82nd Airborne, to whose 505th Regiment my unit was attached. By contrast, we were facing seasoned German troops.

We did not know it at the time but the intelligence forecasts

German Field Marshal Erwin Rommel

were that in the first wave to hit the beach seventy-five out of every hundred men would be killed; in the second wave, fifty out of every hundred; and in the third wave, thirty out of every hundred. Even in retrospect, there seems nothing far-fetched about these estimates. Not knowing where the Allied invasion would take place, the Germans had mined the entire coastline. Behind the personnel mines were two more rows of traps for tanks and other vehicles. Our minesweepers had to cut out lanes through the mine fields, which were then marked by buoys. The landing craft could only move single file in these lanes. On the beaches themselves were electrified fields. Looking down on the beach from impregnable pillboxes were the German gunners, who were shooting down on the unshielded Allied troops. Each of these pillboxes was connected by miles of underground molehills which allowed the Germans to move troops back and forth in response to Allied breakthroughs.

The actual Allied casualties were one-third to one-half those that were projected. This was in large part due to a remarkable concatenation of events in which one cannot fail to see G-d's Providence. War sensitizes one to the workings of Divine Providence, on both the individual and communal level, more intensely than any other human experience. And at no time in our lives was *Hashgachah* (Divine Providence) so real as during the invasion of Normandy.

Though we did not know it, the German defenders were leaderless at the time of the invasion. The supreme commander of the German forces defending the French coastline was perhaps

German electrified fields

the greatest of Hitler's generals, Field Marshal Erwin Rommel, known as the Desert Fox for his campaigns in North Africa. Several weeks earlier, Hitler, *ym"sh*, had removed Rommel's beloved Afrikan Tank Corps from his command so that it was not available to him in the defense of the French coastline.

Realizing that the weather on June 5 ruled out any possibility of a landing, Rommel took the opportunity to return to Berlin and plead with Hitler to place the Afrikan Tank Corps back at his disposal. June 6 was his wife's fiftieth birthday, and he decided to remain in Berlin to celebrate with her rather than rush back to France. So on the morning of June 6, he was still in Berlin.

The German second-in-command retired early on the night of June 5, leaving instructions that under no circumstances was he to be disturbed. When his adjutant first received indications of the impending attack, he was afraid to awaken his commander, knowing his ferocious temper and fearing that he might be hungover from the previous night's partying.

For his part, Hitler refused to believe the first intelligence reports of a likely Allied invasion of Normandy. He had convinced himself that the invasion would take place at Dunkirk, much closer to England, and that any move towards Normandy was at most a feint and diversion. In addition, many of the best German generals had recently been sent to the Russian front where the German forces were suffering heavy losses.

On the day of the invasion, the German forces were left without any air support and the skies belonged completely to the Allies. The major German airfield was further down the peninsula. As the invasion was taking place, only two planes were on base. The rest were elsewhere on training maneuvers and did not become available until the landing for which they were training was a *fait accompli.*

The weather also conspired to aid the success of the invasion and to increase the element of surprise. The strong winds of June 5 abated for only a couple of hours the next day. But when General Eisenhower received weather reports that the gales would stop for those few hours, he decided to go ahead, knowing that the element of surprise would be increased by the bad weather.

Just as in the story of the salvation of the Jews in the days of Mordechai and Esther, so too here every seeming coincidence can be explained by itself, but taken together they constitute an unmistakable pattern of Divine intervention, which anyone with the slightest sensitivity can perceive. Just consider all the apparent coincidences involved:

(1) Who inspired Rommel to choose precisely that day to return to Berlin to present his case to Hitler for the return of his beloved tank corps?

(2) Who prompted Hitler to take command of the tank corps away from Rommel in the first place and thereby occasion the latter's visit to Berlin?

(3) Who brought into the world fifty years earlier a baby girl who would grow up to be Rommel's wife and whose birthday would cause him to remain in Berlin on June 6 rather than return immediately to France on the night of June 5?

(4) Who put it in the mind of Rommel's second-in-command to seclude himself on the night of June 5 and to order his aides not to disturb him?

(5) Who convinced Hitler to ignore the first reports of the invasion?

(6) Who led the German commanders to schedule war games for June 5-7 and leave only two planes in the area?

Truly, "The horse is prepared for battle, but victory belongs to Hashem" (*Proverbs* 21:31).

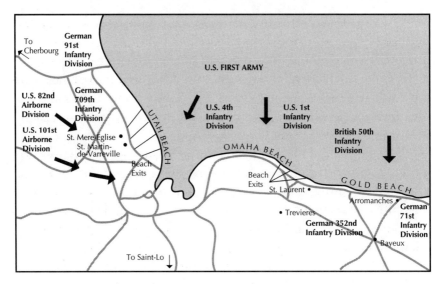

Invasion of Normandy

First Combat

ONLY A SMALL FRACTION OF THE TROOPS WAITING aboard the thousands of ships off the Normandy shore actually took part in the initial fighting. Until we had secured beachheads at Omaha Beach and Utah Beach, there was no way of landing most of the men and equipment. Our unit in fact waited almost a full week offshore before we were able to land. During that time, German artillery fire was aimed at us, but nothing like that which faced the first wave of Allied soldiers.

Though the German defenses had been considerably weakened by the time we landed, it was still our first taste of combat. Among the slender provisions that we carried into battle was what looked like a white mattress cover. Each one of these covers was marked with the soldier's name, rank, serial number, and an "H" or a "C" to indicate whether he was a Hebrew or a Christian. Thankfully, we did not know at the time what these "covers" were, but our blissful ignorance did not last long. Whenever a soldier was killed, they would simply slide his body into the cover he carried with him and zip it up. There was a special unit, which I had never even known about, called the

Graves Registration Unit, which would pick up the dead bodies and take them to a temporary cemetery.

It is impossible to convey to anyone who has not experienced it the sheer terror of soldiers going into battle. I had never before seen a dead body. But in the water, as we raced for the shore, we saw bodies floating towards us. As we hit the shore, the multitude of disembodied limbs or smashed skulls all around terrified us even more than the intact dead bodies. Every soldier carried with him — in addition to his rifle, rations, grenades, and bayonet — a change of underwear. Nothing better conveys the fear that almost paralyzed us than the last item. The fear in battle is so overwhelming that one loses all bowel control.

Meeting an Old Friend

ONCE WE HAD SECURED THE BEACHHEAD AT NORMANDY, more and more forces began to pour in every day in preparation for the upcoming offensive that would take us into Germany. The first town that we reached was St. Mere Eglise, whose total population could not have been more than two hundred. That soon became two hundred Frenchmen and tens of thousands of Allied soldiers. Traffic was murder. There were no street or place names and everybody was lost. Military police were everywhere trying to direct vehicles to their proper destination.

I was stuck with my driver in the middle of a massive traffic jam when I heard someone shouting over the general din, "Mike Birnbaum! Mike Birnbaum!" I turned around and saw my old friend Schmiel Karper sitting on top of a two-and-a-half-ton truck. He jumped off his truck, and we conducted an impromptu reunion in the midst of the turmoil all around us.

"Schmiel, what the heck are you doing here? I always thought you were smart enough to know better." I began.

"If you don't know better, how should I know better?" he countered. Then stepping back a second to get a better look at me, he noticed that I was clean shaven. "Where did you get a *heter* (permission) to shave with a razor?" he asked.

"There's no *heter* to shave with a razor."

"So how come you're shaven?"

"After a while, I began to look like a bum and so I took out my electric shaver, hooked up a couple of batteries and shaved."

"Where did you get batteries?"

"Tomorrow morning you'll have your batteries too. I'll take care of everything for you."

That evening I had one of my mechanics hook up a battery for shaving just as he had for me. The next morning, I saw a vehicle pass by with Schmiel's division number. I stopped the driver and asked him if he knew First Sergeant Samuel Karper. When he told me that he did, I handed him the package and told him, "Well, listen here, Sergeant, I want you to get this to him. It's very important. He requisitioned it."

"I'd love to but I can't," he replied.

"What do you mean you'd love to but you can't? I'm giving you a direct order and I expect you to deliver this to First Sergeant Samuel Karper."

"I'd like to but I can't. Last night he was hit with an .88 and he's loaded with shrapnel. He was sent back to England."

The Sergeant told me that Schmiel had been hit "pretty bad," and I wondered if I would ever see him again. But he survived, and when we first saw each other after the War, I joked with him that I had tried to fulfill my promise but he had made it difficult by getting in the way of the German artillery shell. He showed me his hands, which had been left permanently deformed and twisted, and told me that he had been hit all over his body and that some of the shrapnel was still inside him.

But Schmiel had no complaints. He was glad just to be alive. At the time he was hit, he was carrying his *tefillin* bag over his left shoulder. Some of the shrapnel entered the *tefillin* directly opposite his heart and lodged inside the *tefillin* instead of his heart.

DEATH IS ALL AROUND IN WAR, AND ONE QUICKLY becomes dulled to it. It takes a shock like Schmiel's close call or

My Brother the loss of a buddy in your unit to bring home death's full impact.

About a month or so after Schmiel took a direct hit of shrapnel, my sergeant Rojo came in one day with the mail. When he finished passing it out, he told me that there was a message for me and that I should come with him. We drove for half a mile or so before Rojo stopped the jeep, looked me in the eye, and handed me a pile of letters I had written to my kid brother Elly. They were marked "Deceased."

Elly and I together in uniform

Over 135,000 American soldiers would lose their lives in the European theater from June 6, 1944 to the end of the war, but it took Elly's death for me to fully appreciate what such a number means.

That night I cried until there were no tears. The next morning Rojo and I drove one hundred and twenty five miles to the military cemetery in Bosville, France. I was directed to a makeshift grave where Elly was buried, probably wrapped in one of the portable coffins we carried with us. Rojo led me to the grave and waited quietly while I crouched there reciting *Tehillim* and trying to find a way to commune with Elly, to tell him — now that it was too late — how much I loved him. Pictures of my kid brother from little toddler to recent draftee, looking so proud in his uniform, ran through my mind. I tried to reconcile myself to the fact that the beautiful baby and that tall, smiling young man was no more.

Elly was six years younger than I — two sisters came between us. Unlike me, Elly had a yeshiva background from an early age, and so Young Israel was not as central to his Yiddishkeit as it was to mine. In the summers, though, he used to hang out with me, and always looked up to me as something of a hero. That hero worship had greatly increased in the past two years when I became an officer and he was still in high school. Of course, everybody likes to be a hero, even if only

Reciting Tehillim by Elly's grave

in his brother's eyes, and Elly was my beloved kid brother.

On the few occasions we had seen each other since I was drafted, Elly and I had never spoken of the possibility that we might never see each other again. The possibility of being killed is not something soldiers, even brothers, like to talk about.

We were still in the midst of heavy fighting, and there was no possibility of sitting *shivah* for Elly for more than an hour. When the hour was up, I had no choice but to return to my men and carry on as if nothing had happened.

In a way I was lucky. Going back into combat immediately left me with little time to dwell on Elly's death. I had to keep my mind, for the most part, on the task at hand, letting thoughts of Elly creep in only during the odd moments of rest.

In those moments, I thought a lot of my parents, who would not have combat to distract them from their grief. I knew that they had already been notified of Elly's death, or would be soon, and sat down to write them a letter. I hoped that perhaps their pain would be lessened a fraction by knowing that he had

Elly in basic training

not died completely alone and unmourned on foreign soil, but that I had been there by his grave and been able to recite the prayers for the dead.

I wrote them that Elly's death was a true *Kiddush Hashem*. No other words could describe his volunteering for the army in order to save his fellow Jews. At the time, I did not even know how true my words were. Only later did we learn that Elly had been killed after volunteering for an extremely dangerous mission. Only one of the five comrades who accompanied him on that mission returned alive.

My mother never fully accepted my brother's death. There was a slight misspelling in the telegram notifying my parents that my brother had been killed. After my mother had finished sitting *shivah*, she took the telegram to a *"rebbe"* in the Bronx and pointed out the misspelling. That was sufficient for this *"rebbe"* to convince her that my brother had not been killed but was only suffering from amnesia. The *"rebbe"* also convinced my mother to give him the death benefits she was receiving to distribute to *tzedakah*.

Kiddush Hashem

The following letter is printed here as it first appeared in the January, 1945, issue of the "Viewpoint," published by the National Council of Young Israel. Since it concerns two of our own members who are so well known to us, we deem it a privilege to reprint it in our own Journal.

Dear Mr. Upbin:

Agreeable to our telephone conversation, I am enclosing a letter from one of our members, Lt. Meyer Birnbaum, to his family. In my opinion, this human document is a true example of "*Kiddush Hashem*" and should be spread far and wide. Although the letter speaks for itself, the following points of information may be of interest:

1. The Birnbaum boys have been raised in Young Israel of New Lots from midget age on.

2. The circumstances of Elly's death are not known—and may never be. This much we did learn though—He died a hero's death! He volunteered, along with five others, on a dangerous mission. Only one of them returned.

3. The Young Israel of New Lots is in a painful position. We should like to pay our respects to the memory of Elly Birnbaum through some fitting and permanent memorial, but—! In the notification telegram from the War Dep't the name Birnbaum seems to have been mispelled and the mother clings to the belief that this is all a tragic mistake, and that Elly may be somewhere in a hospital or a prisoner of war. Thus, we at New Lots must withhold any public memorial action.

We join the mother in that faint hope, which G-d grant may prove justified.

With Young Israel Greetings,

IRVING HUNGER, *President*

France
Blessed Be the L--d
Thursday, 8-17-44

My Dearest Mama, Dad and Sisters,

This letter is beyond a doubt the hardest one I've ever attempted to write. I find it so hard to even get started.

To lie to you and tell you that I feel fine, I can't do. To tell you what's wrong with me specifically, I can't either. I have a pain in my heart which no doctor can cure. The cause of it you know by now is my Dear Brother Elly. Again I say this letter is the hardest one I ever tried writing.

A night before last my sergeant came in with the mail. He told me that he had a message for me and that he had to take me somewhere to get it. When he gave out all the mail, we jumped in my jeep and my sergeant drove me out for about a half a mile. He stopped the jeep, looked me in the eye and said, "Lieutenant, I'm very sorry to have to give you this news." He then reached into his pocket and handed me some of my letters which I wrote to Elly. On the envelope was written: "Deceased." I cried myself dry that night and had very little sleep.

Yes, my Brother, the very best brother that ever stepped foot on this earth has gone and left his family here. He fulfilled G-d's will. The Almighty, King of Kings, needed him—therefore your very Dear Son and my very Dear Brother left this earth for an everlasting Peace with the Great of Israel.

Mama Dear and Papa Dear, I know no matter how I may word this letter or no matter what I may say, your grief and sorrow will not be lessened any. I'm no Rabbi or anywhere near as great as one, but I've got my few words and want to tell you and I want you to listen too.

We know G-d giveth life and G-d taketh life from this earth. We know each move G-d makes is a rightful move, and with a purpose. We never question G-d because He is perfect and what He

The letter I wrote following Elly's death

does, is with a reason and for the best always. Yes, I know what you might say now, "Why?" That may dear parents is a question which the Almighty above only knows the answer to. We here on earth are so small and we can't understand the simple things on this earth. How can we understand the more profound things on earth such as life itself? We read in the *Perek*: And Rabbi Yakov said, "This world is like a vestibule before the world to come, prepare yourself in the vestibule, that thou mayest enter into the great hall." The great hall meaning G-d's palace in heaven. Elly, my very dear Brother, is seated amongst Israel's great right now. He was prepared to enter the great hall and so our Creator accepted him. G-d had a purpose for choosing your very Dear Son and my most Dear Brother—he was needed somewhere else more important than here on earth. That somewhere else is in the Kingdom of G-d. He sits amongst our great people. He is now among true friends from heaven. He is there with your *Zade Alya* and your father *Meir*. He is there with our great Jews of old.

The Almighty put Elly forth on this earth for 20 years and a few months and he gave you Mom the honor of being his mother, and you Dad the honor of being his father. I have the great honor of being his only brother. I say "I have" and use the present tense because I still am his Dear Brother. Elly is here with me, he is guarding me through battle and then through life on this earth. He is also with you some 3000 miles away from here on an assignment from G-d.

Elly was chosen by our Creator because he believed in Him so dearly. He fought in G-d's name and left this earth for Him. Many a *Tzadik* (righteous man) lives on this earth for many years but during his lifetime he never comes across an opportunity like our Elly had, and that is to leave this earth for G-d's Holy name. He fought with the fear of G-d in his heart. He made the supreme sacrifice of giving up his life on earth for the Almighty. The next time you visit a Yeshiva you can say to yourself or even aloud: "My dear son gave up his life so people could learn God's Torah. My son Ellya made this possible!"

Mama Dear, tears are rolling down my cheeks right now as I am writing. Our Elly is such a great *Tzadik* and I am so proud of him. We, as Torah-true Jews shouldn't cry, we shouldn't shed a tear but I am a weak one among us. Pick your head up Mama, wipe off those tears; remember, we are very proud of our Elly. Someday we will meet up with him. When the Almighty asks me "Who are you?" I will say, "The brother of the *Tzadik* Ellya."

Yesterday morning I set out to the graveyard which round trip was 250 miles. I arrived there about 4 o'clock in the afternoon. The soldier in charge took me to Elly's grave. For an hour I said all the necessary prayers and in addition some paragraphs from *Thilim*. My tears rolled down my cheeks onto Elly's grave—until tears could come no more. I just couldn't control myself I guess. My sergeant helped me away later. My sergeant took some pictures which I'll send you as soon as they are developed.

Elly is buried in the same cemetery as my unit is attached to. I found out the following information there. He was buried June 28, 1944, which was on a Wednesday, 7 days in *Tamuz*. The day he passed away I don't know yet, but will try finding out. The cemetery is located in Blosvile, France, plot D, row 2, grave 37. Because of military reasons I can't give you the exact name of the cemetery. After the war we have to request his body be sent to us in order for us to get it. There was no embalming done to him and he was buried according to our law in the Torah.

Mama Dear and Dear Dad and sisters, I hope and pray to G-d, *The Ribono shel Olom*, that you have no more *Tza'ar* (sorrow).

"O Merciful G-d, King of Kings, blessed be Thy name, I lift my hands to Thee above and pray to Thee, Grant us Peace on Earth and please Good G-d above, send us *Moshiach* in the very near future. We need Him so much. Bless my family and all good people. Please don't bring any more *Tza'ar* to my family. Amen."

Please don't worry for me for I'll be alright in a couple of weeks. The tragic news got me down a little but I'll be O.K.

My men made me fried eggs this morning which I ate and enjoyed a little.

Don't worry for me Folks, G-d is watching over me. G-d bless you My Very Dear Parents and sisters.

Your Loving Son and Brother,

MEYER.

My mother would go down to Times Square, where large numbers of soldiers were always to be found, but which even in those days was not the most savory spot in the world, to look for my brother. Every time she saw a tall thin soldier she would run over to him to see if it was Elly. She even made plans to go to France to look for him there.

When I returned from overseas and showed my mother pictures of Elly's grave and his dogtag, she was furious with me for depriving her of her hope. As long as she lived, she never marked his *yahrzeit*. When she was living with us in her last years, I always took care to tell her that the *yahrzeit* candle on my brother's *yahrzeit* was for one of my *rebbes*.

Though my mother never fully acknowledged my brother's death, she did at least stop giving the monthly death benefit check to the *"rebbe"* in the Bronx. Instead she saved those payments to purchase a *sefer Torah*. By 1957, she had saved enough money to buy one. My mother was very eager to purchase the *sefer Torah* immediately, but Rabbi Hutner advised me to be careful to take a *sofer* with me to pick out the *sefer Torah*.

For three months, Rabbi Noach Feldman and I went out nearly every night in search of an appropriate *sefer Torah*. In those days, many *shuls* in East New York and Brownsville were closing and selling their *sifrei Torah*. In one *shul* alone there were thirty *sifrei Torah*. Finally, we found a *sefer Torah* in a small *shtiebl* in East New York. As soon as he looked at it, Rabbi Feldman assured me that my search had come to an end and that we had found a scroll written by a true *yirei shamayim*.

My mother was thrilled with the news that we had at last found the scroll for which we were looking. She told me that price was irrelevant. All she cared about was the spiritual quality of the scribe who wrote it.

Rabbi Feldman spent another few months checking the *sefer Torah* from the first to last letter. Much to his surprise, he did not find a single letter missing or in need of correction.

Finally, the joyous day arrived for my mother to present the *sefer Torah* to the Young Israel of New Lots. The privilege of filling in each of the final letters was sold, and my mother bought any that had not been purchased. She wanted to spend every penny

My father carrying the sefer Torah purchased in Elly's honor

of the money that had accumulated from Elly's death benefits.

My mother's *sefer Torah* eventually moved from the Young Israel of New Lots to the Mirrer *minyan* on 16th Avenue in Boro Park. The *baal kriah* of that *minyan,* Rabbi Chaim Shereshevsky, loved that scroll so much that when I subsequently gave it to the Mirrer Yeshiva, where my son Akiva was learning in the *kollel,* he threatened to take me to a *din Torah* for taking away his *sefer Torah.* My mother made *aliyah* with us when she was ninety-five years old, and the *sefer Torah* came with her.

OUR FIRST ASSIGNMENT WAS TO SET UP OUR EQUIPMENT on Hill 310, which means that the hill was 310 feet above sea level.

Accused We were to intercept messages, break down the codes, and relay the information to the ships off the coast from which the big brass were directing the action. We were very successful, despite having to work in foxholes and slit trenches. The Germans had pinpointed our position and kept up a steady artillery barrage in an attempt to take us out of action.

After a day or two, a jeep pulled up and the driver hopped out to give us a present courtesy of the British army: three bottles of whiskey — one of gin, one Scotch, and one Canadian Club. Not being a drinker, I asked him when they'd be passing out the Pepsis and Coca-Colas. I handed the whiskey over to my men, who made short work of it. A couple of days later, my men asked for permission to go into the neighboring village in search of a good time, and I told them to go ahead. I stayed behind, telling them, "It's not my cup of tea."

About two weeks after the invasion, Major Mailman visited us. He asked me how everything was going. I was a little puzzled by the question since I was sure he had been receiving reports on our success in intercepting German communications. As it turned out, his first questions were only by way of pleasantries leading up to the real purpose of his visit, which he got to presently.

"Birnie," he said to me, "I think you should return to England. You liked it there, didn't you?"

"But we've just begun to fight. Why do you want to send me back?" I replied.

Gathering hay for a mattress

"Well, I think it would be good for you."

"Who else is going back?"

"Just you."

"Major, be honest with me. What's going on?"

"All right. You asked for it and I'll talk to you like a Dutch uncle. The men don't want to serve under you anymore. I received a message that they're unhappy and scared of you."

In front of the pup tent in which we slept

"Scared? Why would they be scared of me?"

"Well, Birnie, let me put it to you point blank. They think you're not normal. For one thing, you don't smoke and you don't drink."

"I'm not the only one who doesn't smoke or drink. I give my cigarettes and liquor to the men. Does that make me not normal, as you say?"

"The other night they asked you if you wanted to go into town and have some fun. You told them, 'It's not my cup of tea.' "

"Could be. That's a common expression of mine."

"Well, that's not normal. They think you're strange and that's why they're scared of you. We've got very good doctors in England, and in a few months you can be back here again. I'm going to get orders for you to return to England."

I just stood there, my mouth agape. Mailman knew my moral standards from our days in Fort Jackson, and he had never said then that those standards would disqualify me from being an officer. I felt like I had on the eve of the invasion when Patton spoke to all the officers. Could it really be that trying to live according to the standards of the Torah marked one as such a freak that he could not serve in the American army? Didn't Mailman realize that my *Yiddishkeit*, which kept me from joining the men on their nocturnal adventures, also considered the perversions he was hinting at an abomination?

In the end, Major Mailman persuaded my men to give me another chance. But the idea that I had to defend myself because I didn't smoke, drink, or act immorally floored me. Never had I felt so clearly the extent to which a Torah Jew is set apart from the rest of the world.

CHAPTER SEVEN
On the March

EVERY DAY WE SAW MORE AND MORE ALLIED troops pouring into Normandy in preparation for the next major **The Brest Campaign** campaign. The Allied objective was to break through at St. Lowe and move on to capture Brest, the next peninsula down the coast. Brest was the home base for the German U-boat fleet. The U-boats had wreaked havoc with Allied shipping and supply lines throughout the War, and the goal now was to deprive them of their base of operations.

The major fighting at St. Lowe was on *Tishah B'Av,* and I gave a great deal of thought to how I could fast in the midst of battle. In the end, I realized it was impossible, and that I would be endangering both my own life and the lives of others if I knowingly did anything to reduce my ability to function at top efficiency.

We worked through the night on *Tishah B'Av,* laying communications wires in such a way that they would not be torn up when the massive tanks rolled over them the next day. Our

forces were able to bring artillery into play this time, unlike at Normandy where the artillery had been exclusively German. We succeeded in breaking through, though not without heavy losses. The most painful of these were the boys killed by "friendly fire" when Allied bombers mistakenly identified them as German troops.

As we raced out of St. Lowe, on our way to Brest, — we were warned by an MP directing traffic to be careful passing a nearby farmhouse because there was a German sniper still inside. Tanks had already been called up to destroy the house.

Placing communication lines in a tree. Out of fear of German snipers none of my men would climb up the tree and I had to do it myself.

I told my driver to pull the jeep over to the side. Together my men and I crawled on our bellies in the direction of the farmhouse. When we were about ten yards away, we started lobbing our grenades into the house through the windows. When

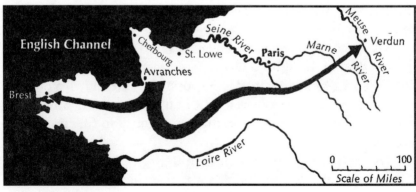

Allied advances

Shooting in combat

the first grenade hit, the German inside came to the window and shot several bursts of random fire. Soon, however, we heard groaning from the house and then silence. That was the first time I knew for sure that I had killed another human being. Though the object of war is to kill the enemy — nevertheless that first time is not easy.

Once through at St. Lowe, we cut the German supply lines to Brest, prior to capturing the German U-boat base itself in heavy fighting. The Germans had cut an underwater port out of one of the mountains on the Brest coastline, which made the U-boats immune to detection by aerial surveillance and invulnerable to bombing. I had never seen anything so interesting in my life. One entered the mountain from the top through an elevator big

Train tracks leading to underground German headquarters

*Concrete reinforced entrance to elevator shaft leading to
underground German headquarters*

enough for just two people. The entire U-boat command had been
sheltered in the bowels of that mountain.

I had one more reason to be well pleased with the survey of
the U-boat command. In the supply room, I found a treasure-

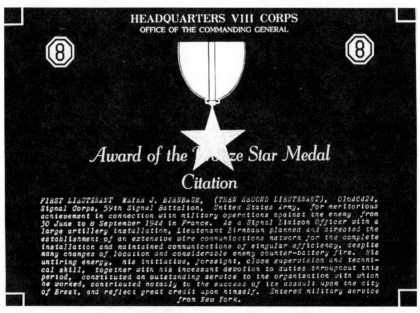

HEADQUARTERS VIII CORPS
OFFICE OF THE COMMANDING GENERAL

Award of the *Bronze* Star Medal

Citation

FIRST LIEUTENANT MEYER J. BIRNBAUM, (THEN SECOND LIEUTENANT), 01640424, Signal Corps, 59th Signal Battalion, United States Army, for meritorious achievement in connection with military operations against the enemy from 30 June to 8 September 1944 in France. As a Signal Liaison Officer with a large artillery installation, Lieutenant Birnbaum planned and directed the establishment of an extensive wire communications network for the complete installation and maintained communications of singular efficiency, despite many changes of location and considerable enemy counter-battery fire. His untiring energy, his initiative, foresight, close supervision and technical skill, together with his incessant devotion to duties throughout this period, constituted an outstanding service to the organization with which he worked, contributed notably to the success of its assault upon the city of Brest, and reflect great credit upon himself. Entered military service from New York.

Bronze Medal citation for the Brest campaign

trove of sardines, which provided some much needed variety to my diet for the next couple of weeks.

I received a Bronze Medal for our efforts in that campaign. It was my second medal of the war. The first — a Purple Heart — was awarded for a shrapnel wound in my hand incurred during the Normandy landing. At that time I had refused to be treated by McVay with whom I still wanted nothing to do.

I HAVEN'T MENTIONED YET HOW I MANAGED TO KEEP kosher in combat, but it wasn't easy. From our rations, the only

Eating Under Fire thing I could eat was a Hershey bar, which was specially designed to replenish our energy quickly, and was supposed to contain some vitamins and minerals along with the sugar.

My corporal and right-hand man was an American Indian from one of the far western states. Rojo was his only name. We became very close in the course of the War, and kept in touch for many years after he moved to California at the war's end.

In any event, Rojo used to go to French farmhouses and ask for rice. We would then cook whatever rice he managed to obtain along with any potatoes, cucumbers, and carrots which I had found. The only cooking utensil we could find that wasn't *treif* was my steel helmet. When you put steel over a fire, it turns all different colors, and my men used to joke that I had the best camouflaged helmet in the army.

OUR THIRD CAMPAIGN WAS THE BATTLE FOR PARIS. THE fighting was not nearly as intense as that at St. Lowe and Brest.

Paris By the time we reached Paris the Germans had fled, and the rest of the Allied forces were held up to allow de Gaulle to enter first at the head of the small Free French Force.

When Shabbos fell during the march on Paris, I instructed my men to lock me inside the sigabra room that we used for coding and decoding, and which was carried on top of a truck. I had only one slight concern. Our orders were to destroy the sigabra machine — if there was any danger of being captured by the

Germans — to prevent our codes from falling into their hands.

In general, my men accommodated themselves to my religious practices with quizzical bemusement throughout the war. On Shabbos, for instance, I was able to give them most of the tasks that were forbidden for me. Though I made little effort to explain why certain things were forbidden on Shabbos, and doubtless would have met with little success if I had tried, they readily complied with my requests. When it was impossible to get somebody else to do something that was prohibited on Shabbos, I was always able to find a *shinui* in order to avoid doing any *melachah d'oraisa*. Of course, without any *rav* to consult, I could never be certain that the *shinui* was sufficient. Some of the more observant among my men noticed that whenever I had to write on Shabbos I always did so in a strange way.

After we captured Paris, Mailman — who had by now been promoted to Colonel — ordered me to take my men into the city and show them a good time. I had heard of the Louvre, a world-famous art museum, and decided to take the men there. Once again my naivete came shining through, and Colonel Mailman ordered me to take them to the Folies-Bergere instead.

One look at the marquee convinced me that this was no place for a religious Jewish boy, and I waited outside while my men went inside.

After a while, a short stubby man joined me where I had remained with the vehicles, and we struck up a conversation. After struggling for awhile in French (we had been taught French and German so that we would be able to interrogate prisoners), my companion and I decided that his broken English was better than my broken French, and we carried on in English. My new friend told me that he had fought in the French Underground, and he had a pack of fascinating stories about his underground work. I countered with stories from the battles I had been in.

"Why don't you go in? Every soldier loves to come here," he coaxed me. He seemed puzzled by my response: "It's not my cup of tea." We stood there in silence for a few minutes before he popped the question that was obviously bothering him: "I hope I won't hurt your feelings, but are you Jewish?" In those days, my hair was still blond and I looked far more like the stereotypical Aryan than the stereotypical Jew.

"Yes, I am, and you're not hurting my feelings," I answered.

"I was afraid that if you were gentile I might have hurt your feelings."

"You could be right, I don't think too many gentiles are happy to be mistaken for being Jewish."

"Are you by any chance religious?"

"Yes, I am. And I'm very proud that I've been able to hold onto everything, even in the army," I said, by way of explaining what I was doing outside and not inside with my men.

"In that case, *shalom aleichem*. My name is Shreiber and I'm the co-owner of this establishment. If you're religious, you've probably heard of my family. I'm from the *Chasam Sofer*."

I didn't want to hear anymore and terminated the conversation by walking away. The thought of a descendant of the *Chasam Sofer* owning such a theater made me sick. I couldn't help thinking how far the apple can fall from the tree when there is an ill wind blowing.

WE HAD NOW FINISHED THREE MAJOR CAMPAIGNS (the maximum that any soldier is allowed to see before being

Under Siege shipped to the back lines is five), and Colonel Mailman ordered two weeks recuperation from battle fatigue in a town in Belgium by the name of Houffalize, which our troops had recently captured. We stayed there in an old hotel, sleeping in a real bed with sheets for the first time in months.

After two or three days of resting, I began to get bored, and suggested to Rojo that we take a trip to nearby Liege and see if we could locate any Jews there.

On arriving in Liege, we discovered that there were several synagogues in the town, each of which had been partly or wholly destroyed by the Nazis. I was directed to one that had no roof. The local children begged us for gum or candy, as they did everywhere we went. In exchange for a few pieces of candy, they offered to locate the gentile woman in charge of the *shul*. When she arrived, she asked me if I was Jewish, and assured that I was, let me take a souvenir from a sack of *sefarim*. I pulled out one

*The LeBrun Hotel where we stayed in Houffalize before the German
counteroffensive at the Battle of the Bulge*

dusty old volume, whose title I could not make out in the wan-
ing light. I asked the woman whether I could return the next day.
She replied that she had nowhere to go, and, in all likelihood,
would be there.

On the way back to Houffalize, I looked at the *sefer* under my
flashlight and recognized it as a book of *Selichos*. Rojo asked me
what it was, and I described going to *shul* late at night or early in
the morning to recite *Selichos* the week before Rosh Hashanah
and during the Ten Days of Repentance. The pages of the old
sefer felt unusually thick. Only after returning to the hotel did I
realize that this was because they were each covered with wax
from candles held during the reading of *Selichos*. The *sefer* was
approximately 400 years old, and you can imagine that it had
accumulated quite a bit of wax over the centuries — before there
were electric lights.

At the old hotel in which we were staying, I ate my usual
dinner of hard-boiled eggs and went to bed early. About 2:30 in
the morning, I heard the loud rumbling of tanks in the streets.
Next I heard machine-gun fire and rifle shots. Until I heard the
machine-gun fire, it never occurred to me that the tanks were

Bombed out Houffalize as it looked after the German counteroffensive.
Bastogne was even more totally destroyed

German and that they were retaking the city.

As I threw on my clothes, I heard Rojo pounding on the door. He burst into the room and told me that the Germans had surrounded us, and we had suffered heavy casualties. "Let's beat it," he yelled at me.

"How are we supposed to do that?" I yelled back.

"I parked in the back and our jeep is still in one piece. You want to make it, we'll jump out the window, grab the jeep and head into the Ardennes Forest."

And that's what we did. There were no German tanks in the forest because the trees grew too close together to allow the tanks to pass. After an hour of furious driving, we reached Bastogne, which was soon to become famous for the brave resistance of Allied troops trapped inside by German forces.

BASTOGNE HAD BEEN ALMOST COMPLETELY BOMBED out, first by the Allies and more recently by the Germans. Within

Bastogne a few days of our entry, the town was completely surrounded by German forces. The German counteroffensive had taken Allied commanders completely by surprise. A Jewish colonel in Army intelligence, Col. Ben Dickson, had warned his superiors that the Germans were still capable of mounting such a counteroffensive, but his warnings were dismissed out of hand.

Trapped inside Bastogne were several thousand Allied troops, with no water, no functioning pipelines, precious little ammunition, and almost no food. The Germans knew that if their desperate counteroffensive failed, the Allied forces would soon be marching through Germany.

We had no water other than melted snow, and for food we ate army hardtack, a very hard cracker that was supposed to contain all the vitamins and minerals we needed to stay alive. It was the middle of the winter, and the inclement weather and low cloud cover made it impossible to drop supplies or to parachute in any reinforcements. The only thing that kept us from being overrun immediately was that the Germans did not know how desperate our situation was.

Morale was very low. We were being subjected to a continuous artillery

Bundled up for the cold just prior to the siege of Bastogne

General Patton's citation of the American troops at Bastogne

bombardment and were almost starving. One day I was trying to
lift Rojo's spirits by telling him a few jokes, when he said to me,
"Lieutenant, I see that you're as scared as I am."

I laughed. "Yeah, I was just trying to humor you. But I guess
we all have pretty lousy morale right now."

Rojo, who was a religious Catholic, grew pensive. After a few

On duty

minutes, he asked me whether I thought it was an omen that I had picked up a book of *Selichos* just a few days before — a warning, perhaps, that we must repent. I replied that he was very likely right.

December 22, 1944, a few days after we were surrounded in Bastogne, a German soldier came marching in with a white flag on his gun and carrying an ultimatum from the German commander: Surrender or be wiped out. Our highest-ranking officer, General MacAuliffe, gave him his famous one-word answer, "Nuts!" and sent the messenger running for his life.

We were trapped in Bastogne for two weeks before the 101st and 82nd Airborne were able to drop in ammunition and food. With the new supplies, we began to fight our way out, while Patton's 4th Armored Division broke the German encirclement from the outside.

Outside Bastogne was a little town called Marmandie where the Germans succeeded in capturing the 106th Infantry Division. The Germans took no prisoners. They simply mowed down with machine-gun fire the surrendering American soldiers. For some reason that particular division had a high percentage of Jews, though the Germans couldn't have known that.

The Germans knew that they were fighting for their lives and used every trick at their disposal. They had a whole group of soldiers who had studied in American universities and spoke fluent English. They would turn around road markers or put up new ones, either sending the driver in the wrong direction or straight into German ambushes. We were told to be careful to always check every sign to see whether it had been recently uprooted.

BY THIS TIME, PATTON AND HIS MEN HAD ALREADY
put the first pontoon bridges across the Rhine, and the invasion

**Finding a
Chavrusa**

of Germany was in full swing. The fresh American units were being sent ahead to push on with
Patton and Bradley. Meanwhile veteran combat
units like my own, which had been decimated by heavy casualties, were regrouping. In the fighting, many men had been separated from their units. Rojo and I, for instance, had no idea where
our unit was located. The Military Police were given orders to
direct all those who had become separated from their units back
to where they were regrouping for the next push forward.

Perhaps because of our heavy casualties, our unit was
assigned a Jewish chaplain for the first time. Colonel Mailman
ordered me to find out who was Jewish and to put up notices in
every company that there would be services on Sunday morning.
As the only Jewish officer in the unit, I was given the assignment
of finding and bringing the fifteen or so Jewish soldiers.

Arriving at the bivouac area that Sunday, I spotted a short,
stocky young man with a white scarf draped around his neck
and hanging down over the front of his uniform. On closer in-
spection, the scarf turned out to be the army-issue version of a
tallis and its wearer was the chaplain. I did not participate in the
service, which was almost entirely in English. After the service,
the chaplain asked me to bring the men back the following Sunday if we had not moved on by then.

From the nature of the service, I assumed that the chaplain
was a Conservative or Reform rabbi. I did not realize that he was
just trying to form some kind of connection with the Jewish soldiers without scaring away the vast majority who had little or
no Jewish background.

By the third week, the rabbi had found out that I was Jewish.
Just as I did not expect to find an Orthodox rabbi in the middle
of France, he apparently didn't expect to find any Orthodox soldiers and assumed, not unreasonably, that I was avoiding par-
ticipating in his services because I was a confirmed atheist. He
started the conversation by telling me that the best-selling book
of the day, one read by almost every soldier, was written by an
army chaplain and entitled *There Ain't No Atheists in Foxholes.*

Chaplain Herschel Schacter conducting Shavuos services at Buchenwald

Having shared this information, he invited me to participate. I again turned down his invitation with my all-purpose reply, "It's not my cup of tea."

For some reason, at that point the chaplain had a sudden flash of inspiration and asked me if I was Orthodox. When I told him I was, he became genuinely excited and for the first time told me his name and a little of his background. His name, it turned out, was Herschel Schacter, and he was a graduate of Yeshiva University. For the next two weeks, while our unit prepared for the push into Germany, Herschel and I found time to learn *Gemara* every day, an unexpected pleasure for both of us.

The night before we crossed the Rhine into Germany was *leil Pesach*. There was no chance to make a *seder* together since we were under strict orders to have no lights on at night, for that would give away our positions to the Germans. But, on *Erev Pesach* Herschel did manage to pass out some *matzos* and wine to the Jewish soldiers and to conduct an impromptu *seder* for those with little familiarity with a real *seder*. Herschel and I crossed the Rhine together the next day in a jeep driven by Rojo. There had been no chance of our staying behind since it would have been impossible for us to catch up to our units.

WE WERE ON THE OFFENSIVE AGAIN AND TAKING A LOT of German prisoners as we went. One of my jobs was to do the

School in Hashgachah

first interrogation before they were sent on to G-2, the Army Intelligence branch. The prisoners were encouraged by my blond hair and always asked hopefully if I was of German descent, apparently thinking they would receive more sympathetic treatment. Had they known I was Jewish, they would no doubt have been even more terrified than they already were.

We were now into Germany, near Aachen, traveling with the advance column of an armored tank corps. As we were moving down an open road, Sergeant Desidero, one of those who had been with me since the invasion, requested permission to go ahead. He was frustrated with the slow pace of the convoy and looking for an opportunity to let off a little steam. As soon as I granted him permission, he put the gas pedal to the floor and sped ahead. Unfortunately, as he raced ahead, a German sniper hiding behind a bush leaped out and shot him, sending the jeep over an embankment and killing all four of those inside. Right in front of my eyes, I saw Desidero killed by a bullet that had been meant for me in the lead car.

Never again would I have such a clear sense of my life resting in the *Yad Hashem* (G-d's hand) at every moment. In war, one is always conscious of the fact that one's own skill makes his survival only marginally more likely at best — whether an artillery shell lands near you or twenty yards down the line has nothing to do with you. The illusion that we control our fate is never harder to maintain than in warfare.

After being released from the army, I frequently heard other ex-GI's bemoaning the four years they "lost" in the army. But I never felt that way. For one thing, the army turned me into a man. But even more important, I learned in war the lessons in *emunah* (faith) that would guide me in everything else I would ever do.

CHAPTER EIGHT
Buchenwald

O N APRIL 11, 1945, MY UNIT RECEIVED ORDERS TO proceed to Ohrdruff, an annex to the infamous Buchenwald con-

Ohrdruff centration camp, the first of the camps to be liberated by American troops. (I learned later from survivors that Buchenwald was a veritable *Gan Eden* (paradise) compared to Ohrdruff.) As I sat studying the maps, my driver Rojo said to me, "Lieutenant, you can put away those maps. I don't need them. I can just follow my nose. The smell of death fills your nostrils!"

When we reached Ohrdruff, we had to get out of our jeep. Bodies were piled everywhere, making passage impossible. When we tried to move the bodies so that we could go on, we realized that they were still warm. Prior to retreating, the Nazis had lined up all the prisoners and mowed them down with machine guns. Those that followed orders and went to the courtyard were killed where they stood. The blood was still pouring out of their wounds.

I was totally unprepared for what we found in Ohrdruff. I

Generals Eisenhower, Bradley, and Patton view bodies piled at the entrance to Ohrdruff

had heard of the concentration camps of course, but until the moment when we entered Ohrdruff and found the bodies strewn all about, I imagined them to be giant work camps employing slave labor — three meals a day and a bed at night in exchange for unpaid labor. In fact, Ohrdruff and Buchenwald were "slave labor camps" — not extermination camps like Auschwitz and Treblinka, whose whole purpose was to process human beings for slaughter — but my picture of slave labor was typically rose tinted. Slave labor for the Nazis meant working Jews to death rather than processing them through gas chambers and crematoria.

On the thirtieth anniversary of the liberation of Buchenwald, Yosef Friedenson, a survivor of Ohrdruff and Buchenwald, described the former in *Dos Yiddishe Vort*:

> *When I remind myself of Ohrdruff, I still break out in a sweat more than thirty years later. Over there you ran. They chased you day and night — with dogs, with sticks, with clubs. They made you run to work in the morning, and they*

The Polish man and Hungarian boy

made you run to eat. They specialized not only in murder and cruelty, but in the art of chasing people. Veterans of the camp compared it to Auschwitz in its first stage [before it became exclusively an extermination camp]. People fell like fleas from the work....

The few survivors still alive when we entered the camp — those the Germans did not have time to gather in the courtyard or who had ignored their orders — were nothing more than living skeletons. They were literally just skin and bones. Their mouths had constricted, and their cheekbones protruded from drawn cheeks. Only their noses appeared to retain anything of their original size and dominated their faces. How any of them were still alive we could not imagine.

I found the thirty-five-year-old Polish Jew and the sixteen-year-old Hungarian Jewish boy, whose story I described in the Prologue, alive in the typhus ward. Their disease had saved their lives by rendering them too feeble to respond to the Germans' order to congregate in the courtyard of the camp.

When the boy finished his story and asked me, "Now, you tell me. Do I have to do *teshuvah*?" I had no words to offer him. I could do nothing but put my arms

The gallows at Ohrdruf from which the boy's father was hung

around his frail shoulders and kiss him. The only way to preserve your sanity after listening to that kind of story was to keep so busy that you didn't have too much time to think.

The first thing I did was to try to respond to their request for bread to eat. Bread was too bulky to be carried by front-line soldiers, who relied on army hardtacks. So I contacted battalion headquarters by radio and asked that they immediately bring in as much bread as possible. The next morning not only bread but cooked meals and other foods were dropped in by parachute.

AS SOON AS THE BREAD WAS DROPPED IN, I RUSHED TO bring it to the two survivors from the typhus ward. I gave my

Revenge bayonet to the Polish Jew to to use for cutting his bread. I warned him not to cut towards himself, but he answered matter-of-factly, "Don't worry, my body can take a beating. After what I've been through, one more cut won't make any difference." We had been told to make sure that the starved survivors eat slowly lest their stomachs burst from the sudden infusion of food, but I could not restrain the Polish Jew from gulping down the bread, without chewing, almost as soon as it entered his mouth.

Outside of the barracks where we were eating, a middle-aged German civilian was being interrogated. He had ostensibly wandered into the camp and offered to show the American personnel around. For all the world, he looked like a respectable burgher from the neighboring town, who just happened to have a good familiarity with the camp. He was explaining the various means employed to dispose of bodies — incineration or caustic acid.

As this interrogation was being conducted, I noticed that the Polish Jew was no longer talking to me but was listening very intently to the interrogation going on outside. He got up as if in some type of trance and started to walk outside. Even as he walked outside, he continued eating his bread. I followed right behind him, afraid that something had snapped inside him. The German civilian was explaining in broken, heavily accented English the operation of the camp — how the prisoners had been

tortured, how their bodies had been disposed of, etc. As he was talking, the Polish Jew drew closer and closer, as if he were sleepwalking. At last he stood in front of the German. Before anyone could stop him, he pulled out my bayonet and plunged it into the German's heart, killing him instantly.

The officers who had been interrogating the German wanted to kill the Jew on the spot, but I was able to restrain them. "Wait a minute, guys," I told them. "Let me find out what's going on here. This man speaks only Yiddish. Let me find out why he did this."

The slain SS man

Then turning to the Jew, I asked him why he had killed the German civilian.

"He was no civilian," he assured me. "I recognize his voice from Auschwitz. I will never forget his voice. He was not a civilian but a Nazi — a Nazi who killed many, many Jews. His voice has been ringing in my ears all the years since Auschwitz."

"How can you be sure?" I persisted. "It's been years since you were in Auschwitz."

"You don't forget the voice that barked commands. Our ears were highly attuned to our Nazi captors. You might not have heard the person standing next to you — even your closest relative or best friend — but you heard the voice of the Nazi guard. If you didn't instantly obey his every command, you were dead."

"Even if you're right," I asked him, "how can I prove to my fellow officers here that you're telling the truth?"

"Simple, just roll up his sleeve and you'll see his SS insignia."

We rolled up the dead man's sleeve, and there it was on his upper arm — the insignia of the dreaded SS.

BEFORE LEAVING OHRDRUFF, I TOOK PICTURES OF WHAT we had seen. One that speaks an entire book is of a body left in

Memorializing the Crimes

the courtyard. The man's arms and legs were literally sticks. But even this half-dead state did not satisfy the Nazis. They were not content until every breath of life had been extinguished. Even though the war was lost, their desire to wipe out every Jew remained unassuaged. Or perhaps they were afraid of leaving alive any witnesses to their monstrous crimes and reasoned that even what we could surmise from the bodies piled in front of us would pale beside the testimony of survivors.

The means of disposing of the bodies of those who dropped dead every day at Ohrdruff were far more primitive than in the extermination camps themselves. One of the techniques was to place railroad ties doused with kerosene beneath a pyramid of

Railroad ties used to burn bodies in Ohrdruff

Charred remains from the incineration of dead bodies

Lye pit — note the undissolved leg

bodies and then ignite them. Individual limbs and bodies that had charred, but not burned, remained. The stench left behind was indescribable, and my men wore bandannas over their faces to try to lessen its effects on them. Little did I dream when I took pictures of the Nazis' means of destroying the evidence that there would one day be those who would deny that the Nazis' crimes ever took place.

The other method they used to dispose of the bodies was to pile up several hundred at a time and pour caustic acid over them. To give you some idea of the power of caustic acid, consider the fact that plumbers in New York City stopped using Drano, which is only five-percent caustic acid, because they found it burned away metal pipes.

Burying My Brothers

AFTER LESS THAN TWO DAYS IN OHRDRUFF, I RECEIVED orders to proceed with three jeeps to Buchenwald. At the entrance to Buchenwald, we were confronted with the same sight as in Ohrdruff — hundreds of corpses of those killed by the Nazis as they were retreating before the Allied advance.

There was a fear that the presence of so many dead bodies would lead to epidemics or even a plague. As a consequence, a mass burial had been ordered for the recently murdered. I realized that virtually all of those slain were Jewish and approached the highest-ranking officer on the scene — a one-star general in the Tank Corps — and requested permission to bury them in individual graves.

"What difference can it possibly make now?" the general

The entrance to Buchenwald

wanted to know. "We have no way of identifying them." I pointed out that each of the corpses had been tattooed and said that I would mark each grave with the concentration camp number. That way if the Nazis had kept records of the inmates, it might someday be possible to identify who was buried there.

Only one more question remained: Where would I find the manpower to carry out such a large task? The war was not yet over, and the general was unwilling to commit a substantial number of soldiers to the task of burial. I answered that I would use German civilians — the same civilians who would later deny any knowledge of what had been taking place right next door to them, despite the smell of death that permeated the air.

Realizing how important this was to me, the general at last relented and gave me permission to provide some semblance of a burial for the Jewish inmates. Rojo and I rounded up a group of Germans roaming around the surrounding countryside and put them to work digging graves.

All around us were reminders of the enormity of the crimes that had been committed in this place. The commandant of Buchenwald, appropriately named "the Butcher of Buchenwald," had fled at the approach of General Eisenhower's troops. He had been tracked down, however, and in his home were found lampshades of a highly unusual texture. Medics subsequently

German civilians viewing lampshades made of human skin

identified them as having been fashioned from human skin. These lampshades were apparently the special hobby of the commandant's wife; more than thirty were found in the house.

General Eisenhower ordered that all the civilians in the region be ordered to visit Buchenwald and see what their fellow "good Germans" had been doing there. Among the exhibits on display were the lampshades, which were set up on a table.

While the German civilians were being forced to tour Buchenwald, — one of General Eisenhower's aides, who had seen me talking to the inmates, mentioned to him that I could translate if he wanted to talk to the inmates. Ike told the aide to fetch me, and I ended up translating for twenty minutes or so while he heard some of the inmates' stories. I could tell that their stories made a strong impression on him. Subsequently, he gave orders that as many Allied troops as possible should be brought to Buchenwald. "They may not know what they're fighting for," he said, "but I want them to know, at least, what they are fighting against."

Indeed, the sight of what the Nazis had done did have a profound effect on the American troops. Rabbi Naftali Hirsch

The ovens in which bodies were burned at Buchenwald

Levaser, who was an army chaplain, recounts in his memoirs being told by Jewish prisoners that when American troops first saw what the Nazis had done in the camps, they took out their guns and shot hundreds of Gestapo men who had not succeeded in escaping. In other cases, Allied soldiers let the inmates themselves take revenge on their former oppressors.

UNLIKE OHRDRUFF, THERE WERE STILL HUNDREDS OF Jews left alive in Buchenwald, and I asked Colonel Mailman for

Administering "Last Rites" permission to remain there to supply the survivors with any assistance possible. Since all that remained of the war in Europe was the capture of Berlin, and it looked like the Russians were, in any event, going to get there first, he agreed.

Shortly after I received permission to remain in Buchenwald, a gentile chaplain came running up to me and wanted to know whether I was Jewish. I told him that I was, and he asked whether I knew how to administer the "last rites" to those on the verge of death. A makeshift hospital had been set up for the survivors, many of whom had little chance of living, and he wanted me to go there with him. In truth, I had little idea of what to do by the bedside of a dying Jew, but I figured no one else in the vicinity would know any better and headed for the hospital.

The first bed I approached held what appeared to be an extremely emaciated adolescent. All that remained, it seemed, were two prominent eyes, cheekbones, and a protruding nose. "*Du bist a Yid* — Are you a Jew?" I asked. He nodded. I asked his name, and he whispered that it was Yosef. I explained that I was a Jewish officer in the American army, and that I had come to help him.

I was at a loss as to how I should proceed. I couldn't just ask him to start reciting *vidui* (the deathbed confession) with me, especially since I did not know it by heart. "When did you last pray to *Hashem Yisbarach?*" I asked.

"I always pray to *Hashem Yisbarach*," was his simple reply, more eloquent than any profession of faith I had ever heard.

He asked me for something to eat, and I gave him some bread. Anything else, we were told, could tear up their stomachs.

In his emaciated state, Yosef appeared to be not more that seventeen or eighteen. I subsequently learned that he was twenty-three and only looked younger because of the starvation. I had no idea what to do next, and so began to recite *Shema Yisrael*, the basic proclamation of faith. But in the middle, he stopped, and asked me with a smile why I was reciting *Shema* with him. I saw that he was fully aware, and having no answer to his question, I switched the discussion to other topics.

I inquired about Yosef's family, and he told me his family name was Friedenson. His father, Eliezer Gershon Friedenson, had been one of the leaders of Agudath Israel in Poland and the editor of the *Bais Yaakov Journal* from its inception in 1923. He was a close associate of Sarah Schenirer, the founder of the Bais Yaakov movement. Bais Yaakov was almost unknown in America when I was growing up — I knew only of the Bais Yaakov which was located in Williamsburg — and so I did not fully appreciate what it meant to be a close colleague of Sarah Schenirer. Nevertheless, I realized that I was talking to the son of someone of considerable stature in the pre-War, Eastern European Torah world.

*American troops patrolling among the barracks in the Buchenwald
concentration camp after liberation*

Fortunately, Yosef Friedenson defied the doctor's predictions,
and that conversation was only the first of many over the years.
We would meet again in the Displaced Persons' camp in Feldafing
and again in New York, where he eventually became the editor
of *Dos Yiddishe Vort* and one of the most prominent writers in the
Jewish world.

Yosef Friedenson has written a moving description of his own
memories of the liberation of Buchenwald. He describes how the
prisoners could not sleep the night prior to the liberation. They
could hear the American forces drawing nearer with each passing
moment. But a rumor started circulating among the prisoners
that the Germans intended to set the entire camp on fire before
the Americans arrived. The prisoners sat cowering in their
barracks — wondering whether they would live to see their
saviors.

In the morning, the sounds of machine-gun fire kept drawing closer and closer but no one had the courage to lift up his
head and look out through the window for fear of being hit by a
bullet. At last one intrepid prisoner looked out, and reported that

the Germans were standing there with their hands raised and their guns on the ground, while the Americans were closing in with guns drawn and bayonets fixed.

Buchenwald was liberated the twenty-eighth day of *Nissan*. As he wandered about the camp on the morning of liberation, Friedenson met an acquaintance. The man told him that every day during Pesach he had tried to recite *Hallel*. But no sooner had he recited the blessing each day than the words of *Hallel* completely escaped him. Now, however, he felt confident that he could remember the words. Five minutes later, Friedenson saw him with his face pressed to the wall trembling as he recited *Hallel*. When he got to the words, "I shall not die! But I shall live!" the man's whole body shook.

This account may partially explain the gratitude of the survivors we met in the days immediately after liberation. I suspect that those who lived to see that joyous day pictured every American soldier as having fought his way into Buchenwald in fierce hand-to-hand combat in order to liberate them. In my case, of course, that picture could hardly have been farther from the truth, but even today I can never shake the idea that I was their liberator from the minds of survivors who remember me from Buchenwald.

No More Tears

ONCE IT BECAME KNOWN THAT I COULD SPEAK YIDDISH, there was always a line of men and boys waiting to talk to me. I must have listened to hundreds of their tales, each one more tragic than the next. It seemed that none of the survivors could recall a single happy moment in their lives. The memory of what they had been through, and the loved ones they had lost, had blotted out everything else.

I began to notice that when they spoke to me there were never any tears in their eyes. I could be crying buckets listening to them, but from them there was never more than a dry sob. Their tear ducts seemed to have dried up; their tears were spent and there were no more to replace them.

It was not long before I felt that I could not bear to hear any more of their stories, but when I saw how desperate they were to share what they had seen with an outsider, who had not gone through the horror with them, I could not refuse.

No matter what the request, it was impossible to refuse. One young teenager approached me with a small sealed vial. "You're an American," he began. "We all envy you. You didn't have to go through what we went through. Would you do me a favor? Please bury this vial in a Jewish cemetery, preferably on *Har Hazeisim*. It's the ashes of my father."

One of the most moving experiences of my life occurred one night in the mess hall. A Jew approached me and asked if I had ever heard of Reb Elchonon Wasserman. "Not only have I heard of him," I replied, "I had the *zechus* of seeing him in person in 1938. Even though I was only a teenager, I saw from the expression on his face that I was looking at a Moshe *Rabbeinu* for our times."

The man told me that he had been a student of Reb Elchonon's and had actually been in hiding with him in the Kovno ghetto until Reb Elchonon was martyred at the hands of Lithuanian anti-Semites. A few days before he was killed, Reb Elchonon told four of his students that he never went to sleep at night until he had an answer for whatever *kashya* (difficulty) one of the students had asked him during the day. Sometimes he would have to stay up all night working on the problem, but by the next morning he always had a solution for the *bachur*.

Only one question had he been unable to answer: Why? When he was approached and asked: "Why my *zeide*?" "Why my *bubbe*?" "Why my mother and father?" "Why my wife and children?" he had nothing to reply. "I still don't know the answer to that question," Reb Elchonen told his students, "but at least I understand why the question cannot be answered." He then proceeded to relate the following *mashal* (parable).

> *Once a man who knew nothing at all about agriculture came to a farmer and asked to be taught about farming. The farmer took him to his field and asked him what he saw. "I see a beautiful piece of land, lush with grass, and pleasing to the eye." Then the visitor stood aghast while the farmer*

plowed under the grass and turned the beautiful green field
into a mass of shallow brown ditches.

"Why did you ruin the field!" he demanded.

"Be patient. You will see," said the farmer.

Then the farmer showed his guest a sackful of plump
kernels of wheat and said, "Tell me what you see." The visitor
described the nutritious, inviting grain — and then, once
more watched in shock as the farmer ruined something
beautiful. This time he walked up and down the furrows and
dropped kernels into the open ground wherever he went. Then
he covered the kernels with clods of soil.

"Are you insane?" the man demanded. "First you
destroyed the field, and then you ruined the grain!"

"Be patient. You will see."

Time went by, and once more the farmer took his guest
out to the field. Now they saw endless straight rows of green
stalks sprouting up from all the furrows. The visitor smiled
broadly.

"I apologize. Now I understand what you were doing. You
made the field more beautiful than ever. The art of farming is
truly marvelous."

"No," said the farmer. "We are not done. You must still
be patient."

More time went by and the stalks were fully grown. Then
the farmer came with a sickle and chopped them all down as
his visitor watched open mouthed, seeing how the orderly
field became an ugly scene of destruction. The farmer bound
the fallen stalks into bundles and decorated the field with
them. Later, he took the bundles to another area where he
beat and crushed them until they became a mass of straw
and loose kernels. Then he separated the kernels from the chaff
and piled them up in a huge hill. Always, he told his
protesting visitor, "We are not done, you must be more
patient."

Then the farmer came with his wagon and piled it high
with grain, which he took to a mill. There, the beautiful grain
was ground into formless choking dust. The visitor
complained again. "You have taken grain and transformed it

into dirt!" Again, he was told to be patient.

The farmer put the dust into sacks and took it back home. He took some dust and mixed it with water while his guest marveled at the foolishness of making "whitish mud." Then the farmer fashioned the "mud" into the shape of a loaf. The visitor saw the perfectly formed loaf and smiled broadly, but his happiness did not last. The farmer kindled a fire in an oven and put the loaf into it.

"Now I know you are insane. After all that work, you burn what you have made."

The farmer looked at him and laughed. "Have I not told you to be patient?"

Finally the farmer opened the oven and took out a freshly baked bread — crisp and brown, with an aroma that made the visitor's mouth water.

"Come," the farmer said. He led his guest to the kitchen table where he cut the bread and offered his now-pleased visitor a liberally buttered slice.

"Now," the farmer said, "now, you understand."

G-d is the Farmer and we are the fools who do not begin to understand His ways or the outcome of His plan. Only when the process is complete will the Jewish people know why all this happened. Then, when Mashiach has finally come, we will know why everything — even when it seems destructive and painful — is part of the process that will produce goodness and beauty.

THERE WERE ONLY A DOZEN OR SO JEWS IN OUR OUTFIT and, with the exception of myself and Rabbi Herschel Schacter,

Rabbi Herschel Schacter

none spoke Yiddish. Reb Herschel spoke a beautiful Yiddish. He not only listened but tried to encourage the survivors and give them some hope for the future. He spoke of the fact that though the ultimate redemption had not yet come, nevertheless the *Eibishter* had spared them and they must use that gift of life.

Reb Herschel procured a small office in Buchenwald — barely larger that a phone booth — where he spent the day talking to

Rabbi Herschel Schacter breathing life into the survivors

survivors. There were almost always a few people lined up to see him since there were few rabbis among the survivors. In those conversations, Reb Herschel had ample opportunity to witness the astounding tenacity with which the survivors were determined to hold on to their *Yiddishkeit*. A sixteen-year-old boy once asked to borrow Reb Herschel's *tefillin*. Informed that they were in his headquarters in Weimar five miles away, the boy did not hesitate to walk there and back.

When Reb Herschel expressed astonishment to an older Jew at the eagerness with which survivors ran after a pair of *tefillin*, the man replied, "What's the alternative — to be a *goy*?" A widely circulated story at that time concerned a *Rebbe* who was being led out into a forest with his chassidim to be shot by the Nazis, *yimach shemam*. As they approached the forest, he turned to his flock and said, "*Kinderlach*, it is time to recite the blessing 'that You did not make me a *goy*.'"

A few weeks after arriving in Buchenwald, Reb Herschel received a large shipment of *siddurim* from the Jewish Welfare Board. He announced in Yiddish over the camp loudspeaker system that he would be distributing the *siddurim* in a large hall, originally designed as a movie theater. A large crowd quickly gathered. Among them was a Polish Jewish Communist by the name of Ignatz. It was May 1, and he was outraged to see this group of Jews rushing to receive *siddurim* instead of celebrating the workers' holiday. He kept shouting at them, "*Meshugenneh kinder,* G-d threw your mothers and fathers into the ovens, and you want to pray!" But the crowd just ignored him, further fueling his wrath.

For *Pesach Sheni* that year, Reb Herschel was able to procure a large quantity of *matzah.* The survivors reacted to these *matzos* as if they were precious diamonds. Rabbi Yitzchak Avigdor, who had been the *rav* of the large Polish city of Borislav, took his *matzos* in hand and, in a voice trembling with emotion, made three blessings over them: "*hamotzi,*" "*al achilas matzah,*" and "*she'hechiyanu.*"

There was one survivor named Chaskell Tydor who attached himself to Reb Herschel. He had survived six years in concentration camps, including three in Auschwitz. Others who had known him in the camps told stories of how this *tzaddik* had shared his last piece of bread with his fellow Jews. He never asked anything for himself, but would take Reb Herschel from one survivor in need of assistance to another.

Studies done on camp survivors after the war revealed something remarkable. Those who took the attitude that it was every man for himself had much lower rates of survival than those who insisted on preserving some sense of communal responsibility even in the inhuman conditions of the camps. Reb Chaskell was the living embodiment of this principle.

There was a large group of survivors who dreamed of going to Palestine. Their ranks ran the gamut from Agudists to Bundists. Reb Herschel managed to obtain a German farm for them through G-5, the army procurement division, which became known as Kibbutz Buchenwald. When he first asked G-5 to requisition the farm, they wanted to know why these Jews could not simply return to Poland. Reb Herschel explained that it was impossible for Jews to return to a country whose ground was watered with the blood of their loved ones.

Reb Herschel made it a condition for being allowed to join

the farm that everyone agree that the sanctity of Shabbos be preserved at the communal level and that the communal kitchens be fully kosher. Still, any cooperative venture involving such an ideologically disparate group of Jews was not going to be an easy matter. The one thing all could agree upon was the appointment of Reb Chaskell Tydor as secretary of the "kibbutz." Though he was religious, he enjoyed the absolute trust of everyone.

Reb Herschel was also able to use his position as a U.S. army officer to assist the survivors in various ways. He took down the names, birthdays, and places of birth of the survivors and sent these to the chief Jewish chaplain in Paris, who gave the lists to the Jewish Telegraph Agency, which then circulated them in camps where there were still survivors, like Bergen-Belsen and Dachau. As a consequence, many of the survivors were reunited with their relatives. There were only men in Buchenwald, but women began to come into the area too in search of missing fathers, husbands, sons, and brothers.

Perhaps Reb Hershel's most important contribution concerned a children's transport to Switzerland. As knowledge of what had taken place in the concentration camps became widely publicized, a number of Western nations attempted to do some minimal penance for not having done more to save Jews. The Swiss government agreed to admit several hundred Jewish children under the age of sixteen. The problem, of course, was that very few children under sixteen were left alive since they would have had to be under eleven when the Nazis first invaded Poland.

The Swiss dispatched a nurse to Buchenwald to examine children to determine that they were young and healthy enough to be allowed into Switzerland. This nurse seemed to have understood her mandate to be to keep the number of children allowed in to an absolute minimum, despite the Swiss government's professed humanitarian goals. She brought back painful memories of the *selektsia* in the concentration camps, as she handed out transit papers to some children which would allow them to be admitted and designated others as too old or too unhealthy.

Reb Herschel asked one of those who had received a Swiss

Child survivors of Buchenwald depart from the concentraion camp by train

entry visa to loan it to him, and he took it into Weimar where he found a German printer who was able to duplicate the document. In the end, the Swiss nurse issued one hundred and sixty passes, and Reb Herschel issued two hundred more.

A train was to take the children from Buchenwald to Basel, and Reb Herschel was appointed to oversee the operation on behalf of the U.S. Army. As the boarding of the train got underway, the nurse was beside herself with fury at the sight of so many Jews to whom she had not issued passes boarding. Among those to whom Reb Herschel had issued documents was a forty-two-year-old mother and her two daughters. He told the mother to hide in a bathroom and not to come out during the entire long trip over the bombed-out tracks to Basel.

When the train finally arrived in Basel, the nurse ran up to the Swiss official in charge and told him that a massive fraud had been perpetrated and that the whole train should be turned around and sent back to Germany immediately. He seemed inclined to agree with her until Reb Herschel approached him wearing his officer's uniform and identified himself as the U.S. army officer in charge of the transport. The Swiss official told him that there appeared to have been serious irregularities, with many aboard the train not entitled to enter Switzerland, having obtained fake entry documents.

"Is it my fault Hitler didn't leave five hundred Jewish children under sixteen alive in Europe?" Reb Herschel asked him. "If this train or any of its passengers is sent back, there will be a press conference here in a half hour — with representatives of all the international media — for the whole world to see the true face of Swiss hospitality." Apparently the thought of being at the center of an international cause celebre did not appeal to the Swiss official, since he quickly reconsidered his decision to send the train back to Germany.

By the time Reb Herschel arrived back in Weimar in early July, the Russians had already taken over. A huge sign over the gate to Buchenwald proclaimed, "Long live Stalin, liberator of Europe." The only Jew left in Buchenwald when Reb Herschel went back for a last view of the camp was Ignatz, the Jewish Communist. He had remained behind when the others went south with the departing American troops, expecting to receive a hero's welcome from the entering Russian forces. Those hopes had been quickly dashed. Ignatz now realized that his faith in the Soviet Union had been badly misplaced and begged Reb Herschel to take him with him when he went south to rejoin his unit.

When Reb Herschel reminded him of the ardor of his former enthusiasm for the Soviet Union, which he had proclaimed the true Jerusalem, he pleaded with him not to rub salt in his wounds. "What I am suffering is a *kapparah min hashamayim*," Ignatz told him. While not doubting the sincerity of Ignatz's *teshuvah* concerning the Soviet Union, there was no way Reb Herschel could take him out of the Soviet zone.

A FEW DAYS AFTER ARRIVING IN BUCHENWALD, I WAS sitting in my tent filling out reports when one of my sergeants **Close Call** told me that there were two German boys who wanted to talk to me. What he neglected to say was that they had specifically asked to speak to a Jewish officer. Without even looking up, I told him, "Take them into the forest and dispose of them. We'll relieve the world of two more anti-Semites." We were so hardened by what we had seen in Buchenwald that we thought nothing of killing a German. We assumed that they all had been accomplices in the atrocities there.

Fortunately, these were bright boys, and they realized that it did not make much sense that they were being marched out into the woods at gunpoint. One of them asked my sergeant, "Did you speak to a Jewish officer?" He replied that he had and was following his orders.

"But did you tell him we were Jewish?"

"You didn't tell me you were Jewish, and you spoke to me in German."

"How could we speak to you in Yiddish? You're not Jewish. So we spoke to you in German."

My sergeant brought the two boys back and told me, "Those two boys claim they're Jewish. Do you want to see them?" I was overwhelmed by what I had almost done. After surviving for years in the Nazi concentration camps, these boys had almost been killed by a fellow Jew. If that had happened, I don't know how I could have lived with the guilt.

When the boys were brought in, their first request was to borrow a pair of *tefillin*.

"How do you know I have a pair of *tefillin*?" I asked them.

"All Jews have *tefillin*," they answered.

Their naivete was touching. Even after all the evil they had seen, they still could not imagine a Jew anywhere in the world without *tefillin*. They remained the same pure chassidic boys they had been in their parents' home.

I gave them my *tefillin* and went back to my reports. Out of the corner of my eye, I noticed that they were passing the *tefillin* back and forth without putting them on. I went over to them and warned them, "Listen, this is not a game. *Tefillin* are not a toy to be passed back and forth."

They looked at me, with sadness in their eyes, "But we don't know the *halachos* (laws) of *tefillin*. We were in the camps long before our bar mitzvahs, and we don't even know how to put them on or what blessing to recite."

The thought of little boys growing up in concentration camps caused tears to well up in my eyes, and I apologized for not having realized that they could not possibly know how to put on *tefillin*. I helped each one wrap the *tefillin* and say the *berachah* and gave them my little *siddur* to *daven* from. When they had finished, I gave them some dried *kichel* that my mother had sent me and sardines I had requisitioned from the house of a nearby German.

The two boys, it turned out, were cousins, Yosef and Laibel Borenstein. They were not as emaciated as most of the other prisoners because they had worked in the camp kitchen. Though they never dared to take any of the food intended for humans, they had taken potato peels that were saved and sent to a nearby pig farm. They had also worked in the pigsties where they had access to potato peels intended for the pigs.

One of them told me a remarkable story concerning his older brother. They were Gerrer chassidim, and lived in Gur near the *Rebbe*. When the Nazis entered Gur, the *Rebbe* had still not managed to escape and was in hiding. As the leader of the largest group of chassidim in Poland, he was at the top of the Nazis' most wanted list and they were very eager to capture him.

The older brother — no more than sixteen himself — approached the Nazis. He told them that he knew where the *Rebbe* was hiding and would take them there. He led them on a long walk into the deep forest near the town. At long last, he showed them the purported hiding place. The *Rebbe* was not there nor were there any signs that anyone had been hiding there. The boy looked perplexed and told the Nazis that he must have gotten confused. He then led them to yet a second spot where he insisted the *Rebbe* was hiding. Here, too, the *Rebbe* was nowhere to be found. Once again the boy pleaded confusion, but assured them that he now realized what his mistake had been. After the third attempt to locate the *Rebbe* proved no more successful than the first two, the Nazis realized that they were being taken for fools and killed the young boy on the spot. His efforts, however, were not in vain. He had succeeded in buying enough time for the *Rebbe* to make his escape on the journey that ultimately brought him to *Eretz Yisrael*.

The Russians Are Coming

IN LATE JUNE, WE RECEIVED NOTICE THAT THE RUSSIANS would be taking over Buchenwald on July 4. I would be staying in the camp until the Russians arrived in order to hand over our communications setup to them, but the last train taking civilians from the camp was leaving on Shabbos. For fear of what might happen to those left behind, I was determined that Yosef and Laibel, who had become particular favorites of mine, be on that train. I told them that they had to get on the train, which would take them to Switzerland, where they would be met and placed in a yeshiva. "You have a lot of catching up to do in your learning," I emphasized, "and this train is pulling out soon."

They were equally adamant that they would not get on the train. "No, it's Shabbos. We were *mechalel Shabbos* long enough, and now it's not a question of life or death. We'll go tomorrow."

"You have to go today. Tomorrow this place will be in Russian hands, and who knows whether they will let you go!" I practically shouted at them. But they were obstinate, and I realized that I was not going to be able to persuade them to get on the train. They were both underweight and I was able to pick up one under each arm. And that is how I boarded the train with them. I stayed with them until the train started to pull out of the station. When the train was going fast enough that I was sure they would not jump off, I jumped off and waved goodbye.

I had no idea as the train pulled away whether I would ever see these two wonderful boys again. But as it happened I was subsequently to renew my contact with both of them. About six months after their train pulled out of Buchenwald, Yosef sent me a picture of himself from the yeshiva in which he was learning.

MANY TIMES DURING MY FOUR YEARS IN THE ARMY I
was asked whether I was an Orthodox Jew. Invariably I
Not So Proud responded that I was. Frequently, I added
for good measure that I had succeeded in
observing the *mitzvos* even in battlefield conditions. The truth is
that I was pretty proud of myself for not having let warfare
become an excuse to depart from the standards of behavior I
followed at home and for having been open about being an
Orthodox Jew even among non-Jews.

An incident that took place one day in Buchenwald, however, helped me to put my own achievement in proper perspective. One day as I was interviewing survivors to help them track
down family members in America, one of them approached me
and said, "I see that you are Jewish." I nodded. He continued,
"From your *yarmulke,* I assume you are a *frumme Yid.*"

"I like to think that I'm a religious Jew," I replied.

The man stood there for a moment with a look of pity in his
eyes, and then he shocked me by spitting right in my face. "I
hope your G-d had a good *shluf* (sleep)," he said, "because my
bobbe and *zeide,* they're sleeping. My *momme* and *tatte* are sleeping. My sisters, my brother, all sleeping. My wife and children,
all sleeping. And your G-d, He was sleeping. So I hope He had a
good sleep."

My first reaction was fury. I wanted to take out my gun and
shoot him on the spot. And no doubt, I would have felt proud
for about five seconds that I had not stood by and let him blas-
pheme.

But as the man went on he became gradually more hysterical. He reached out his arms towards me and I saw the number
from Auschwitz with which the Nazis had marked him for life.
As the recognition of what he had gone through flashed before
me, I realized that I had no right to judge him — that no one who
had not suffered what he had suffered and witnessed what he
had witnessed could pass judgment on his loss of faith or dare to
say that he would have done better in a similar situation. The
three years I had gone through were nothing compared to what
these survivors had been through.

At the same time, I began to fully appreciate for the first time the heroism of those who emerged with their faith intact and who had the courage to pick up the broken shards of their lives and begin anew — marrying again, raising children, and sending those children to yeshivos and Bais Yaakovs.

One woman told me that she had been married before the War and had one small baby. When the Nazis entered Warsaw, she clasped her baby close to her, but the Nazi soldiers snatched him away. In front of her eyes, they threw her baby back and forth in the air, until one German placed his bayonet into the air and another flung the child onto the bayonet bringing to an end their grisly game.

I listened to hundreds of such stories. At first I couldn't bring myself to believe them completely; something inside me did not want to acknowledge that human beings could do what the Nazis had done. But after listening to account after account — which all served to confirm the savagery to which human beings can descend — I knew they were telling the truth. That is why I stand out of respect for anyone who survived the war and remained a believing Jew. They are my heroes.

My second son Akiva Yosef is married to a woman whose parents, Mr. and Mrs. Menachem Moskowitz, both lost their first spouses and young children to the Nazis. And somehow they had the courage to bring forth a second family of wonderful children. I wonder if my *mechutanim* even notice that I rise for them whenever they enter a room. They probably think I'm just being courteous and getting up to greet them. But the truth is that I get up because to me they are the greatest heroes of the spirit.

CHAPTER NINE

Feldafing Block 5A

T HE WAR IN EUROPE WAS OVER. I HAD accumulated 175 points on the basis of the five campaigns I had **Staying On** been in, my time spent overseas and the five combat stars I had won. (Every six months overseas was worth five points and every medal another five.) One hundred and sixty points entitled you to return to the States immediately, but I had already decided that I wanted to continue working in the Displaced Persons' camps helping survivors to find relatives and ensuring that they were provided with what they needed. Having someone in uniform inside the camps greatly facilitated the work that had to be done. As a soldier, I could send letters from the camps under my name without postage and I could be traced easily wherever I went through my army postal number. As an officer, I could requisition needed supplies from the German civilian population.

I approached Colonel Mailman and asked for permission to stay on for another six months in Europe, and he granted my request. He went even further and placed an army jeep at my

With Rojo, August 1943

disposal and provided me with a special letter that I was entitled to bring as much army rations as I wanted into the DP camps. Rojo, who was by now a sergeant, had also accumulated enough points to return home to his wife and young child. But to my amazement when I told him that he was eligible to ship out for America, he pretty much repeated the words of Ruth to Naomi, "Where my lieutenant goes, I'm going." He did, in fact, stay with me the entire time I was in Germany.

Accompanied by Rojo, and furnished with the jeep and Colonel Mailman's letter, I headed south for the Munich area where there were four camps for displaced persons — Feldafing, Fernwald, Landsberg, and Dachau — in close proximity. That was early July and I serviced these camps for the next five months before returning to the States on Thanksgiving Day.

THE FIRST CAMP THAT I CAME TO WAS FELDAFING, which had been until recently a German army base. Towards the

Feldafing

end of the war, the Germans wanted to hide the enormity of their atrocities and had started to transport Jewish prisoners from camps like Dachau and Bergen-Belsen to the Tyrol. The conquering Allied forces had overtaken one of these transports. Having no place to put the liberated Jewish prisoners, they decided to use the nearby German army base for that purpose. Fernwald was an outgrowth of Feldafing, as the former became filled to capacity.

Block 5A of Feldafing was a large building providing temporary housing to hundreds of *frum* Jews. The block was cosmopolitan — there were Jews from Russia, Poland, Lithuania, Hun-

*Seated (left to right): R' Yosef Gelernter, me, R' Yitzchak Meir Ziemba,
Aviezer Burstyn, and Mordechai Leib Glatstein.
Standing (center): R' Avraham Ziemba.*

gary, Czechoslavakia. Whatever the country, it was represented
in Block 5A. Everyone there was clean shaven, though many of
the chassidim were just beginning to grow back the beards that
had been shaved by the Nazis.

The accommodations for the survivors were far from deluxe.
The world was certainly not consumed by guilt for not having
done more to rescue the Jews of Europe from their fate. When I
arrived, they were sleeping on hard benches, without any mattresses. Eventually they took the body bags that soldiers had carried into action, and which fortunately had not been needed, and
began filling them with hay to use as mattresses.

Next to Block 5A was a makeshift hospital. Many of those in
Block 5A were still in very poor health after their ordeal but not
in need of hospitalization. The hospital was run by Dr. Rosenauer,
who had been one of the most prominent eye specialists in Poland and a general in the Polish army prior to the War. As soon
as the American authorities discovered who he was, he was immediately taken to New York, where he ended up on the staff of
Mt. Sinai hospital. After returning home, I visited him several
times with my mother to see if he could help save her remaining
eye, because her vision was deteriorating.

R' Yosef Friedenson imitating Hitler

I decided to sleep in Block 5A rather than the more comfortable army barracks nearby. Every day Rojo and I would drive to the nearby army base to pick up my mail, which by the end of our time there was a veritable truckload, and send all our letters to Mike Tress and others involved in helping the survivors.

Living in Block 5A were many great Jews, including the Klausenberger *Rebbe*, the Stoliner *Rebbe*, the Sulka Rav, and Rabbis Yitzchak Meir and Avraham Ziemba, two surviving nephews of Rabbi Menachem Ziemba, *Hy"d*, perhaps the greatest rabbi of pre-War Warsaw, who perished in the Warsaw Ghetto. I also became reacquainted with others like Yosef Friedenson whom I had met previously in Buchenwald. To keep his sanity in the concentration camps, where he had been unable to study Torah, he had memorized many of the speeches of Hitler, *ym"sh*, which had been ceaselessly broadcast to the prisoners. Now in Feldafing, he often entertained us with his imitations of Hitler's insane orations about conquering the world and other such insane delusions of grandeur.

IN BOTH BUCHENWALD AND AFTERWARDS, MY MOST
tangible service for the survivors was to bring them into contact
with relatives in America. I interviewed the

A Shadchan survivors and took down their names, their
hometown, names of parents and grandparents, and the names
and addresses of any known relatives in America. When I had
finished gathering the information, I forwarded it all to my friend
Mike Tress in New York. Where there were known relatives, he
made contact with them, and where there were not, he took out
full-page newspaper ads with the names of those in the camps
and all identifying information, in the hope that unknown relatives in America would come forward. Mike would then write
back with the names of relatives in America and frequently en-
close letters from them to their relatives in one of the DP camps.
I picked up my mail every day. In time, I was receiving hundreds of letters a day.

I also began to receive packages to distribute to the survivors. Initially, I received five or six packages a day in Buchenwald,
but that soon increased to ten and then fifteen. By the time I
moved south to the DP camps around Munich, a thousand packages a week were being delivered. By far the largest number of
these packages came through Mike Tress and Zeirei Agudath Is-

Passing out mail in Feldafing

One of the many "thank-you" letters...

Lt. Meyer J. Birnbaum
Hq. 59th Signal Bn.
APO - 403
c/o PM - N.Y.C.

18 September 1945

Refugee-Immigration Division
Agudath Israel Youth Council of America
113 West 42nd Street
New York 18, N. Y.

Gentlemen:

I wish to express my appreciation and also acknowledge receipt for the more than 3,000 kosher food packages that your organization sent to me during the past month for the Jewish refugees in the displaced persons centers in my area, of which I received 1,000 packages during the course of one week. I also wish to assure you that I dealt with the innumerable letters and cabled messages for these Jews through your organization.

From first-hand experience. I can unhesitatingly state that you are the American Jewish organization that has been bringing substantial aid and succor particularly kosher food - to our destitute fellow-Jews in the liberated concentration camps.

Words cannot suffice to express their undying gratitude for your outstanding relief work. I express to all the unbounding appreciation and thanks of all our brethren in Feldafing, Dachau and Landsberg, who are being aided through your organization.

With Torah Greetings,

Meyer J. Birnbaum

Lt. Meyer J. Birnbaum

THE YOUNG MEN'S CHRISTIAN ASSOCIATIONS · THE NATIONAL CATHOLIC COMMUNITY SERVICE
THE SALVATION ARMY · THE YOUNG WOMEN'S CHRISTIAN ASSOCIATIONS
THE JEWISH WELFARE BOARD · THE NATIONAL TRAVELERS AID ASSOCIATION
U S O IS FINANCED BY THE AMERICAN PEOPLE THROUGH THE NATIONAL WAR FUND

A letter of thanks from me to Agudath Israel

rael. *Talmidim* of Torah Vodaath and Chofetz Chaim of Queens would come down to the Zeirei offices after their night learning *seder* and stay there all night preparing packages.

In almost every package there was also a personal note. "Dear Lieutenant," a typical letter began, "my name is so-and-so. Please give me a blessing and ask whoever receives this to give me a blessing." I'll never forget the packages from one young man in Torah Vodaath named Yankele Goldstein. "Please give me a blessing that I *shteig* in my learning. Please give me a blessing that I find an appropriate *shidduch*. I'm your partner. I send these packages and I hope they arrive in good condition," he would write me. Today, Rabbi Goldstein is a very dear friend.

The number of packages was so overwhelming that eventually the army decided that I must be running a black market ring. Shortly after I returned to the States, my friend Moshe Gibber, who had finished the service as a captain, called me up to find out whether I had yet been discharged. Told that I had, he was clearly relieved. "G-2, army intelligence, is looking for you. They

Girls from the Ohel Sarah girls' home at Landsberg

suspect you of having run a black market operation," he told me.

"Well, I did receive over a thousand packages a week. But those went straight to the refugees."

"I know that, but the U.S. Army doesn't know it."

"That's crazy. If I was running a black market operation, how come I'm penniless? I left behind my electric shaver and batteries, which was the only thing I owned by the time I shipped out. And I didn't even have enough money to buy a new one when I got home."

"Well, anyway, that was the rumor going around. *Baruch Hashem,* they didn't catch you and give you a rough time."

Even in those first few months after the liberation, the remarkable resilience of the Jewish spirit was evident. In Feldafing, a group of Polish Jews led by Rabbi Yitzchak Meir Ziemba established a branch of Agudath Israel. They created a girls' home called Ohel Sarah and Kibbutz Chofetz Chaim for those interested in going to *Eretz Yisrael.* Bais Yaakov seminary girls put their training to use and set up schools first in Feldafing and then in the other DP camps.

The Agudah branch in Feldafing began to organize the other

Teacher at the Feldafing DP camp instructing pupils in Hebrew.
On the board the "Shema" is written.

DP camps, and even held a conference for representatives from camps from all over Germany. Feldafing became the center for the distribution of kosher food and *tashmishei kedushah*, and I was the contact person for the Agudah leaders in the camp with Zeirei Agudah in America.

THE DOMINANT FIGURE IN FELDAFING WAS UNQUES-tionably the Klausenberger *Rebbe*. What he did for our broken

The Klausenberger Rebbe

brothers and sisters no one else could have. He had lost his wife and eleven children to the Nazi murderers. Yet he was a constant source of strength to his fellow survivors. He befriended everyone and gave them the courage to start over again. He himself eventually found his second Rebbetzin there and started a second family. Russian, Litvak, chassid, he didn't discriminate. If you were Jewish, he would do everything he could for you.

One incident revealed to me the *Rebbe's* greatness more than

*Klausenberger Rebbe accompanied by students and followers
at the D.P. camp in Fernwald*

any other. A group of Hungarian Jewish girls in Fernwald were
conducting themselves in a way far removed from the traditional
standards of modesty that have always characterized the daughters of Israel. Treated as animals for much of their formative teen-
age years, they had simply lost all sense of the Divine spark in
themselves. This situation was brought to my attention by an
American commander in the area, and I in turn spoke to the
Klausenberger *Rebbe* about it.

The *Rebbe* did not hesitate a moment when I described the
situation to him. He went with me straight into the area where
these girls were living and started speaking to them in Hungarian, which was their native tongue. His love and concern for them
was so overwhelming that ninety percent returned with him to
Feldafing, where he established a school for them. These girls
would cry their hearts out to him, and he would listen to them
and offer consolation. Most of these girls had come from religious homes, and the majority of them eventually returned to
the fold solely because of the Klausenberger *Rebbe's* concern.

One of the first things the Klausenberger asked me after we met was whether I had kosher *tefillin*. I told him that I thought they were, and that I remembered going with my mother to a *chassidishe sofer* who wrote the *parshiyos* and obtained the *batim*. The Klausenberger *Rebbe* was thrilled that he would for the first time in many years be able to put on *tefillin* with a blessing. Until that time, he had been able to obtain pairs of *tefillin*, but in each case there had been doubts about whether they were kosher, and so he had not made a blessing.

As soon as word got out that I had kosher *tefillin*, the whole block wanted to put them on. Every morning, they would line up under the watchful gaze of the Klausenberger *Rebbe*, who would make sure that no one tarried. He used to stand there saying, "All right, put on the *tefillin*. Faster, faster. Make your *berachah*. Finishing putting on the *shel Rosh*. Say *Shema*. Take off the *tefillin*. Next."

IT WAS NEARING THE TIME TO BEGIN RECITING THE *Selichos* prior to the *Yamim Noraim*. I had succeeded in obtaining

The Wrath of Rojo many *Selichos*, and went to ask the Klausenberger *Rebbe* if there was anything else I could do. He told me that he had managed to procure a proper *chalif* (knife for performing *shechitah*) from a Jewish chaplain who had passed through the camp, and that there was a qualified *shochet* (ritual slaughterer) among the survivors. Could I possibly obtain any sheep, the *Rebbe* wanted to know.

Rojo and I commandeered a two-and-a-half ton truck and requisitioned seven sheep from farmers in the region. There was great rejoicing in the camp when we drove up with the sheep. They were led out of the truck and slaughtered right there on the grass. As a little boy, I had seen chickens slaughtered, but this was the first time I had ever seen the *shechitah* of a large animal.

Of the seven sheep, only four were found to be kosher. That was, however, sufficient to prepare a feast for the coming Shabbos to which the entire camp was invited. For the survivors it would be the first taste of meat in many years.

Rojo and I were invited as the guests of honor to the *simchah*.

Everything proceeded smoothly on Shabbos night until it came time for *Kiddush*. There was no kosher wine, but I told the *Rebbe* not to worry because I had plenty of wine that I had made myself.

Part of our army rations was a small package of raisins, and I would save these and put them into a canteen with a little water and sugar and allow them to ferment. With this "wine," I made *Kiddush* and *Havdalah* every week. Using my wine, the *Rebbe* made *Kiddush* and sat down to drink. No sooner had he placed the first sip in his mouth, however, than he spit it out, saying, "That's not wine, that's vinegar, and I made the wrong *berachah*. You can't say *boreh pri hagafen* on vinegar." I had been drinking this vinegar for so long that I had ceased to notice its sour taste and just assumed that's what wine tasted like.

Shabbos day was the eagerly awaited feast. A huge *cholent* had been prepared, and was placed before the *Rebbe*. The *Rebbe* tasted the *cholent* and then took another big spoonful and passed it to me as the guest of honor. Standing behind me was Rojo, my faithful companion and cook for the past year. As the spoon was being passed to me, Rojo reached out and knocked it out of the *Rebbe's* hand, sending the *cholent* flying through the air. I was in total shock and horror.

"No one does any cooking for my lieutenant. I'm the only one who cooks for him. Don't you know that he eats kosher and only kosher?" Rojo exclaimed.

"*Vus haht der meshugenner gezugt* — What did the crazy man say?" the *Rebbe* wanted to know. I tried to explain to him how Rojo did all my cooking using my helmet for a cooking vessel and showed him my helmet of many colors. All that was left was to explain to Rojo that the Klausenberger *Rebbe* was a very holy man and we could rely on the fact that anything he served us was kosher. I'm not sure, however, whether Rojo was completely mollified by my explanation. I think his feelings were hurt at no longer being my exclusive cook.

I WAS VERY GRATEFUL FOR THE OPPORTUNITY THAT I had to help the survivors in some small way. The opportunity to live with and observe such a giant as the Klausenberger over many months was one that I wouldn't trade for anything. The

The Stoliner Rebbe's Modesty

truth is that my *emunah* was strengthened by every single person that I met in the DP camp. Each one of them was, as I said, a hero to me.

The gratitude of the *sh'eiris hapleitah* (refugees) for what we were trying to do for them was boundless. One day I was approached by two young girls who asked me whether I had been able to obtain *shemurah matzos* for Pesach. I told them that I considered myself lucky to receive any kind of *matzos* through the mail from my mother, but had been unable to obtain *shemurah matzos*. The next day they presented me with two "*shemurah matzos*." True, it was long past Pesach and the "*matzos*" bore precious little resemblance to *matzos* of any kind, but these young girls obviously remembered how dear the preparation of *matzos* had been in their father's home and wanted to give me a present of great value. I did not fully succeed in holding back my tears when they gave me this precious gift.

I have always been puzzled by the feelings of gratitude of the *sh'eiris hapleitah* — both then and even today after all these years. From the point of view of the religious soldiers who were in the camps, everything we were able to do seemed such a pitiable drop in the bucket in relation to what our fellow Jews had suffered. And no great *mesiras nefesh* was required on our part. I once mentioned my feelings to Moshe Greenwalt, a storekeeper in the Geulah neighborhood of Jerusalem who I first met as a teenager in Block 5A. He explained that I was looking at it from the wrong perspective:

"Think of it from the point of view of a sixteen-year-old boy who had watched his parents taken away, and was certain that neither of them were alive. We had already seen the prisoners from Western European countries repatriated, and it seemed to us that we were going to be completely abandoned. Then all of a sudden you appeared in Block 5A, and everyday you were with us for four or five hours passing out pants and shirts and food. Can you imagine what that meant for us?"

One of the men in Block 5A about whom I had written to

Mike Tress was named Perlow. Mike wrote back that I should ask him if he was related to the Stoliner *Rebbe*. I approached the man and asked him if he was related to the Stoliner *Rebbe*, and he shook his head that he was not. Eventually someone in America became suspicious that it was the *Rebbe* himself, and Mike instructed me to ask him outright whether he was the Stoliner *Rebbe*.

This time he acknowledged that he was the Stoliner *Rebbe*. What had tipped them off in America was that the *Rebbe* had once asked me if I could obtain a fiddle for him, and I had mentioned this in one of my letters

The Stoliner Rebbe, Rabbi Yochanan Perlow, as he appeared in his passport picture upon leaving the D.P. camp

to Mike Tress. Someone in America remembered that the Stoliner *Rebbe* had played the fiddle.

I was overwhelmed by the Stoliner's modesty. After all that he had suffered, he could have had a semi-privileged position among the survivors by revealing who he was. But he refused to be treated any differently from any of the others. Thus, when I had asked him if he was related to the Stoliner *Rebbe*, he had answered truthfully that he was not, without adding that he *was* the Stoliner *Rebbe*.

Sleeping on a bench not far from the Stoliner *Rebbe* was a man named Yechiel Roth, on whom the effects of his ordeal were still pronounced. He had a relative in Crown Heights to whom I had written, and we were waiting to receive some kind of response.

I never smoked, but I loved the aroma of pipe tobacco, and used to occasionally fill a pipe and blow out the smoke just to savor the delicious smell. One day, I happened to pass Yechiel Roth as I was blowing my pipe, and he asked me if he could smoke my pipe for a moment. His enjoyment of this little luxury was so palpable that I gave him the pipe and the next day picked up a few more for him at the army PX.

While he was enjoying his first smoke, we started talking and I asked him where he was from. He told me he was from Sulka, which was in Czechoslovakia. Mention of Czechoslovakia brought to mind my friend Gedaliah Schwartz from London, and I asked Yechiel Roth if he had ever heard of him. He fairly shrieked, "What do you mean? That's the name of my dearest and closest friend!" Until that moment, he had no idea that Reb Gedaliah was still alive, much less that he had spent the War in the relative safety of England. His joy was without bounds.

I immediately wrote a letter to Reb Gedaliah that his dear friend and *chavrusa* (study partner), the Sulka Rav, was alive. I had thought it ridiculous when Reb Gedaliah had asked me on the eve of the Normandy invasion to keep an eye open for Yechiel Roth, and now I was the intermediary for reuniting these childhood friends. No incident better captures the thrill of the work I was doing and the feeling that the *Ribbono Shel Olam* had provided me with an immeasurable *zechus* in being able to bring the survivors back in touch with family and friends.

Survivors at the DP camp in Feldafing.

Farewell party tendered in my honor by Zerei Agudah DP group

In center a young boy I helped smuggle out to Switzerland

CHAPTER TEN

Yom Kippur in the Camps

ELUL WAS APPROACHING AND I VISITED ALL THE four camps in which I was working to ascertain what they needed

Mission Across the Channel

for the upcoming *Yamim Noraim*. A man I knew only as Hillel Lichtenstein was in charge of organizing the *kehillah* in Landsberg, which was an annex of Dachau where many of the survivors of Dachau had settled. He gave me a detailed list of the necessities which were lacking in Landsberg.

List in hand, I flew from Munich to London. In London, I went straight to the house of Harry Goodman. That great *baal tzedakah* was immediately on the phone to every Jewish community in England describing the plight of the survivors and their needs for the upcoming holidays. My goal was to fly back with an army transport filled with everything from *sifrei Torah, shofuros, talleisim, machzorim, siddurim,* and *selichos,* to *yarmulkes, gartlach, bekeshes,* and *shtreimlach.*

I also contacted my friend Moshe Swerdloff, who was still in London. He asked me what the survivors desired most, and was

Loading the plane with religious supplies for the flight back to Germany

shocked when I told him "*arbah minim* and *gartlach*." He had naturally assumed that food or clothing would be at the top of their list. While working for Lend Lease, Moshe had established a good relationship with the senior Jewish chaplain stationed in London, and he prevailed upon the chaplain to order as many sets of *arbah minim* as he could. Eventually an army transport was dispatched from the United States carrying a number of sets of *arbah minim* with its other cargo.

All night long, volunteers worked in communities throughout England collecting everything on my list and transporting it to London. We gathered everything together, and twenty-four hours after my arrival I was on my way back to Munich with a full plane. The day I was in London was VJ Day, the day of Japan's unconditional surrender, but the joy I felt at that news was nothing compared to what I felt because of the treasures I was taking back with me.

Rojo was parked at the airport waiting with a truck to meet me. We went first to Dachau, then Feldafing, and then Fernwald to drop off our treasures. Our last stop was Landsberg, where I looked for Hillel Lichtenstein to hand over the items on his list. He was nowhere to be found so I just left a message that the *talleisim* and *shofars* had all been checked and he did not need to check them again. It would be another thirty years before I would meet Reb Hillel again, albeit under a different name than I had known him in the DP camps.

ON BOTH ROSH HASHANAH AND YOM KIPPUR, I divided my *davening* between the various *minyanim* set up in **The** Feldafing. Yom Kippur, I *davened Kol* **Klausenberger** *Nidrei* and *Maariv* with the Klausen- **Rebbe's** berger *Rebbe* and survivors from Hun- **Kol Nidrei** gary, Romania, and Czechoslovakia. **Drashah** *Shacharis* and *Mussaf*, I *davened* with the small *Litvishe minyan*, and for *Minchah* and *Ne'ilah*, I was with the *Polisher minyan*.

After *Kol Nidrei*, the Klausenberger *Rebbe* got up to speak. I had never heard so powerful a speech in my life, and I never will again. When he had finished, more than two hours later, I was both emotionally drained and inspired for the best *davening* of my life.

The *Rebbe* stood there with his *machzor* in his hand, flipping through its pages. Periodically, he would ask rhetorically, "*Wehr haht das geshriben* — Who wrote this? Does this apply to us? Are we guilty of the sins enumerated here?" One by one, he went through each of the sins listed in the *Ashamnu* prayer and then the *Al Chait* and concluded that those sins had little to do with those who had survived the camps.

"*Ashamnu* (We have become guilty) — Does this apply to us? Have we sinned against Hashem or man? I doubt it. Let's go on.

"*Bagadnu* (We have betrayed) — Have we been ungrateful for the good Hashem has done us? Are we disloyal to Hashem? Have we betrayed our loved ones? No. *Bagadnu* does not apply to us.

"*Gazalnu* (We have stolen) — From whom could we have stolen? Definitely this does not apply to us. There was no such thing as theft in the camps. There was nothing to steal. This does not apply to us!

"Wait. *Gazalnu* does apply to me. I have to *klop chatasi* (beat my chest to atone) for *gazalnu.* One day I came in from work and lay down on the wooden slats to rest. While I was sleeping, my skin got caught between two of the slats. Remember, we consisted of nothing more than skin and bones, and our sweat over the years had eaten away the slats so that there were places in between in which your skin could get caught.

"I wiggled one way and another, but I could not free myself. Finally, I gave a hard push to free myself from between the slats. When I did, some skin ripped off and I started bleeding. As I freed myself, I called out *'Oy.'* I thought I had only groaned softly, but my cry was enough to wake up one of the fellow prisoners. *Gezeilah,* I stole sleep from this man.

"This is the only theft I remember for which I must *klop 'chatasi.'* There was nothing to steal. No one had anything to steal. Even if we had wanted to steal, we couldn't have.

"*Dibarnu dofi* (We have spoken slander) — We didn't speak any slander. We didn't speak at all. If we had any strength to speak, we saved it for our SS guards so that we would have enough strength to answer them.

"*He'evinu* (We have caused perversion) — No one caused me to deviate from the right path and I did not cause anyone else to go off the path.

"*Vehirshanu* (We have caused wickedness), *zadnu* (We have sinned willfully), *chamasnu* (We have exhorted), *tafalnu sheker* (We have accused falsely) — No, these don't apply to us.

"*Latznu* (We have scoffed) — Who wrote this *machzor?* Who put it together? We were so serious in the camps. There was no such thing as smiling or making a joke.

"*Moradnu* (We have rebelled) — Who should we have rebelled against? Against Hashem? We weren't able to rebel at all. If we had tried to rebel against the Nazis it would have been our last rebellion."

When the Klausenberger *Rebbe* had finished the entire *Ashamnu* prayer in this fashion, he continued with the *Al Chait.*

"*Al chait she'chatanu lifanecha b'ones uveratzon* (For the sin we have sinned before You under duress and willingly) — Certainly nothing we did in the camps was with *ratzon* (will), and it was even beyond the category of *ones* (by compulsion).

"*B'imutz halev* (with hardness of heart) — Our hearts were soft. The Nazis saw to that.

"*Bev'li daas* (without knowledge) — Our minds were in such a state that we did not have knowledge of anything.

"*B'gilui arayos* (through sexual impropriety) — Our bodies were so weak that *gilui araiyos* was the furthest thing from our thoughts.

"*B'dibbur peh* (with harsh speech) — We spoke only in whispers.

"*B'tipshus peh* (with foolish speech) — That's a *gelechter* (something funny). Who spoke foolishly or lightheartedly in the situation we were in?

"*B'yetzer hara* (with the evil urge) — To sin with the *yetzer hara* you must first have possession of your physical senses — a desire to touch or see or hear or taste something forbidden.

"We didn't have any sense of touch. We were skin and bones incapable of touching. The only thing we could feel was the corpses that we carried out every morning. Each morning, we looked around to see who was no longer moving and would have to be carried out from the barracks.

"We heard only one thing. The commands of our guards. We had ears for nothing else. Our eyes were only for looking around to see whether our guards were watching when we wanted to take a rest. Otherwise we were as blind men seeing nothing.

"Smell — Yes, we had a sense of smell. The unforgettable stench of death was constantly in our nostrils making us nauseous. We never got used to that smell. The dead lay everywhere.

"Taste — The only taste we knew was the thin soup they gave us so we would have enough strength for another day's work. Oh yes, I forgot, we did have the *yetzer hara* for food — for the slop that we saw thrown to the pigs. What the SS officers would not eat they threw to the pigs. How we envied the pigs, especially for the potato peels that were thrown to them. How we would have loved to eat those potato peels."

Once by one, he eliminated every *al chait*. I can no longer remember what he said about each one, but the effect on me as an American soldier, whose experiences were so far removed from that of these survivors, was to emphasize just how much these sins did apply to me and how much breast-beating was required.

The *Rebbe* had closed his *machzor* and I was sure that he had finally finished. But then he asked again, "Who wrote this *machzor*? I don't see any-where the sins that do apply to us — the sins of having lost our *emunah* and *bitachon* (faith and trust in G-d).

Klausenberger Rebbe

"What is the proof that we sinned in this fashion? How many times did we recite *Krias Shema* on our wood slats at night and think to ourselves: '*Ribbono Shel Olam*, let this be my last *hamapil*. I can't carry on any longer. I'm so weak. I have no reason to carry on any more. Is there no end to our suffering? *Ribbono Shel Olam*, please take my *neshamah* so that I do not have to repeat once again in the morning, "I'm thankful before You, the living King, who has re-turned my soul to me. . . ." I don't need my soul. You can keep it.'

"How many of us went to sleep thinking that we couldn't exist another day, with all *bitachon* lost? And yet when the dawn broke in the morning, we once again had to say *Modeh Ani* and thank Hashem for having returned our souls.

"None of us expected to survive. Yes, we tried to survive, but none of us expected to. Every morning, we saw this one didn't move and that one didn't move, and as we carried the dead out, we looked upon them with envy. Is that *emunah* in Hashem? Is that *bitachon* in Hashem?

"Yes, we have sinned. We have sinned and now we must *klop* "*al chait*." We must pray to get back the *emunah* and *bitachon* we once had, the *emunah* and *bitachon* that went to sleep these last few years in the camps. Now that we are freed, *Ribbono Shel Olam*, we beg You to forgive us. Forgive everyone here. Forgive every Jew in the world, *Ribbono Shel Olam*, our Father."

I *DAVENED SHACHARIS* AND *MUSSAF* THE NEXT morning with the *Litivishe minyan.* There were very few men there,

A Difficult Quandary which only increased the mournful air. When time came for *Yizkor,* I did not realize at first that it was *Yizkor* since not a single person left the room.

After *Mussaf,* General Eisenhower came to visit the camp. Another religious officer from Williamsburg named Lieutenant Silver and I escorted the Klausenberger *Rebbe* and Rabbi Yitzchak Meir Ziemba to meet Eisenhower. The entire camp was there, and I served as the interpreter.

General Eisenhower spoke first and said how proud he was to have had a part in the liberation of the concentration camps. Then the Klausenberger *Rebbe* and Rabbi Ziemba thanked him for having been G-d's appointed emissary to bring them to freedom. Though it was Yom Kippur, and everyone was fasting, they presented Eisenhower with a *challah* that had been specially baked for him. I learned later that *challos* are a traditional offering of appreciation to gentile authorities.

When the ceremony was completed, Eisenhower looked at me and said, "Lieutenant, I know you from somewhere." I reminded him that I had also served as his translator when he came to visit Buchenwald.

I was shocked at *Minchah* in the *Polisher minyan* when Yosef Friedenson and a friend of his bought *Maftir Yonah* for me for three bottles of beer. After *Minchah,* Yosef Friedenson's friend approached me to help him with a problem — confronting him. He told me that he knew his wife's *yahrzeit* from a survivor who had seen her going to the gas chamber, and that he had said *yizkor* for her and their young daughter, who he presumed had been with her until the end. But someone who had been in Auschwitz when it was liberated and returned to Poland afterwards had just recently crossed over from the Russian to the American side of the border. That man told him that his daughter was still alive: "He gave me the name of a *goyishe* woman who had been taking care of her the whole war, and she gave him the message, 'If you run into this girl's father, tell him I have his daughter.' "

He wanted to know whether I thought he should take the

chance of returning to Russian-held territory and perhaps being arrested and even sent to Siberia, especially in light of his doubts that his daughter was still alive.

I couldn't understand what he wanted from me. "I'm just a young *bachur*. You have in this camp the Klausenberger *Rebbe*, the Ziemba brothers, the Stoliner *Rebbe*, the Sulka Rav. These men are giants, and they can answer your question," I said. But despite my trying to push him off, he returned after *Maariv*, as I was breaking the fast, and once again asked me for help in deciding what to do.

"I still think you should talk to one of the *rabbanim* here," I told him. "But if you ask me my opinion, it seems to me that if you don't go back you'll never have a night's sleep again. You'll spend the rest of your life wondering: Was that my daughter? It will drive you crazy as long as you live." With that our conversation concluded.

Six months later, after I had already returned to the States, I received a phone call one day from Friedenson's friend. He had made it to America and was then living with his brother-in-law, the Boyaner *Rebbe*. He wanted to come over immediately to talk to me. I gave him my address and told him that he'd better take a cab because it would be too complicated to come by train.

About an hour-and-a-half later, he walked into my parents' house with a blonde four-year-old girl. "Is this your daughter?" I asked him.

His reply was a shock: "This is the monster called my daughter." I admonished him for calling his daughter a monster, and he replied, "Here, take a look at my fingers. Every one of them has bite marks. Every time I'm not looking for a moment, she comes up and bites one or two. Now look at my shin and see how she kicks me." He rolled up his pants leg to reveal a black-and-blue leg.

"I can't go on like this. I don't know what to do," he complained. He then told me the story of how he had returned to Poland and found his daughter. The gentile woman who had been keeping her from infancy provided clear proofs as to her identity and demanded a substantial ransom for her return. That ransom had been supplied by the Boyaner *Rebbe*, who was the girl's uncle. Since the girl had been raised almost all her life by the Polish woman, she had no desire to leave her. She cursed her father in Polish, called him a kidnaper, and continually attacked him.

"Last time I asked you for advice, you advised me well. You were surely right that I would have been plagued forever if I had not gone back for my daughter. But I'm twenty-nine years old. I want to start over. Who will marry me with such a daughter? Please tell me what I should do," he pleaded with me.

"My advice is that you talk this over with the Boyaner *Rebbe*. He is a very wise man. Speak to him, and I'm sure he'll come up with an *eitzah* (proper advice)."

"No, I want to hear from you an *eitzah*."

"Since she is the Boyaner *Rebbe's* niece, he has an obligation to bring her up, just like any uncle would. His children are grown up. I suggest that you leave the house completely, and let the *Rebbe* raise your daughter. She has no animosity towards him or her cousins so just leave her there."

My mother served tea, and I took the opportunity to run out and go to the corner candy store, where I bought a little Kewpie doll. I put it down on a chair near the little girl and watched out of the corner of my eye. She drew closer and closer to the doll, all the while looking at me to make sure I was not going to object. Finally, she picked up the doll, held it, and started to play with it.

Seeing the way she behaved with the doll, I told her father, "I don't know too much about children, but this looks like a perfectly normal child to me. The only thing you have to do right now is get out of her life. You'll always know she's your daughter, and you'll participate in all her *simchas*. But meanwhile let her grow up normally in the Boyaner *Rebbe's* home."

To make a long story short, this little girl grew up to be a real princess. Today she has a beautiful family. I was lucky enough to be at her wedding and to meet her again recently after many years. Seeing how well things had turned out after her first four years in a gentile house was a very moving experience for me.

CHAPTER ELEVEN
Meeting Again

IN EARLY NOVEMBER, I RECEIVED WORD THAT a delegation from America headed by Mike Tress, and including my old *Rebbe* Rabbi Shmuel Shechter, would soon be visiting the DP camps, and I decided that I was no longer needed. Before I left, the Agudath Israel group in Feldafing threw a beautiful going away party for me. There was one young teenager in the camp with no relatives, and I was asked to try to smuggle him out to Paris, which I succeeded in doing. On Thanksgiving day, I boarded ship for the return trip to the United States. Though I was leaving the camps behind, my contacts with many of those I met there were to be renewed over the years.

It's already a standing joke with my children that any time they go out with me they are likely to be present for a surprise reunion with someone I met in Buchenwald or one of the DP camps. On my son Shlomo's first visit home after the start of a new *zman* at the Mirrer Yeshiva, I asked him the name of his *chavrusa*. He assured me that I would not know the boy's family since they were from Kew Garden Hills in Queens and not from

Left to right: R' Chaim Teiter, Yitzchak Friedman, Yisrael Kutner

Brooklyn. But when he told me the boy's name was Kutner, I took out the pictures from my farewell party in Feldafing, pointed to one of those in the picture, and told him to take the picture to his *chavrusa* and ask him whether that was his father. Unfortunately, the boy's father had just passed away, but he was very excited to see a picture of his father as a young man just after the war.

One day I was walking through the New York diamond district when one of the storeowners suddenly darted out of his store and dragged me in. It was none other then Yosef Borenstein, whom I had put on the last train out of Buchenwald. After a long talk in his office, he took out a heart shaped pin surrounded by slivers of diamonds, and asked me how I liked it. I told him that it was exquisite but beyond my price range. Two nights later, Yosef came over to my house and insisted that I take the pin. To this day, it is my wife's favorite piece of jewelry. Yosef's cousin Laibel remained in Switzerland where he became successful in the watch business. Both of the cousins come to Jerusalem frequently to spend the festivals with the Gerrer *Rebbe*, and when they do, we often get together.

By now my children often recognize that one of these impromptu reunions is about to take place even before I do. One time, I picked up a *chassidishe* fellow at the Williamsburg entrance to the Brooklyn-Queens Expressway. A few minutes into the drive to Boro Park, my son Shlomo noticed that the man was staring at me and said something about it to me. "Let him stare at me, I don't owe him any money," I told him.

Shlomo was right about the man staring at me because a few minutes later the man admitted that he was trying to place me from somewhere. After a few minutes of guessing, Shlomo, already a veteran of such encounters, solved the mystery by asking the man whether he was one of the *sh'eiris hapleitah* (survivors) and whether he had been in Feldafing. When the chassid answered that he had, in fact, been in Feldafing, Shlomo asked him whether he remembered having less than two minutes every morning to put on the pair of kosher *tefillin* that was circulated among the survivors. The man asked Shlomo how he could possibly have known that, and Shlomo told him, "Because you were wearing my father's *tefillin*." The man looked at me and exclaimed, "*Oberleutenant* Birnbaum. I didn't recognize you immediately because you were sitting down, and I didn't see how tall you are."

I SUBSEQUENTLY DISCOVERED HOW MUCH THOSE *tefillin* meant to the residents of Block 5A. A few years ago, Rabbi

Precious Tefillin

Shalom Klein, a neighbor in Mattesdorf, asked me whether I had an extra pair of *tefillin* for a *baal teshuvah* from Russia, who was too poor to buy his own. After thinking about his request for a moment, I remembered my *bar mitzvah tefillin* and went searching for them. "I don't know if these are still kosher," I told him, "but you can take them to a *sofer*, and I'll pay to have them looked over and for any repairs that are needed." I told him these were my army *tefillin* and that they were the first *tefillin* the Klausenberger *Rebbe* and many other survivors made a blessing on after the war.

Rabbi Klein brought the *tefillin* to a *sofer* in Kiryat Sanz, which is about five minutes from my house. The *sofer* found the *parshiyos* in perfect condition, though the *batim* needed some minor repairs. In passing, Rabbi Klein mentioned that the Klausenberger

Rebbe had used these *tefillin* after the war. The *sofer* stared at him, mouth agape and asked, "You mean the owner of these *tefillin* was in Feldafing? Are these the *tefillin* that we used to put on in a minute and a half? If you can prove to me that these are the same *tefillin,* I'll pay you a thousand dollars for them."

The *sofer* then made a call to the Klausenberger *Rebbe's* community in Netanya, Kiryat Sanz, and talked to someone who remembered that the *tefillin* had belonged to *Oberleutenant* Birnbaum. The man on the other end of the phone immediately offered two thousand dollars for the *tefillin.* As soon as Rabbi Klein heard this, he raced back to my home to tell me that I had obviously made a *mekach ta'us* (a sale or gift voidable by one of the parties on the basis of his lack of information) since I didn't have any idea of the value of the *tefillin.* I told him to keep the *tefillin,* but he refused. We left it that he would have all the necessary repairs made, and we would then decide what to do. When I mentioned the incident to my children they were very upset with me. Such *tefillin* should be a legacy for them, they argued. That convinced me and I ended up buying a brand new pair of *tefillin* for the Russian boy and keeping my *bar mitzvah* pair for my children.

Since moving to *Eretz Yisrael,* these "coincidental" meetings seem to be taking place even more frequently than before. The summer we moved to *Eretz Yisrael,* I went to *daven Minchah* across the street in the *minyan* of the Kaliver *Rebbe.* As I entered, a man walked over, gave me a warm greeting, and asked good-naturedly, "Meyer Birnbaum, don't you know your old friends? You were at my *sheva berachos.*" I had to confess my embarrassment. Thankfully, he finally introduced himself as Yitzchak Friedman.

I had known him as a young Gerrer chassid in one of the DP camps. After the war, he had made it to Hartford, Connecticut, where he developed a successful glass and mirror business. He married a *frum* American girl, and Rabbi Avraham Ziemba made *sheva berachos* for him in Brooklyn, to which I was invited. It was more than thirty years since I had seen him at that *sheva berachos,* but we soon became good friends again.

When I say that my true heroes are those who lost their en-

tire families and somehow found the courage to begin again —
and in many cases even managed to become successful business-
men despite coming to America without a word of English —
Yitzchak Friedman is one of those I have in mind.

❧   ❧   ❧

About six years ago, I was standing on the main street in the
Geulah section of Jerusalem when someone walked out of a store
and gave me an exuberant *"Shalom aleichem."* I looked at him in
surprise and asked if I knew him. He answered, equally surprised,
"What, don't I know you from Hungary?" I assured him that I
had never been to Hungary in my life and that I also didn't know
him from yeshiva in Czechoslovakia, which was his next guess.
By this time, I had learned that the most likely bet was from
Feldafing or Fernwald, and I asked him if he had been there. My
guess was on the money — he had been in both places.

When I told him my name was Birnbaum, he shouted,
"Oberleutenant Birnbaum" and gave me a big bear hug and a kiss
and dragged me down a few steps to his store to introduce me to
his wife and son. "You know who this man is?" he asked them.
"He is our liberator." Even today, whenever he sees me on the
street, he always gives me a big hello and tells whomever hap-
pens to be standing nearby, "This was my liberator. This was the
one who freed me."

Geulah has been the location for a number of these impromptu
reunions. One Friday morning, I was returning from the *Kosel*
with my friend Morley Auerbach, and we decided to stop in
Geulah and pick up *challos* for Shabbos. Suddenly out of nowhere
a well-dressed middle-aged man ran up to me, threw his arms
around my neck and started kissing me. Finally, he backed off
and asked me in a sort of hurt tone, "Don't you remember me?"

From the expression on my face, it was clear that I did not. But he
soon consoled himself: "I guess that's no surprise. The last time you
saw me I was still wearing a striped inmate's uniform. You were the
first one to give me some food after the liberation of Buchenwald." The
three of us must have made quite a scene on the main street of Geulah
at six o'clock in the morning as we stood there crying in unison.

Many of my meetings with those I met in the camps seem to take place at weddings. My son Aharon lives on a religious kibbutz named Be'erot Yitzchak. At his wedding to Shulamit Shne'or, one of the old-timers on the kibbutz approached him, pointed at me, and asked him, "Who is that man? I know him from somewhere."

Aharon replied, "That's my father."

The man looked confused. "Oh, I must have made a mistake. I don't know any Gals (the name my son took when he moved to Israel)."

"His name isn't Gal. It's Birnbaum."

"He looks just like *Oberleutenant* Birnbaum."

"That's him. Why don't you go over and talk to him?"

Recently my grandson Chananya married the daughter of a Gerrer chassid from Bnei Brak. Our whole family went to Bnei Brak for Shabbos *sheva berachos*. After *davening* on Shabbos night, one of the chassidim approached to give me a *mazel tov*. As we were talking, he asked me if I was from Lodz. I told him that I was an American and had never been in Poland. "But I know you from somewhere," he insisted. "What's your name?"

"Birnbaum," I replied.

"You're *Oberleutenant* Birnbaum. I slept on the bench next to you on Yom Kippur night in Feldafing. I remember when you escorted the Klausenberger *Rebbe* and Rabbi Yitzchak Ziemba to meet Eisenhower."

Though my son and grandson had no doubt heard the story of Yom Kippur in Feldafing dozens of times, it still gave them a chill to see what the memory of that Yom Kippur means to those who were there and how strong the feelings are between all those who share those memories. For my son's *mechutan*, of course, this was a previously unknown aspect of his daughter's new family.

Actually, I'm extremely embarrassed whenever I meet one of the *sh'eiris hapleitah* and they overwhelm me with their expressions of gratitude for what I am supposed to have done for them. For my part, I consider it the greatest privilege of my life to have been given the opportunity to help my Jewish brothers and sisters who survived the concentration camps. Anytime one of them remembers *Oberleutenant* Birnbaum with thanks, I think to myself that it is I who should be thanking them. Above all, they taught me more clearly than anyone else the power of faith in Hashem and the true nature of Jewish heroism.

One of the most incredible of these reunions took place on the production line of Empire Kosher Poultry. Empire supplied my company, Mauzone Home Kosher Products, with all our chickens, and I periodically visited the Empire plant to check on the operations there. On one of those visits, I was wearing fairly decent clothes, which I wanted to keep clean, something that is not so easy to do walking down the line of *shochtim* while the chickens are being slaughtered. Finally, Joe Katz, the president of Empire, suggested that I borrow his son Murray's army uniform. Murray had just been released from the service and was using his uniform in the plant.

Walking down the line of *shochtim* with Joe Katz and my partner Rabbi Moshe Leib Levovitz, I noticed Rabbi Simcha Buchman, one of the Empire *shochtim* and Reb Moshe Leib's brother-in-law. We had met perhaps a dozen times at various Levovitz family affairs and knew each other fairly well. As I approached him, he suddenly rushed over and started hugging and kissing me.

"*Oberleutenant* Birnbaum! *Oberleutenant* Birnbaum! What are you doing here? How many years is it since I saw you in Buchenwald?" he said excitedly. His brother-in-law standing right next to me was flabbergasted by this effusive greeting since he knew that Rabbi Buchman and I had met many times in the past without any such displays of affection. On those occasions, I had always been dressed in a suit and tie, and so Rabbi Buchman had only thought of me as his brother-in-law's partner. Now, however, seeing me in uniform, he suddenly remembered me as the young lieutenant from Buchenwald. Every time we saw each other after that, it was a different type of "*Shalom aleichem*" that I received.

PERHAPS THE MOST MOVING OF THESE REUNIONS took place at the wedding of the son of Shlomo Weiss, a Satmar chassid who worked for me in my Boro Park store. Neither my wife nor I had been too eager to go since we surmised — correctly it turned out — that we would not know anyone else there. The

The Krasner Rebbe

mesader kiddushin was a very bent old man in a wheelchair. It was clear that he was not well, and a ring of chassidim stood around him to make sure that no one disturbed him. Somehow he looked very familiar to me, and I asked one of the chassidim who he was. His response — the Krasner *Rebbe* — meant nothing to me.

After the *chuppah*, I went over to give the father of the *chasan* a *mazel tov* and a present

The Krasner Rebbe

for the newlyweds. "By the way," I asked, "what is the name of the *mesader kiddushin*? He looks familiar." When he told me the Rebbe's name was Lichtenstein, I asked whether his first name was Hillel.

"Yes, but we don't call him by his first name. We call him *Rebbe*."

I had last seen the *Rebbe* more than thirty years earlier when he was the leader of the survivors in Landsberg, and I knew him only as Hillel Lichtenstein. At that time, he was just beginning to grow back the beard the Nazis had cut off, so it is no wonder that I didn't immediately recognize him. Seeing that he was planning to leave, I asked a young chassidic boy standing nearby to bring the *Rebbe* a message that *Oberleutenant* Birnbaum sends regards. I made him repeat it to make sure he got it right. I watched as the boy broke through the circle of guards around the *Rebbe*. A moment later, he emerged again from the circle with the message: "The *Rebbe* wants to speak to you."

The circle split and I walked over to the *Rebbe* and gave him a "*Shalom aleichem.*" Instead of the traditional response, "*Aleichem shalom,*" he responded, "*Yasher koach.*" I asked him what the "*yasher koach*" was for.

The *Rebbe* explained, "Don't you remember when you went to London and brought back all the *machzorim, seforim, tefillin, shofros, bekeshes,* and *gartlach* and left them in Landsberg?"

"I looked for you, but couldn't find you," I told the *Rebbe.*

"No, but when I came back and found everything you had left, I wanted to thank you. Now, at last, I can say *yasher koach* for all that you did for us then."

Needless to say, that *yasher koach* was well worth waiting for.

PART II

OUT OF UNIFORM

CHAPTER TWELVE
A Civilian Again

I ENTERED THE ARMY A RELATIVELY inexperienced, unworldly young man of twenty-three. I was then working days and studying accounting two nights a week. My low-paying job did not weigh too heavily on me because I had as yet no familial responsibilities and was confident that a bright future lay ahead upon the completion of my studies. I returned home four years later light years removed from the youth I had been in terms of life experiences and maturity, but no more prepared to earn a living than when I left. Nor could I content myself any longer with dreams of a rosy future. I wanted to marry and start a family, and that meant putting food on the table.

BEFORE I COULD EVEN START THINKING ABOUT HOW I was going to support a family, I received a call from Mike Tress.

The Value of a Uniform "Are you still legally allowed to wear your uniform?" he asked. I told him that I was. Because I had never taken any kind of vacation during my army years, I was entitled to three months of paid leave, and during that period I was still officially in the army.

"Fine," said Mike. "I bet you have a bunch of medals and ribbons." I told him that I had several medals, which pleased him greatly. Having assured himself that I would cut a sufficiently dashing figure in my uniform, Mike explained why he needed me — or at least my uniform.

The major focus of the Vaad Hatzalah and the other rescue organizations had become the bringing of the *sh'eiris hapleitah* (surviving remnants) from Europe out of the DP camps and to America. (Entry to Palestine was still blocked by the British.) Strict immigration quotas — originally designed to disfavor immigration from countries with large Jewish populations — constituted the major obstacle to bringing in these refugees. The almost total unwillingness of the American government to waive these quotas in the face of the Nazi's Final Solution had already cost hundreds of thousands, if not millions, of Jews their lives, and now they were being used to prevent the survivors of the Final Solution from entering the United States.

Mike told me there was only one way to circumvent the quotas: by obtaining affidavits from American sponsors insuring that the immigrants would not become wards of the state. In order to sign an affidavit, the sponsor had to first demonstrate that his resources were sufficient to support the immigrant for whom he was signing the affidavit.

At that time, few Orthodox Jews were capable of signing affidavits. Thus, if enough affidavits were to be secured, the majority would have to be obtained from affluent Conservative and Reform Jews. That is where my uniform came in. Mike wanted me to go around with him to Reform and Conservative Temples to describe what I had seen in Buchenwald and the DP camps. He felt that my firsthand experience and beribboned uniform gave me a certain credibility that no one else would have. "If you can draw a tear or two from them," Mike said, "they'll sign an affidavit."

My first reaction was to turn Mike down. I had never spoken to a large audience in my life, and had little desire to start civilian life by making a clown of myself. But I soon learned that it was almost impossible to say no to Mike. I knew how he had worked for years around the clock on behalf of European Jews, and it would have taken someone a lot tougher than me to refuse him. His passion and sense of mission were simply irresistible.

Irving Bunim

"This is *pikuach nefesh* (the saving of lives)," Mike said. "That means you have no choice. You'll simply have to learn how to speak. You'll see, once you start, the *Ribbono Shel Olam* won't let you fail."

Mike and I started together at Temple Sinai in Manhattan. Fortunately, no rhetorical skill was needed on my part. All I had to do was give a simple and straightforward account of what I had seen in the camps and tell the survivors' stories of what they had been through. When I finished, Mike would get up and make an appeal for volunteers to sign affidavits for "our brothers and sisters stuck in Europe." We would start with around two hundred affidavits, and gradually whittle the pile away in the course of the day, as we went from one temple to another. We did this four or five times a week for three months.

At the end of the day, Mike would take me to Eden Textiles, owned by Irving Bunim, another one of the legendary figures of that generation. Mr. Bunim would ask us how many affidavits we managed to obtain that day. Usually the number came to forty or so.

"That's not too bad," Mr. Bunim would reply. "How many do you have left?" We would tell him, and he'd instruct us to stand on either side of him with the pile of remaining affidavits. One of us would put down an affidavit for his signature and the other would pick it up as the next one was being slapped down on the table.

No one knew better than Irving Bunim what it was to save a life. Each affidavit subjected him to thousands of dollars of potential liability, and if the government had known how many affidavits he signed, he would probably have found himself the subject of a major fraud investigation. Yet I personally witnessed him signing thousands of affidavits as if he were practicing writing his signature.

When he had finished going through the stack of affidavits, it was time for me to collect my pay for the day. Mr. Bunim would take Mike and me to a kosher restaurant and insist that we order whatever we wanted. For dessert, I'd order one of everything, not that it helped much: I remained as skinny as ever.

THE RANGE OF RESCUE ACTIVITIES IN WHICH MIKE TRESS was involved was simply unbelievable. All over Europe, Jewish

Save a Child

parents had hidden their children from the Nazi murderers in Catholic convents and orphanages. In 1948, Mike established the Save a Child Foundation in order to rescue such children located in Belgium.

The success of the entire operation depended on finding someone bright, absolutely trustworthy, and French speaking. Mike called me and asked me whether I thought my friend Moshe Swerdloff would be suitable. I told Mike that both Moshe and his wife Estelle knew French and that it would be hard to imagine two more capable people. As for their willingness to go, Mike would have to speak to them directly.

Moshe and I met with Mike and some of the activists in Zeirei Agudath Israel, including Rabbi Moshe Sherer, who had just started working full-time with Mike. At that meeting, Mike outlined how the operation was to work. Moshe and Estelle were to go to Belgium and try to locate Jewish children in various Catholic institutions and with private families. If they succeeded in convincing the families or institutions to turn over the children, they were to take them to Paris where they would meet Herman Treiser. From there Herman Treiser would take them to Switzerland and place them with religious families.

Moshe and Estelle undertook this assignment with enthusiasm even though their undercover activities were obviously fraught with risk. Estelle was expecting their first child at the time and they did not even tell their parents what they were doing for fear that they would attempt to stop them from going.

Before leaving for Belgium, Moshe and Estelle gave me a valuable lesson in the meaning of friendship. I had just started a business at the time, and we were struggling and suffering from a continuous lack of adequate cash. Moshe gave me power of attorney over his bank account, which contained a few thousand dollars, and told me that I could use the money whenever I needed it. Eventually, I borrowed the entire sum. It took me five years to repay the full amount. During that

Together with Moshe Swerdloff

entire time, Moshe and Estelle never said a word to me about the money.

Moshe and Estelle remained in Belgium a little over a year. The work proved both difficult and heartbreaking. Most of the children who had close relatives still alive had already been reclaimed by that time. Those that remained had by then been with gentile families or in Catholic institutions for six or seven years, and most had no memory of their real parents. The attachments that had formed were deep, and few families or institutions were willing to part with the children. While the secular Jewish agencies in Belgium were willing to provide names of Jewish children, they took the position that the children were better off not being uprooted again and refused to help the Swerdloffs in any way. Even where families or the Catholic institutions were willing to part with the children, they often demanded to be compensated for their expenses, and the Swerdloffs frequently found themselves without sufficient funds to do so.

Despite these frustrations, Moshe and Estelle did succeed in rescuing a dozen or so children in the little more than a year they spent in Belgium. During that time their first child was born, a boy named Elya Chaim, and Rabbi Reuvain Rabinowitz flew over from Birmingham to perform the *bris*. A couple of months later, Moshe was arrested, along with Herman Treiser, and charged with kidnaping. Mike Tress called me up and told me that we had to raise a large sum immediately to pay their legal expenses. Eventually they were released on condition they leave Belgium immediately and never set foot again in the country.

I cannot help but feel that Moshe and Estelle have merited children who are all recognized *talmidei chachamim* or married to *talmidei chachamim* as a result of their *mesiras nefesh* to save Jewish children.

About ten years after his activities in Belgium, Moshe and I were standing together at a wedding when Moshe mentioned that a girl standing by the *mechitzah* was staring at him. I told him he was imagining things, but he was insistent. Finally, he persuaded me to go over and speak to the girl who was talking to some friends by the bandstand.

I was still far from convinced that Moshe was right, but I went over to the girl and told her, "My friend thinks you're staring at him, and he is very embarrassed."

She did not deny that she was staring at Moshe. "I'm sure I know him from somewhere, and it's bothering me," she said. "Is he European?"

"No. Why do you ask?"

"Because I remember his face from when I was a kid. I was born in Europe and brought to Switzerland after the War. Now I'm studying in Bais Yaakov here."

"Were you in a convent in Belgium during the War?"

"How did you know?"

"Because the man you are staring at is the one who took you out."

MY THREE MONTHS OF PAID LEAVE (AND WITH IT THE right to wear my uniform) was up, bringing the speaking tours in search of affidavits to an end. The time had come to settle into the workaday world. One day, Alan (Avraham) Schreiber, an old friend from the Young Israel of New Lots, came to see me. His first question was whether I knew anything about veterans' rights. I told him that part of my duties as an officer had consisted of informing my men of the various benefits they were entitled to receive under

Kill or Be Killed

the G.I. Bill. Alan told me that the National Council of Young Israel was looking for a director of veterans' affairs, and he had recommended me for the job. I went down to the national headquarters for an interview and was hired.

A short while later, I was also appointed the head of Young Israel's employment service. Both the office of veterans' affairs and the employment bureau were the first Orthodox organizations of their kind.

With the donning of a coat and tie, I assumed that my days of excitement and cloak-and-dagger work were over. But about six months after I started working with Young Israel, Mr. Edward Silver, the National President of Young Israel, approached me secretively to talk about what we could do to help the various organized Jewish fighting forces in Palestine. These paramilitary groups — the Haganah, Irgun, and Stern Gang — were busy preparing for the inevitable war if the United Nations agreed to remove the British Mandate over Palestine and recognize an independent Jewish state. One of their most pressing needs was trained intelligence operatives.

Such training was impossible in Palestine, where the British had outlawed all paramilitary activity and made even the possession of a weapon punishable by death. As a consequence, it was decided that young Jews from Palestine would be trained in America. The instructors were to be Americans with a background in intelligence work. The location of the school, Mr. Silver told me, was to be the National Council of Young Israel building on West 16th Street in Manhattan. It was assumed that no one would suspect the existence of such a school in the classrooms of an Orthodox institution. I was placed in charge of the organizational details connected with running The School, as it came to be called.

The most important teacher in the school, Geoffrey Mott-Smith, was not even Jewish, but a retired OSS cryptologist from Schenectady, New York. He taught the fifty or sixty participants in the course the use of ciphers and codes in the transmission of information. He would sit in the classroom with an unfamiliar *kippah* on his head and a *sefer* of some kind open in front of him, rocking back and forth like any yeshiva *bachur* over his Gemara, while trying to impart the most advanced techniques in cryptology in a sing-song Gemara *niggun*.

Down the hall from Mott-Smith, I taught a class appropriately called "Kill or Be Killed." Among the charming subjects included in the curriculum were the use of piano wire to strangle someone from behind, judo to disarm a knife-wielding attacker or someone with a gun to your back, and the placement of piano wire across a road so as to decapitate enemy drivers who might be approaching in an open jeep.

The Young Israel headquarters also became a depot for arms being collected from all over the United States. Appeals were made to Jewish war veterans to contribute any weapons they still possessed. I was in charge of this effort. We would pack the weapons in crates ourselves, and then I would drive down to Hoboken or one of the other seaboard ports in the middle of the night. There the guns would be loaded onto ships which would hopefully manage to get them to Palestine.

All this work was, of course, completely illegal. The Neutrality Act forbade the participation of Americans in foreign military acitivity and there was an arms embargo on shipments to Palestine. One of the most crucial and dangerous tasks was transmitting coded communications to Tel Aviv. Reuben Gross, an amateur ham radio operator and young attorney, volunteered for the job. One night he was surprised to see a large sedan bearing three FBI agents pull up to his house. As it turned out, the FBI's interest in him had been piqued by the fact that he and his contact in Tel Aviv were using Greek call letters, and the FBI suspected that he might be involved in aiding Communist rebels in Greece. When they learned that he was in communication with Tel Aviv their interest waned, though not before Reuben spent a number of sleepless nights.

AFTER WORKING FOR ABOUT NINE MONTHS AT THE National Council of Young Israel, I was promoted to Executive

An Unwitting Messenger
Director. My salary, unfortunately, was not commensurate with my fancy title. Young Israel in those days was a debt-ridden organization, and my take-home pay was no more than sixty to

*Young Israel dinner. Right to left: Irving Bunim, Hyman Goldstein, me,
Rabbi Dr. Samson R. Weiss, Esther (Rubens) Sugerman, J. David Delman, Edward R.
Silver, Elijah Stein, Jacob D. Zabrowsky, Moshe Krumbein, and Harry Fromberg.*

sixty-five dollars a week. But at least my mother was proud to
see her son dressed up in a suit and tie and working in a fancy
air-conditioned office. (Air-conditioning was still a rarity in those
days.)

My only superior was Rabbi Dr. Samson Raphael Weiss, the
National Director. He was a truly remarkable man. Despite having fled from Nazi Germany only a few years before, he had already risen to the top of one of America's largest Orthodox organizations. He was both a *talmid chacham* and extremely erudite,
eloquent in both speech and writing in three languages. And all
this was coupled with a rare nobility of character and sensitivity
to others.

One day I was in Rabbi Weiss' office discussing some matter
with him when I received a phone call from a woman we'll call
Mrs. Cohen. I started to tell her that I would call back when my
meeting was over, but Rabbi Weiss signaled to me that I should
take the call.

Mrs. Cohen proceeded to launch into a tirade directed at me.
"Why didn't you let me sleep last night? You disturbed me all
night long. I didn't think you were the kind of person who would
wake people up in the middle of the night," she ranted.

I realized that she was hysterical, but had no idea what could have triggered this attack. I knew Mrs. Cohen well, and she had always struck me as a very nice woman. I tried to calm her and tell her that I had no idea what she was talking about and certainly had not been anywhere near her house the previous night. But my denials had no effect.

"As if I didn't have enough on my head, I need you coming in to disturb me. Every time I fall asleep, you come into my room and wake me up," she insisted.

"Mrs. Cohen, you must be making a mistake. We don't live near one another, and I never left my room last night so how could I have been waking you up?"

"Well, you did, you did!" she said vehemently. "Don't I have enough *tzares* as it is without your coming to rob me of my sleep? And especially now, when I need to get my sleep so I can think clearly about what to do."

I continued trying to humor her and asked if there was anything else I could do for her.

"You can't do anything for me. Just let me rest. If I fall asleep, don't bother me," she replied. With that she hung up the phone.

Rabbi Weiss had heard the shouting on the other end of the line and seen the bewildered look on my face. He asked me what the call had been about. When I told him, he was as puzzled as I was.

Half an hour later, I received another call from Mrs. Cohen. She was even more hysterical than the first time. She had tried to lie down and take a nap, she said, but I had prevented her from doing so. I explained to her that I had been in my office working the entire time. I tried to bring the conversation to a close as speedily as possible: "Mrs. Cohen, I'm in my office working. I never bothered you. I like you very much. You're a wonderful person. But I have absolutely no idea what you are talking about. I'm sorry, but I'm busy now and must get off."

Her reply surprised me: "I see you're too busy for me also."

I assured her that I would be glad to help if she would only tell me what was bothering her.

"You can't do anything for me. It's my daughter Leah. I have such trouble with Leah right now." She told me that Leah had

had some kind of nervous breakdown and been committed to a mental hospital. Her case was coming up for review, and Mrs. Cohen was afraid that the review board would recommend her for long-term institutionalization some place upstate. She was convinced that if her daughter were sent upstate she would never again see her.

"I want to argue my daughter's case. And I can't think straight. I must rest, and you won't let me rest."

"Listen, I feel badly about Leah. She's such a sweet girl. I'll *daven* that everything turns out well for her."

"You can't do anything for me. Only the *Eibishter* can help me."

"You're a hundred percent right," I agreed, prior to hanging up the phone.

I received yet a third call from Mrs. Cohen later in the morning, which followed the same pattern as the first two.

About two o'clock that afternoon, Rabbi Weiss called me into his office and asked me to find someone to replace Dr. Rafael Gold in that night's Jewish Philosophy class in our adult education program. Dr. Gold was a prominent Orthodox psychologist, who also lectured on Jewish thought.

A short while later, Dr. Gold himself dropped by the office. I mentioned that I had been given the assignment of finding a substitute for him that night and asked if he had any suggestions. In the course of our conversation, he explained why he was unable to teach that night: He was on the State Board of Psychiatric Examiners and that night he had to be at Kings County Hospital to review the cases of several mental patients to determine their disposition.

It hit me in a flash that Dr. Gold's participation in these hearings might be related to the strange phone calls I had received all morning from Mrs. Cohen. "Dr. Gold, I know this is going to sound wild to you," I said to him, "but if I give you a name, can you tell me whether you have that name on your list?"

Dr. Gold's first reaction was to tell me that the names were confidential, but I kept pressing him that I only wanted him to confirm whether one particular name was on the list. Finally, he consented, and I asked him whether he was going to review Leah

Cohen's case that night. He ruffled through his files until he found a folder marked Leah Cohen.

I told him about the weird phone calls I had been receiving all morning from Mrs. Cohen. "There is something very strange going on," I said. "Why in the world did Mrs. Cohen suddenly get this bug in her head that I was disturbing her sleep? There must be a hundred people she knows better than me. But now it's beginning to make a little sense. Maybe I was the *shaliach* (messenger) to ask you to have *rachmones* (mercy) on Leah Cohen, and that's why her mother was calling me. If she hadn't called me, I would never have thought of asking you if you were reviewing Leah Cohen's case."

I concluded by asking Dr. Gold to do me a personal favor: If he found Leah's case to be borderline, he should not have her committed to the hospital upstate.

That night Mrs. Cohen called me at home. This time she was very excited but no longer hysterical. "You'll never guess what happened. The *Eibishter* answered all my prayers, and I want you to be the first to know after the way I bothered you all day. My daughter is to be released on the cognizance of a Dr. Gold, who was one of those reviewing her case. He signed for her, and she is going to live with his family while he treats her. He knows I have no money for such intensive treatment, but he's very sympathetic. Isn't that wonderful? Did you ever hear of anything like that?"

"No, I never heard of anything like that, and I'm thrilled for you," I replied.

"I'm very sorry that I bothered you all day. I was so nervous and tired, and for some reason you kept coming into my mind."

"That's quite all right. I'm just happy that it all worked out so well."

"Yes, this is the greatest thing that ever happened to me. I see that *Hashem Yisborach* is really watching over me very carefully."

"Yes, I agree with you a hundred percent," I told her.

This story has a happy postscript. Dr. Gold was completely

successful in helping Leah overcome that traumatic breakdown. She went on to marry and raise a beautiful family of *bnei Torah*. To this day, she remains one of my closest friends. And her mother, used to cry every time she saw me and say, " You were a *shaliach* from Heaven. You brought *nachas* to my home. As long as I live, I'll never forget what you did for me and my family."

CHAPTER THIRTEEN
Going into Business

Y FRIEND ALAN SCHREIBER APPROACHED ME in January 1948 and told me that he was interested in going into business and wanted me to be one of his partners. An advertisement for a chicken-barbecuing machine had sparked the idea of going into the business of selling kosher barbecued chickens, and he wanted my opinion of this brainstorm.

I told him that it sounded like a promising idea provided all the details were worked out and there was sufficient start-up capital available. Alan replied that he already had another partner by the name of Shaul Stern. Stern's father-in-law owned a little store and adjacent garage on Rockaway Beach Boulevard that he was willing to lease for forty dollars a month. Neither the price nor the location thrilled me. Rockaway in those days was a popular area during the summer months, but devoid of Jews the rest of the year. That meant we could not rely on local sales for the bulk of our business. The forty-dollar-a-month rent was also quite a bit of money for those days.

Nevertheless, I realized that my economic prospects at Young

Israel were not too bright, and given the state of the organization's budget there was no chance of a raise. I told Alan that before I could consider going into partnership I'd have to meet Shaul Stern. Partnership, I reasoned, is akin to marriage, and just as you don't marry without seeing the bride, neither should you enter a partnership blindly. When I first met Shaul Stern a week later, I was very favorably impressed. I felt at once that he was honest and that our approach to doing things would be compatible. We went to a lawyer to draw up a partnership agreement, and I gave notice at Young Israel.

One person who definitely was not happy with this venture was my mother. She had been poor all her life and giving up a steady salary, no matter how inadequate, was anathema to her. In addition, she had much *nachas* from my working for an important Orthodox organization, especially since I had a fancy-sounding title and my own office. There was certainly nothing elegant about barbecuing chickens all day, which is what I was planning to do.

Our plan was to be the first to offer kosher eviscerated chickens. In those days, housewives bought whole chickens from a kosher butcher, and then cleaned out and *kashered* the chickens themselves. In the early days, one of the most frequent questions heard from potential customers was: "What will I do with the salting board and pail I use to *kasher* the chickens?" My standard reply was, "Buy from us, and I'll purchase your salting board and pail." On the other hand, there were others who did not know how to *kasher* chickens who now, for the first time, had easy access to kosher meat.

We would drive down to Vineland, New Jersey where there was a fine young *shochet* by the name of Rabbi Dreyfus. We would then pile the slaughtered chickens into ice chests and drive back up to Rockaway, where we cleaned and *kashered* the chickens. This work was done by Moshe Nosson Alt. I first met Moshe in the DP camps after the war, and I had promised to help him find a job if he managed to reach New York. Meanwhile, I spent most of my time on the phone trying to drum up business.

By the time we had installed a walk-in freezer and the necessary electrical wiring and purchased the barbecue machine, we had exhausted our entire original capital. After only two months, we were bankrupt. Luckily, Shaul Stern's unmarried brother Moshe decided to join us and invested enough extra capital to keep us going for another few months.

At the same time, Alan Schreiber decided that he could no longer take the pressure or bear to watch his carefully saved money disappear, and he dropped out. Though we had all lost our original investments, Shaul and I returned Alan's original investment to him. He was very moved by this gesture, and told us, "I wish you every *hatzlachah* (success). If you should succeed, as I hope you will, I will never have anything but joy in your success after the way you treated me." And, in fact, Alan remains one of my closest friends to this day.

Rabbi Hutner — Mashgiach

DESPITE WORKING SEVENTEEN-HOUR DAYS, THE business was still going nowhere. To infuse a little more capital into the venture, we took on a third Stern brother — Sid — as a partner. Sid had a real head for business, but it still did not seem to help.

After about five months in business, I happened to meet Rabbi Yitzchak Hutner one day, and he asked me how business was. "*Baruch Hashem*," I replied. Apparently my reply did not satisfy him because he asked me a second time, "How's *bizyonos* (humiliation)?" — a pun on the word business, which, unfortunately, hit too close to home. Again I answered, "*Baruch Hashem*." This time Rabbi Hutner told me with the slightest trace of annoyance in his voice, "I didn't ask how pious you are! Tell me how is the *gesheft* (business)."

I had no choice but to confess that business was not so good — in fact, it was lousy. He wanted to know what I thought the problem was, and I explained that our inability to afford a reliable *mashgiach* was a major limitation. Every time someone called to order, they would invariably ask whose supervision we were under. When I told them that we could not yet afford supervision, they usually hung up and never called back.

"But I'm your customer," Rabbi Hutner said.

"I know the Rosh Yeshiva is, but I can't ask the Rosh Yeshiva to give me his *hashgachah*."

"Listen, I give you permission to tell anyone who wants to know that I'm one of your customers. And if they don't believe you, let them call me at home."

From then on whenever I was asked about our *kashrus* supervision, I would answer that everyone working there was someone who could be fully relied on in matters of *kashrus* and I would cite as proof the fact that Rabbi Hutner, the Rosh Yeshiva of Mesivta Chaim Berlin, was

Rabbi Hutner

one of our customers. A few people even went so far as to call Rabbi Hutner at home, but he never complained about it. Our *mazel* changed immediately from the time of my chance meeting with Rabbi Hutner.

Six or seven months later, we were no longer losing money, though we were still far from making any either. I felt terribly guilty about having turned Rabbi Hutner into our de facto *mashgiach,* and at that point hired Rabbi Yisroel Kaplinsky to be our *mashgiach.* We explained to him that we could not yet pay a salary and that the only thing we took out of the business was the chickens we brought home to eat.

Rabbi Kaplinsky agreed to struggle along with us on a salary of chickens — up to five a week for his growing family. He had a beautiful sense of humor. One Friday, he called me and said in a voice of mock disappointment, "Meyer, I thought you told me that you brought me every chicken on which there was any doubt whatsoever."

"One hundred percent," I responded.

"Well, on every one of the three chickens you sent me for Shabbos, there are major questions, and I can't even find the answer in *Shulchan Aruch.*"

"What's the question, Rabbi Kaplinsky?"

"How is it that three chickens have fifteen necks?"

I laughed and told him that we threw in extra *pupiks* and necks that we figured his wife could use. "Oh," he said, "the *pupiks* I didn't see. That only makes the *shaylah* more difficult."

Rabbi Kaplinsky continued to struggle along with the rest of us until we were finally able to pay him a salary, albeit a meager one.

Rabbi Yisroel Kaplinsky

STARTING OUT AROUND THE SAME TIME AS US WAS AN outfit by the name of Empire Poultry. We were looking for an-

New Partners
other reliable supplier besides Vineland, and so I called up Joe Katz, the president of Empire, and asked him who his *shochet* was. He gave me the name of Rabbi Moshe Leib Levovitz.

I spoke to Rabbi Hutner and asked him if he had ever heard of this particular *shochet*. Rabbi Hutner told me that he was the son of Rabbi Yerucham Levovitz, the great *Mashgiach* of the pre-War Mirrer Yeshiva, and that we could trust him completely. At the same time, Rabbi Hutner told me that he knew nothing about his abilities as a *shochet* and that we would have to clarify this for ourselves.

Alan Schreiber, who was still with us at that time, was a nephew of the head of Mesivta Torah Vodaath, "Mister" Shraga Feivel Mendlowitz. Reb Shraga Feivel had been a *shochet* in his youth in his native Hungary and was an expert in checking a *chalif* (the knife used for kosher slaughtering). So Alan asked him if he would mind driving down to the Empire plant in Pennsylvania to give us his opinion of Rabbi Levovitz. When I think about this today, I can hardly believe that in those years the *heimishe olam* in America was still so small that we thought nothing of enlisting Reb Shraga Feivel for such an expedition. Here was the person who had done more than any other to make the idea of a yeshiva education acceptable in America, and we were taking a full day of his time to obtain his opinion of a particular *shochet*.

In those days, Empire Poultry operated out of a garage big enough to hold maybe ten cars in Bethlehem, Pennsylvania. The *shochet*, Rabbi Levovitz, also served as a rabbi in nearby Sunberry, Pennsylvania. When we arrived, he was busy slaughtering the chickens, and we just stood there observing him for awhile. After a few minutes, Mr. Mendlowitz greeted him, and Rabbi Levovitz handed him his *chalif* as a courtesy. Mr. Mendlowitz checked the *chalif* and asked him to *shecht* another twenty chickens. When he finished, he once again returned the *chalif* to Mr. Mendlowitz, who this time asked him to *shecht* fifty chickens.

The test over, Mr. Mendlowitz pronounced himself amazed with Rabbi Levovitz's proficiency. "The *chalif* was good when he first showed it to me," he said, "but after *shechting* so many chickens you would expect it to need resharpening. It's amazing how this man *shechts* and even more amazing how exact he is in handling his *chalif*."

Mr. Mendlowitz's son Moshe Yitzchak, who had accompanied us, asked his father, "*Tatte*, can they buy from them?" He answered without hesitation that we could. Next Moshe Yitzchak wanted to know whether his father would personally eat from Rabbi Levovitz's *shechitah*.

"If he grew a beard," Mr. Mendlowitz replied. Rabbi Levovitz overheard this last remark, but remained silent. As we were leaving, however, he approached Mr. Mendlowitz to thank him for his compliment on the handling of his *chalif*. Then he added, "My *rebbe* taught me that you *shecht* with a *chalif*, not with a beard." Reb Shraga Feivel laughed.

Eventually we began purchasing all of our chickens from Empire. One factor was that Rabbi Levovitz was so well known because he was the son of Reb Yerucham.

Initially, Empire sold only dress poultry — i.e, poultry that the purchaser still had to clean and *kasher*. On one of our visits to

Bethlehem, we asked Joe Katz whether he could clean and *kasher* the chickens as well. He hesitated at first, because they were operating out of such a small space, before turning to Rabbi Levovitz and asking him, "Rabbi, can we do that?" Rabbi Levovitz told him that it was possible and proceeded to work out a system for doing so.

Now we were receiving our chickens already *kashered,* which enabled us to sell them wholesale as well as retail. I started approaching caterers to see whether they would be interested in purchasing our chickens. To my surprise and delight almost all of them recognized what an advantage it would be for them to work with prepared chickens.

One of the caterers whom I met through our wholesale business was Yisroel Hoffman, who ran a catering hall named Israel Manor. He was an expert chef, and as we became friendly, he began teaching me how to make a variety of dishes: *knishes, kishke, kashe varnishkes,* chopped liver. I learned quickly. We installed an oven in the area which we had formerly used for *kashering* chickens and began producing a whole line of side dishes as well. Our only problem was learning how to package the various items so that they did not fall apart by the time they reached our customers.

Besides teaching me how to cook, Yisroel Hoffman also helped me out with a big *mitzvah.* Yeshivas Chaim Berlin was struggling financially at that time, and the *rebbes* were often not paid for months at a time. I realized that my *rebbe* from the Young Israel of New Lots, Rabbi Yaakov Moshe Shurkin, who taught the highest *shiur* at Chaim Berlin, was having a hard time feeding his family, and I hit upon the idea of him becoming the *mashgiach* at Israel Manor. First, I convinced Yisroel Hoffman that he would attract a much wider clientele if he had a highly respected *mashgiach* on the premises.

That was the easy part. Far harder was convincing Rabbi Shurkin that a *rosh yeshiva* could also double as a *mashgiach.* Only when I pointed out to him that I was at Israel Manor every Saturday night and Sunday and could do most of the supervision myself did he agree to take the job. Having taken it, however, he treated his responsibilities with all the seriousness one would expect from a *talmid* of the Chafetz Chaim. He would never let me or anyone else, for instance, *kasher* the livers, but insisted on doing it himself.

One Sunday morning, I was awakened by Yisroel Hoffman screaming on the phone, "I never want to see that man in my place again." It took a number of minutes before I could calm him down enough to find out what had happened. There had been a wedding at Israel Manor the previous night. After survey-

Rabbi Shurkin

ing the guests, the officiating rabbi had apparently been less than excited about the qualifications of anyone present to serve as a witness, and he had asked that the *mashgiach* be summoned to serve as a witness along with him. Rabbi Shurkin's response was: "But I don't know the *chassan* and I don't know the *kallah*. How can I serve as a witness?" No amount of cajoling or threats could get him to budge from his position. It was his refusal, and the embarrassing delay in the wedding which resulted, that had provoked Yisroel's wrath.

Joe Katz approached us in 1953 with the idea of opening a store in Boro Park offering a full range of kosher take-out foods. I was delighted with the idea. With the opening of the first store, we re-incorporated as Mauzone Home Kosher Products. At the first meeting, I was elected president of our fledgling corporation — a title I retained until we liquidated the business with my move to Israel in 1981.

We were the first manufacturers of *glatt* kosher take-home foods, and the idea really took off. Within five years, we had ten stores in Brooklyn and Queens and were supplying other stores on the Lower East Side and Washington Heights. We were producing close to sixty different products every week.

THE *GEMARA* RELATES AN INCIDENT WHERE BOTH MAR Ukvah and his wife jumped into an oven to avoid being identi-

A Unique Opportunity fied by someone to whom they were giving *tzedakah* anonymously. Miraculously, only Mar Ukvah's feet were singed. His wife, however, was completely unscathed. Mar Ukvah explained that his wife's merit was greater than his because when poor people approached him for *tzedakah* he gave them money to purchase what they needed in the marketplace. But she gave them food, which they could eat immediately. Since we were in the food business, we were in a unique position to emulate Mar Ukvah's wife.

With the creation of Mauzone, Rabbi Levovitz became my partner. He was the one who pushed me constantly to use the business to help those in need. He would come to me and say, "You know so-and-so just became an *almanah* (widow). See what you can do. Tell her we have specials. Give her any price you want as long as she buys from us."

In such cases, I would have a third party inform the widow that we had great specials for those who bought their chickens by the case. If she had no room for a case, we would mark the case with her name and keep it in our freezer, and I would deliver the chickens as she needed them. Thus, the widow never had to come to the store at all.

We also tried to give breaks to *bnei Torah*, though this was not always easy. One day, I saw Rebbetzin Kotler in one of our Boro Park stores. The counterman tried to give her a reduced price, but she caught on immediately. Despite his insistence that the price was correct, she had multiplied in her head the price per pound by the weight on the scale and was not fooled. She told the embarrassed salesman, "You're taking money from the owner of the store," and insisted that he reweigh the chickens and do his price calculations again. We finally figured out a way to fool her. We used big, clumsy scales in those days, and it was impossible for the customer to see exactly how many chickens were on the scale. So when Rebbetzin Kotler bought three chickens, the counterman would put two on the scale and leave the third on the side.

Individuals who had nothing to eat would come in early in the morning before the other customers appeared. All the sales-people had instructions that anyone who asked for food was to be fed. Institutions would also approach us for help. There wasn't a week when a free case of chickens wasn't sent out to one ye-shiva or another. We also used to contribute the side dishes for many of the free lunch programs that different organizations ran.

Rabbi Levovitz taught me that the word "no" was not in our vocabulary, and it was a lesson well learnt. He did not involve himself directly in these matters, but pushed me to take care of them. I have no doubt that our success was largely a reward for our generosity, and I thank G-d that we went along with Rabbi Levovitz in this matter.

CHAPTER FOURTEEN
Remarriage

I N 1965, MY FIRST MARRIAGE SOURED AFTER seventeen years and seven children. It is far from my intent to rehash in any way the details of my divorce, and I only mention the fact at all as a prelude to the story of my remarriage and how I came to be the father of sixteen children. The latter story deserves to be told for what it reveals about the marvelous *Hashgachah* (Providence) of Hashem and how that which appears at one moment to be our greatest tragedy may be recognized, with the passage of time, as our greatest blessing.

AT THE END OF 1965, RABBI SHMUEL BRUDNY, MY SON Akiva's *rebbe* in the Mirrer Yeshiva in Brooklyn, strongly recommended to my son that he go study in the **Rabbi Cheshin** Mirrer Yeshiva in Jerusalem. I was very uncertain about this step. But after meeting the Mirrer Rosh Yeshiva, Rabbi Beinush Finkel, who was in America to raise funds, and hearing that my son would be in Rabbi Nachum Perzowitz's *shiur*, I consented to his going.

About six months later, I decided to visit Israel for the first time. I was delighted with Akiva's enthusiasm for his studies, as well as the glowing reports I heard from his *rebbeim* in the Mir. While visiting Akiva, I also intended to visit the various holy sites to pray for a reconciliation with my wife and the restoration of my *shalom bayis* (marital harmony).

One of the first people I contacted in *Eretz Yisrael* was Rabbi Shmuel Schecter, my old *rebbe* from Mesivta Chaim Berlin, who had settled in the new Mattesdorf neighborhood of Jerusalem. I filled Reb Shmuel in on recent developments in my life, and he suggested that we pay a visit to Rabbi Binyamin Ze'ev Cheshin. Reb Shmuel explained that Rabbi Cheshin was one of Jerusalem's most famous *mekubalim* — a seventh-generation descendant of the followers of the Vilna Gaon, who had led the return to *Eretz Yisrael* nearly two hundred years earlier.

I was intrigued by Reb Shmuel's description and suggested that he call Rabbi Cheshin to set up an appointment. Reb Shmuel told me that he could not do that since Rabbi Cheshin had no phone. My amazement at hearing of someone in this day and age who eschewed a telephone as a matter of principle was nothing compared to Reb Shmuel's next shocker: "He doesn't even have a bathroom in the house. All he has is an outhouse in the courtyard." Rabbi Cheshin, it seems, preferred living much the same way as his father and grandfather before him.

I drove over to Shaarei Chesed, one of Jerusalem's oldest and most picturesque neighborhoods, together with Reb Shmuel and Akiva. This was before gentrification had overtaken the neighborhood, and it was still inhabited, for the most part, by old Yerushalmi families. Living in the same narrow winding lane as Rabbi Cheshin were, I learned, a number of other Torah giants.

We found Rabbi Cheshin at home and were invited into his tiny house. The kitchen was outside in the courtyard, and was so narrow that only one person at a time could fit into it. Every room in the home had more that one function. All the furniture in one room was cleared out at night and mattresses moved in for the girls to sleep on. And the tiny study in which Rabbi Cheshin spoke to me also doubled as his bedroom.

Rabbi Cheshin seemed very interested in hearing about my

life, and I started talking to him about some of the great figures I had met in the DP camps after the war, particularly the Klausenberger *Rebbe*.

While I was speaking, I saw that he was staring intently at my hand. At first I thought I must be boring him or that he had fallen asleep because he was no longer looking directly at me. Suddenly, he reached over and took hold of my wrist and held it for a moment. I had absolutely no idea what was going on and became very self-conscious about my hands. It occurred to me that perhaps they were dirty and that I had a made a blessing without washing them properly.

"Open and close your hand," Rabbi Cheshin said. I felt like I was in a doctor's office preparing for a blood test or to have my blood pressure taken. At this point, I asked Rabbi Cheshin what he was looking at. He did not answer me directly, but asked Rabbi Schecter and Akiva to leave the room.

Once they had left the room, Rabbi Cheshin told me very gently but firmly that I must work on strengthening my *emunah* and *bitachon*. He assured me that the *Eibishter* would pull me out of the *Gehinnom* in which I now found myself. "It is very sad, very sad," he repeated, "for I see that there are seven *korbonos* (sacrifices)." I had told him almost nothing about my personal life, and certainly nothing about my children, so I could not figure out what he was talking about. I asked what he meant by seven *korbonos*.

His only response was cryptic: "It makes no difference. I know more than you imagine. In two more years you'll meet your true *zivug* (spouse). Until then, you'll just have to be patient and trust in Hashem."

Now I was really confused. I had come to ask this holy man to pray that *shalom bayis* be restored to my home and here he was telling me that I had not yet met my destined spouse.

"But I'm married already. Don't you understand? I have a *zivug*. I'm not looking for another one," I protested.

"What is happening to you is a *gezeirah min hashamayim* (a Heavenly decree)," he replied. "But your first wife is not your true *zivug*. That one is yet to come."

"How is that possible?" I pleaded with him. "I have seven children."

"Yes, I know without your telling me."

It is almost impossible for me to describe how I felt at that moment. I could not dismiss Rabbi Cheshin's words out of hand as the mumbo-jumbo of a witch doctor. I had never before met anyone like him, and an aura of holiness surrounded him and permeated his home.

On the other hand, what he was telling me seemed foreign to my whole concept of the

Rabbi Cheshin

sanctity of marriage in Judaism. My understanding until then had always been that for better or worse a person marries the person destined for him, and it is up to him to try to make the marriage work, no matter what. Now, Rabbi Cheshin was telling me that a person may have more than one *zivug,* and that although it is a great blessing if that true one is one's first wife, it does not always work out that way.

"We often don't know who our true *zivug* is," he told me, "but your wife is definitely not yours. You'll have to wait two years. In those two years, you'll suffer very much, but have faith. Be strong."

While I did not dismiss his words, neither was I prepared to accept them. In an effort to drown out what I had just heard, I yelled for Rabbi Schecter and Akiva. They came running in, and I started shouting at them in English, "This man is telling me that I have not been married to the right woman for the last seventeen years. That my seven children are not from my true *zivug.*"

Rabbi Schecter did what he could to calm me down, but I continued yelling. (Nothing has the power to enrage like the truth.) "I came to *Eretz Yisrael* to pray at the holy places for a restoration of my marriage, and he tells me I'm married to the wrong woman," I kept repeating.

While I carried on, Rabbi Cheshin spoke softly to Rabbi Schecter on the side. He explained that there is sometimes more than one *zivug* for a man and that while I had to marry my first wife, my true life partner was yet to come.

ABOUT A YEAR AND A HALF AFTER MY MEETING WITH Rabbi Cheshin, I was sitting at home alone. Though the divorce

An Insurance Policy was not yet finalized, my wife had long since departed taking with her all but my second and third oldest sons. I received a phone call from Rabbi Yisroel Perkowski, who was, and remains, something of a *rebbe* of mine. Reb Yisroel was the *rav* of the Young Israel of New Lots for seven or eight years before becoming the *rav* of the 16th Avenue Agudah in Boro Park.

After the usual exchange of pleasantries, Reb Yisroel surprised me by asking whether I had any life insurance. I assured him that I did and inquired as to why he was interested in my insurance coverage. "Because I've become an insurance agent," he replied.

Knowing that Reb Yisroel spoke barely a word of English, this news occasioned more than a little surprise, but I figured that he was working under someone else's brokerage license and servicing an exclusively Yiddish-speaking clientele. I told Reb Yisroel that I would be over as soon as I finished eating my supper.

I walked the three blocks from my house to Reb Yisroel's and found him eating in his kitchen. I told him I would wait in the dining room. While sitting there, I glanced around the room, but didn't see any evidence of Reb Yisroel's new profession as an insurance agent. There were several volumes of *Gemara* on the table, but no insurance policies.

When Reb Yisroel finished his dinner, he entered the dining room and gave me a very warm *Shalom aleichem*. I mentioned that I had looked around for a policy without success. "Are you selling term or straight-life insurance?" I asked him. From the look on his face, it was clear that he had no idea what I was talking about. Finally, I asked him precisely what kind of policy he was selling.

"*Arichus yamim* (length of days)," Reb Yisroel replied with a straight face.

"I've never heard of that policy," I said nervously, like one who suspects he is being made the butt of a practical joke but decides to play along rather than be considered a spoilsport.

"But I have such a policy," Reb Yisroel insisted.

"In that case, I guess you're going to be a very popular man."

Until now, we had both been standing. Reb Yisroel then took both my hands in his and asked me to sit down. "Reb Meyer," he said, "when you're ready for another *shidduch*, remember one thing — an *almanah* (widow) with small children."

"What does that have to do with an insurance policy?" I wanted to know.

"Reb Meyer, the *Gemara* says in many places that when *kinderlach* (children) become orphans, Hashem takes the place of their father. That is why there are so many special laws concerning how one may treat an orphan. You have to be very careful dealing with a *yasom* (orphan) because you are dealing with one of Hashem's children.

"Now Meyer, if you were to take a few orphans off the *Ribbono Shel Olam's* hands, how do you think He would react? Don't you think He would say, 'Who is this wonderful person who is taking responsibility for My children?' Can you imagine a better insurance policy than that?"

Reb Yisroel then showed me a number of places in the *Gemaras* lying on the table that discuss the great *mitzvah* involved in helping a broken widow and children who don't know what a father is. He assured me that there is no greater *mitzvah* than ensuring that orphans have a proper upbringing.

Finally Reb Yisroel said to me, "Many people would be scared to raise someone else's children. But you're a *gibbor* (strong person), and you can do it." He made me promise him that when the proper time came to remarry that I would seriously consider what he had said.

From Reb Yisroel's impassioned plea, I suspected that he must have a particular widow in mind for me, but that turned out not to be the case. He really wanted nothing more than to sell me an insurance policy for a long and happy life.

MY FRIENDS COULDN'T HELP BUT NOTICE THAT I WAS
becoming more and more despondent as my domestic situation

**The
Magic
Car**

continued without any resolution. Mr. Neuhaus of
Camp Torah Vodaath invited me to spend the summer up in the country at camp. He gave me a room
adjacent to the infirmary where I spent every Shabbos
and a couple of nights during the week.

Moshe Swerdloff, my oldest and dearest friend, and his family had rented a bungalow on the other side of the mountains for
part of the summer, and when the time came to leave, Moshe
asked me if I could drive over and pack up my car with some of
his wife's nicer things and take them back to the city.

At that time I was driving a maroon Buick Electra — the type
of gas guzzler that has long since become extinct — which my
partners had bought for me. The car was equipped with all manner of electric gadgetry. When I pulled into Oakwood Cottages,
where Moshe and his family were staying, I spotted a group of
children nearby and decided to give them a little afternoon entertainment. First, I pushed a button to lower the car's radio an-
tennae.

In this group of children was a little five-and-a-half-year-old,
who went wild over this trick. He stood there laughing and asking me, "Mister, can you do that magic again? Can you make
that thing go up and down?" Something about this child's smile
got to me and I called him over and showed him how the electric
windows worked.

"Look, I've got even more magic," I told him. I put him onto
the front passenger seat and started pressing all the buttons adjusting the position of the seat. He went forwards and backwards,
up and down. The boy couldn't stop laughing and talking about
the "magic car, with an elevator inside."

In the middle of the show, Moshe came outside and called
me in for dinner. As we were loading the car after dinner, who
should come over but that same sweet little five-and-a-half-year-
old! This time he had a whole platoon of other children behind
him, whom he was lecturing about the "magic car."

His infectious enthusiasm had really gotten to me and I could
not turn him down when he asked me to show his friends how

the seat worked and to give him another ride in the elevator. The elevator ride completed, I asked him to get out, explaining that I wanted to get back to the other side of the mountains while there was still daylight. This didn't seem to concern him at all, and he refused to get out until I had given him a ride in the car. Once I agreed to his request, I had no choice but to pile in the other fifteen children he had brought with him and drive across the road to Camp Ohr Shraga, where I treated the children to sodas.

I assumed that the ride and the soda were sufficient treats, and with one crucial exception I was right. The children each thanked me and got out of the car. My original "fan," however, had not yet had enough. My entreaties proved unsuccessful in dislodging him from the car, and in desperation, I turned to Moshe to find out where the kid's parents were. Moshe pointed to a woman reading on a nearby beach chair, with three little children gathered around her, and told me she was the little boy's mother. When I explained my plight to her, she yelled, "Shloime, get out of that car immediately." The kid promptly got out, muttering something under his breath. I thanked his mother and made my escape.

ABOUT A WEEK AFTER MY RETURN FROM THE mountains, I received a call from Moshe Swerdloff. He asked me

Return of the Stranger

for a case of chickens — the tops for his family and the bottoms for a widow. As my accountant, Moshe was well aware of our policy of giving chickens to widows at reduced prices and wanted to be sure that I would not forget to do so with this particular widow. I asked him the name and address of the widow so I could deliver the chickens to her.

I called the woman up to make sure she would be home at the time I intended to deliver the chickens. As soon as she opened the door, I recognized her as the mother of the kid who had been so infatuated with my car. While we were standing at the door, I heard shouting from the stairwell outside: "The man with the maroon car came back. The man with the maroon car came back." With that, my nemesis from the mountains burst through the door.

He kept repeating, "I knew you'd come back. I knew you'd come back," and then turning to his mother, "You see, Mommy, I told you he would show up. He promised me before I left the car."

This last statement was news to me. Shloime then proceeded to insist that I had promised him another ride as well. Somehow this too had escaped my memory, but I realized that I was not going to get away scot-free and agreed to take him around the block in the car. That ride did not satisfy him in the least and he refused point-blank to get out of the car. Once more, I had to turn to his mother for assistance. "Please, lady," I pleaded, "take him out of the car. I know he's glued to it, but I've got work to do."

"No, no, no," Shloime whined. "He gave me such a short ride. He just went around the block. Ask him if he's coming back."

Coming back was the last thing on my mind at that point. But then I thought about what Moshe had told me about this young widow being left with four small children, and asked, "What day do the kids have off? Maybe I could take them for a longer ride then. I see how much Shloime enjoys this."

She told me that they had half a day off on Columbus Day, and I promised to return then to take the three oldest children out for a longer drive. My only stipulations were that the baby, who was still in diapers, stay at home, and that the Swerdloff's daughter Yonina, who had known the kids over the summer up in the mountains, agree to come along with me.

A Day at the Zoo

THE SWERDLOFFS READILY CONSENTED TO YONINA coming along, and I showed up on the appointed day together with her to take the three oldest kids to the Staten Island Zoo. As we arrived, the mother was preparing to take the baby, Yissachar, to the park. Even though he was only two, he was not too pleased with being left behind. Finally, I turned to the mother and asked her if she wanted to come along with the little one.

Once again I made two conditions with her: that she not interfere in my treatment of the children and that she not talk to me. My divorce had still not been finalized, and I felt in those circumstances that it would not be appropriate for me to be seen talking to an unmarried woman.

It was a beautiful autumn day as we walked around the zoo. The three oldest children hung close to me so that I could explain to them about the different animals. In the snake house, we saw some of the larger snakes being fed, and watched with fascination the way they swallowed the mice and rabbits they were fed in one gulp. I pointed out the way the snakes constricted their stomach muscles in such a way that their prey was moved along the length of their body as if on a conveyor belt. I told the children how the *Ribbono Shel Olam* had punished the first snake for deceiving Chava and cursed him that neither he nor his descendants would enjoy eating their food. Everything would taste like dust. That is why snakes swallow everything whole, without chewing. Nevertheless, Hashem, in His infinite wisdom, has so constructed them that they derived all the nourishment they needed without chewing or breaking down their food in any way.

After a short while, I noticed that the mother was having a lot of difficulty holding the baby. He was short, but built like a tank. I offered to carry him around. And that's how we walked around — the three older children at my side and Yissachar in my arms. At the end of the day, I bought each of the kids a soda and a little souvenir. Their mother protested, but I reminded her of my condition that she not interfere with my handling of the kids.

When we arrived back in Brooklyn, the kids were very appreciative for the day at the zoo. In fact, to this day they still remember the first time I took them out.

SHORTLY AFTER THAT FIRST TRIP TO THE ZOO, ALL THE lengthy negotiations surrounding the termination of my first

Courting marriage were finally completed, and I was free to start seeing Goldie.

Nine months later, I told my son Akiva, who was once again learning at the Mirrer Yeshiva in Brooklyn, that I was seriously considering marrying a young widow with four small children. That Shabbos, he joined me at her house for the Friday night meal.

As we left, he said to me, "Abba, you're talking about starting all over from *aleph* again. The youngest one isn't more than two-and-a-half, and they're all young."

"Yeah, I realize that. But maybe that's just what I need," I answered.

"Well, I'm not going to tell you what to do. All I can say is *kol hakavod* if you go through with it. It's a big undertaking."

A few nights later, Akiva had difficulty falling asleep and for some reason took out a Jewish calendar to look at. I had told him the story of how I had met Goldie for the first time, and as he looked at the calendar, he had an amazing flash: The date of our meeting was almost two years to the day from the meeting with Rabbi Cheshin at which he predicted that I would meet my true *zivug* in another two years. The next morning Akiva called me excitedly to share his insight. All he could say was: "This is no coincidence."

ONLY ONE MORE OBSTACLE HAD TO BE CLEARED BEFORE we could get married: securing the approval of Goldie's family.

Convincing the Family My wife is the youngest of four sisters, and they were extremely protective of her, especially after the terrible tragedy in which her first husband passed away suddenly as a young man. The fact that I was nearly twice her age did nothing to allay their concerns or those of her parents, Mr. and Mrs. Herschel Berliner.

Fortunately, one of Goldie's brothers-in-law had formed a favorable impression of me, though I was unaware of ever having met him. At the time we decided to get married, Goldie's brother-in-law Rabbi Alexander (Sandy) Adams and her sister were on vacation in *Eretz Yisrael*. They returned to New York at 11:00 p.m. one night, and Goldie immediately called me up to know whether I could come right over to meet them. I protested that they must be exhausted from their trip and that we could wait until the next day, but she was very eager that we meet as soon as possible.

It was nearly midnight when I arrived at the Adams' home. Rabbi Adams greeted me warmly and asked me several questions as if he and I were old friends. This struck me as strange, and I mentioned that as far as I knew we had never met.

"I know you very well," he said.

"That's funny, I don't remember ever meeting you."

"Oh sure, you know me. You once lent me five thousand dollars."

"I'd like to take the credit, but you've got me confused with someone else. I never lent you five thousand dollars."

"Wait a minute. Aren't you the one from East New York?"

"Yes."

"And aren't you friendly with Joe Schechter?"

"Very friendly."

"Do you remember his son Avraham?"

"Of course. I know him very well."

"And didn't you loan him money?"

"Yes, but that was a long time ago, and he paid me back."

"Do you remember what the loan was for?"

"He had a camp in Connecticut, and he and his partner were in trouble. So he asked me to loan him some money."

"Well, I'm the partner and I'm the one who paid you back. And do you remember that you didn't even ask for so much as an IOU from us, even though you didn't know me at all?"

With that he turned to Goldie and said, "You see how this man helped me without even knowing who I was." With the Adams' stamp of approval, the *shidduch* was clinched.

SHORTLY AFTER OUR MARRIAGE, GOLDIE AND I TOOK A vacation to *Eretz Yisrael*. The first person I wanted to introduce her to

Meeting Rabbi Cheshin Again

was Rabbi Cheshin, who had so accurately predicted my eventual salvation. Knowing he did not have a phone, I called his daughter as soon as we arrived in Jerusalem and she told me that he was giving a *shiur* in the Beis Yisroel neighborhood, near the Mirrer Yeshiva, until 11:00 p.m.

My wife and I drove over to where the *shiur* was being given. Rabbi Cheshin noticed me as soon as he finished the *shiur* and came over to give me a warm welcome.

"Is your wife with you?" he immediately wanted to know.

"How did you know that I'm married?" I asked.

"*Ich veis schon* — I already know," was all he would say in response to my question.

When he heard that my wife was with me, he suggested that we go to the *kever* (grave) of Rachel *Imeinu*, despite the lateness of the hour. I mentioned that it would probably be

Meyer and Goldie Birnbaum

locked, but Rabbi Cheshin brushed aside my objection — he had the key. We arrived at *Kever Rachel* around midnight, and Rabbi Cheshin spent a long time praying for the success of our marriage. Both Goldie and I were very touched by his concern. From that night on, we grew closer and closer to Rabbi Cheshin.

Rabbi Cheshin had correctly seen that my true *zivug* was yet to come. But even he did not predict that in the process of finding her I would gain a whole new family. Goldie's four children were still all very young at the time of my marriage. The youngest, Yissachar, had no memory of his father at all, and even the memories of the older ones — Avraham, Shloime, and Leah — were fading fast. The kids immediately began calling me Abba and treating me as their father in every respect. Today those who know my family in Israel are often unaware that I am not the biological father of all nine children.

The tone of my relationship with Goldie's children was set shortly after our marriage. The principal of the yeshiva in which the boys were studying called me in for a conference, and told me that he understood that the boys were not my children and therefore did not expect me to pick up the full tab for their yeshiva costs. I set him straight immediately: "You're mistaken. These are my children. I neither want nor will accept any reduction on their tuition."

Our last year in the States, Shloime, who was then eighteen (and who continues to seek *shadchanus gelt* from me to this day), talked to his brothers and sister about officially adopting the name Birnbaum, which they had been using since I married their mother. On their own initiative, they went to a lawyer in Boro Park, who arranged for a court hearing, at which they explained to the judge their reasons for a name change. That day was one of the happiest of my life.

In Search of Mitzvos

HE PERIOD BETWEEN THE BREAKUP OF MY FIRST marriage and my second marriage was surely the worst of my life. But it was also one of the most productive. I racked my brains constantly with the same question: What terrible sin had I committed to deserve this fate? At times this question left me too depressed to do much more than go through the motions each day. But I am by nature a high-energy person, and moping around is foreign to me. Therefore I begged *HaKadosh Baruch Hu* to send me some special *mitzvah* that no one else was interested in or capable of doing and in that way let me atone for whatever I had done. I learned that when you seek out *mitzvos* of this nature Hashem sends them to you.

THE FIRST *MITZVAH* HASHEM SENT ME WAS DURING MY trip to *Eretz Yisrael* in the summer of 1966. Despite the blowup at my first meeting with Rabbi Cheshin, he agreed to accompany me on a tour of holy places in the Galilee. Joining us were Rabbi

Schecter, my son Akiva, my partner's son Nachman Levovitz (then a *talmid* in Brisk, who subsequently married a daughter of the Mirrer Rosh Yeshiva Rabbi Beinush Finkel), and Avraham Meir Hershowitz, the son of Rabbi Dovid Hershowitz, my first mentor in the Young Israel of New Lots.

Exposing the Autopsy Scandal

Even though Rabbi Cheshin had told me that what was happening to me was a Heavenly decree, I still hoped that a combination of prayer and *chesed* might win me a reprieve. We visited every place that the kabbalistic works mention as especially suited to prayer. In Tiberias, we went to the graves of Rabbi Akiva, Rabbi Meir Baal HaNes, and the Rambam; in Tzefas, those of Rabbi Yosef Caro, the Arizal, Rabbi Moshe Cordevero, and the Mabit; in Meron, that of Rabbi Shimon Bar Yochai and his son Rabbi Elazar; and elsewhere in the Galilee, those of Hillel and Shammai, Rabbi Yonasan ben Uziel, and Rabbi Yochanan HaSandlar. At the cave of Eliyahu HaNavi in Haifa, a Sephardi woman took one look at Rabbi Cheshin and came running over to ask him to say *Tehillim* for her sick son. Rabbi Cheshin also took me to see a *mekubal* known as the Raanana Tzaddik, who lived in a tiny hut. Everyone in our group asked him for a blessing, but when Rabbi Cheshin's turn came, the Tzaddik told him, "It seems to me that it is I who should be asking you for a *berachah*."

In the course of the trip, I learned that Rabbi Cheshin was also fluent in Arabic and Spanish. He had grown up in the Old City of Jerusalem, which in his youth was a polygot of peoples and tongues, and had picked up the languages of the various groups living there.

We returned to Jerusalem on Friday morning, and I profusely thanked everyone who had accompanied me and joined their prayers to my own. That Shabbos was spent in Bnei Brak with Rabbi Dovid and Esther Hershowitz, two friends from my youth. At their house, I met Rabbi Yosef Liss, one of the greatest of the survivors from the pre-War Mirrer Yeshiva. He could not stop talking about the proliferation of autopsies then taking place in Israel. As he told it, there was almost no one who was not subjected to an autopsy, even where the family of the deceased was opposed on halachic grounds and there was no medical justification.

Under the Anatomy-Pathology Law of 1953 a doctor was given the right to "dissect a body to determine the cause of death, or to use the parts of the body for healing purposes." Nowhere did the statute make any mention of the wishes of the deceased or his family concerning the disposition of his body. Nor did the doctor performing the dissection have to make any showing that determination of the cause of death would be of any benefit in terms of saving the lives of others. Neither then nor now did any other country in the Western world permit autopsies without the consent of the deceased or next of kin, except in cases of suspected foul play or a threat to public health.

The rate of autopsies in Israel was spiraling rapidly, and had reached eighty percent in most of the major hospitals. (Only two groups, I learned later, had any success in evading the post-mortem scalpel: doctors themselves and the politicians responsible for the law.) Because of the unrestricted availability of autopsies in Israel compared to any place else in the world, Israeli hospitals received large grants from abroad to conduct epidemiological studies on deceased patients. Research conducted at Hadassah Hospital in 1959-60 on the degree of artherosclerosis in 895 autopsied patients, for instance, was conducted under a grant from the National Institutes of Health of the United States government.

A 1963 Hebrew University Research Report noted: "The above-mentioned law provides a unique opportunity to research into the morbid anatomy of these cases because in most countries these chronic cases are not brought to an autopsy, neither in hospital or forensic medicine institutes." The Report continued that the different ethnic groups in Israel made it an ideal laboratory to test theories on environmental and ethnic factors in various common diseases.

All this research was being undertaken at a time when it was becoming increasingly recognized in the medical profession that such research on dead patients was of little value. Already in 1956, an editorial writer in the Journal of the American Medical Association argued: "If any research of importance is coming from studies being made at the routine autopsy at present I am not aware of it…. Huge stacks of records and files of cards have accumulated, apparently with the hope that someone will someday dig up gold nuggets of valuable information. But in recent years no one has and, in my opinion, no one will. It seems ridiculous to continue gathering routine information of this kind."

Under the Israeli Anatomy and Pathology Law even the bodies of foreign citizens became the property of Israeli hospitals if they were so unlucky as to die in Israel. When the wife of Rabbi Zvi Hirsch Cohen, a prominent New York rabbi, took ill and died while on a visit to Israel, her husband was powerless to stop the hospital from conducting an autopsy. That case caused a particular uproar in the United States.

Mrs. Bela Maza, another American citizen and the mother of a rabbi, was hospitalized in Hadassah Hospital for a prolonged period with a known kidney condition. Her son flew to Israel to be with her, and only returned to the United States after having been assured that if she should die, no autopsy would be performed since the cause of her illness was fully determined. Nevertheless, when she passed away an autopsy was performed, without informing the family's appointed representative in Israel. Mrs. Maza was opened from head to foot and all her vital organs removed. When the family demanded her organs be returned for burial, the *Chevrah Kadishah* received a sack with a conglomeration of organs taken at random — three lungs, no heart, etc.

Autopsies to determine the cause of death almost never require removal of internal organs. But Israeli doctors had been so calloused by the routine nature of autopsies that they cut up the whole body as a matter of course and removed all the organs. By contrast, the parallel New York State statute at the time required familial consent before an autopsy could be performed. Even where such permission was granted, the physician still had to fill out a form in advance specifying the area to be examined and the number of incisions necessary.

Of course, Rabbi Liss did not relate all these facts to me that Shabbos. Most of the specifics of the issue only became known to me over the next couple of years as I became actively involved in the United States mobilizing opposition to the statute. But he did describe in highly emotional terms a general situation in which families were either avoiding hospitals altogether or bringing terminally ill loved ones home to die in order to avoid having them subjected to autopsies. Where that was impossible, they organized around-the-clock vigils at their hospital beds to prevent autopsies from being done after the death. Even in the latter case, they had no legal authority to prevent autopsies. As a consequence, seriously ill patients often spent their last hours wondering what would be left of them for burial after the doctors had finished cutting them up.

Even where doctors assured patients that they would not order an autopsy if they died in the hospital, they routinely failed to honor those promises. By a June 7, 1966 order of the Ministry of Health, hospitals were ordered not to respond to requests from patients not to be dissected. When one sick old man, admitted to the Tel Hashomer emergency room, asked the nurse on duty for some assurance he would not be dissected, the supervising doctor ordered him to be sent home if he attempted to make any stipulations.

Frankly, I greeted Rabbi Liss' descriptions of the situation with more than a little skepticism. Americans of my generation grew up with a general feeling of optimism about the essential goodness of most people. We also believed our high school civics lessons about government being the servant of the people. Somehow, despite the horrors I had witnessed in Europe, something of this optimistic view remained. I told Rabbi Liss that it was very hard for me to believe that anything like he was describing could happen in a civilized country. I found it even more difficult to believe that this was taking place in the Jewish State, with the full sanction of the government and the medical establishment, given Judaism's emphasis on the sanctity of the dead. His stories, as far as I was concerned, were wild exaggerations based on perhaps a few isolated cases.

I asked Rabbi Liss why, if something like this were really taking place, the religious community didn't just protest to the government and get them to put an end to it. "You don't understand how things work here," he told me. "The doctors present themselves as the voice of reason and progress. They claim these autopsies are necessary to ensure the advance of Israeli medicine, and the protests are nothing more than the work of religious fanatics still dwelling in the Dark Ages. The Israeli government is eager to present itself as the most progressive and enlightened in the world, and so it permits doctors to ignore the wishes of families and to carry out autopsies to an extent not permitted anywhere else in the world."

Seeing that I was still not convinced, Rabbi Liss challenged me to come and see for myself. It would not be difficult to arrange such a tour, he told me. All I had to do was dress up in a long *kapote*, like any other member of the *Chevrah Kadishah*, and they would take me with them on their rounds to the various hospitals. There I would see precisely how indiscriminately autopsies were being done.

"Are you afraid of dead bodies?" he asked me. I assured him that I had, unfortunately, seen more dead bodies during the war and at the liberation of the concentration camps than a thousand average people see in a lifetime.

The next night I went around with the *Chevrah Kadishah* in Tel Aviv. We visited Tel Hashomer, Ichilov, and a small branch of Hadassah hospital. We had only one purpose in mind: that I view as many bodies in each morgue as possible. I carried with me

A pile of organs removed from autopsied patients

what was then a new type of camera, in which four flashbulbs could be put at one time. The flash bulbs would pop out automatically as the pictures were taken.

We started taking out the bodies that were in cold storage, and I couldn't believe what I saw. The first body they removed had been cut open from the top of the head through the chest to the groin. In others, the thighs had been sliced open as well.

My guides did not try to color my view of what I was seeing, but just waited for me to ask questions. When I asked what this man had died of, I was told, "That's just the point. If he had something in his stomach, why was his head cut open, and if they suspected something in the brain, why was the rest of the body carved up?"

As we pulled out more bodies, we saw one example after another of these head-to-toe autopsies. I pulled out my camera and started taking pictures as fast as I could, completely forgetting about the flashbulbs that were being ejected onto the floor. In every hospital we visited that night, I saw the same situation repeated.

By the time I reached Jerusalem the next day, the Brisker Rav's son Rabbi Refoel Soloveitchik, who was spearheading the campaign against autopsies, had already heard about my pictures. He asked me for the film so that it could be sent back to America that night for developing. He was afraid to risk developing it in Israel, and did not want to leave the film with me for fear that the police might succeed in identifying me and confiscate it.

I did not yet know it, but the Israeli papers were already full of stories of some maniac who was going around from one hospital morgue to another snapping pictures. I had been given away by the used flash bulbs found at each of the three hospitals we visited the previous night.

Before I left Israel there were wall posters up all over Jerusalem showing pictures of desecrated bodies. The first time I saw the poster I was struck by how familiar the pictures looked. It took me a few minutes to realize that they were mine. In time these posters were plastered all over Israel, with the caption, "This is what they will do to your relatives; this is what they will do to your loved ones."

Years later, I asked Reb Refoel why no one had previously taken photographs of what was being done given the power of such graphic evidence. He answered with the typical Brisker truthfulness: "We didn't think of it."

When I returned to America, the Jewish media was very interested in my story. My photographs and the attendant publicity helped to galvanize the American Orthodox community. I was asked to give a report to Agudath Israel of America on what I had seen. When I had finished showing my slides, Rabbi Moshe Feinstein came over to give me a kiss and a *"yasher koach."* I also arranged a number of parlor meetings where I spoke about the situation and showed the evidence of what was going on.

Soon after returning to America, I met with Mr. Joseph Gross, the Treasurer of the Hadassah Medical Organization, in his office and explained to him in detail what I had seen in Israeli hospitals. He did not believe what I told him, just as I had not believed Rabbi Liss when he first spoke to me. Confronted with my pictures, he could only shake his head and say, "Well I don't know what to think, but I can't believe this is taking place in Israel."

"Well, I'm not crazy," I replied. "This is my camera and here are my photographs. What you see in those photos is exactly what I saw. If you don't believe me, here are the negatives. You can see for yourself that there wasn't any trick photography involved."

A large number of mass meetings were held over the next year, at which all the leading *gedolei Torah* spoke. As a result, a great deal of pressure was brought to bear on the Israeli government. At a mass rally on September 20, 1967, Rabbi Moshe Feinstein threatened to place a ban on Jews living or traveling to Israel unless the Pathology Law was repealed.

In Israel, too, the pictures had the desired effect of giving credence to the charges of the Orthodox community. The tumult in the press about the madman who had snuck into the hospitals to photograph dead people and the pictures themselves had brought the issue to the fore. In the Sephardi community, particularly, there were tens of thousands who, while not fully observant, were horrified by the thought of bodies being so indiscriminately cut up.

Reb Refoel Soloveitchik called me several times from Israel to ask me if I was prepared for an even bigger *Kiddush Hashem.*

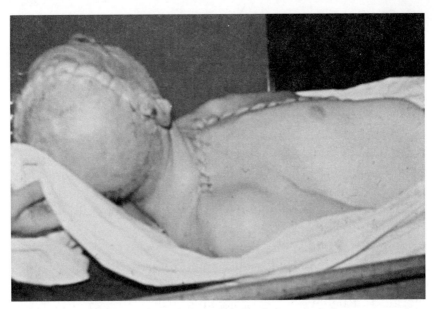

A view of a typical autopsy that I photographed

In response to my question how I could do so, he replied, "Simple. The police are looking for you. If you fly back here, I'll tip off the police in advance and they'll arrest you as soon as you land. Your arrest will create a furor and keep the issue in the forefront."

I was not then in a position to spend weeks, and perhaps months, in an Israeli jail or entangled in the legal system and politely turned down the request for my martyrdom.

INTERESTINGLY, THE SECOND *MITZVAH* THAT HASHEM sent me, less than six months after the first, also involved *kavod hameis* (the honor of the dead). The last week of December 1966, the gravediggers in New York City went on strike. As a consequence, no one could be buried.

The Gravediggers' Strike

Coffins were simply being left above ground, so that the Biblical injunction, "to dust you shall return," remained unfulfilled.

This situation continued on until the first week in January with no end in sight. By that time, in the Jewish cemeteries alone there were already hundreds of coffins without proper burial. The despair of those grieving for lost relatives was increased immeasurably by their awareness that their loved ones were still languishing without a proper burial. To make matters worse, reports began circulating that squirrels were eating through the coffins that had been left above ground.

I was feeling very restless at this time and greatly in need of something to do to distract my thoughts from my own personal problems. One day, I came up with the idea of organizing a group of *yeshiva bachurim* to dig the graves. I approached Rabbi Shmuel Birnbaum, the Mirrer Rosh Yeshiva, for permission to organize a group of boys, and with the help of Mordechai Abramson, a good friend of my son Akiva, succeeded in rounding up a good-sized contingent.

None of us had any idea about how one goes about digging a grave. On the other hand, we didn't imagine that it would be terribly difficult. I purchased pickaxes, shovels, and other equipment I thought we might need, and we headed for Beth David Cemetery in Elmont, New York.

When we got to the cemetery that first time, we found a picket line near the front gate. The pickets were not what one would call a terribly *heimish*-looking group, and I decided that buttering them up would be the better part of valor. It was an unusually bitter-cold winter that year, and the poor men on the picket line were practically freezing. So I hopped back into the car to purchase hot coffee and rolls for all of them as a kind of initial peace offering.

I explained that we had come to bury an important rabbi whose family was suffering great anguish due to the failure to bury him. The gravediggers took one look at us and burst out laughing at the thought that a group of yeshiva students and I were planning to dig the grave. They made no effort to stop us since they realized what we did not know: There was simply no way that we were going to be able to dig in the frozen ground.

The ground was frozen solid. No matter how hard we struck the ground with our pickaxes, they bounced back in our faces twice as fast. We were obviously not going to get anywhere in this fashion so I decided to shmooze with the pickets a bit and see if I couldn't extract a few hints. Leaving the boys in the car trying to get some circulation going again in their frozen hands,

I purchased refills on the coffee and went to talk to the pickets.

As I explained our predicament, they just laughed at the idea that one could get a pickaxe into the ground in the dead of winter. But they did in the end reveal the secret. First one gathers leaves and branches and places them on top of the gravesite. That allows the top six to eight inches of topsoil, the frozen part, to thaw out. Then one can begin digging. Using this technique, we were able to dig a number of graves that first day.

We returned every day that week to Beth David, until the gravediggers' strike was finally settled. Before leaving for the cemetery every day, I loaded up on sandwiches and danishes for the pickets. The strikers came to look forward to our arrival as a temporary relief from the tedium of standing there in the bitter cold all day, and we became quite friendly with them. They never bothered us as we went about our digging and even gave us a few pointers from time to time.

Several years after the gravediggers' strike, I was paying a *shivah* call when a young man asked if he could speak to me privately. We stepped over to the side of the room. He introduced himself as Rabbi David Fein and said to me, "You're Meyer Birnbaum, aren't you? You buried my grandmother during the New York gravedigger's strike, and I just want to give you a *yasher koach* on behalf of my whole family. I can't tell you how much it meant to us." In one of those interesting coincidences that seem to be always happening to me, it turned out that Rabbi Fein's grandmother was the mother of Mrs. Lou Fish, a neighbor of mine in Mattesdorf, and Abe Halperin, who used to manage our Bensonhurst store, as well as the grandmother of Rebbetzin Plitnik, the house mother at the Bais Yaakov Seminary, where I lecture frequently.

AKIVA WAS LEARNING IN PONEVEZH IN 1967 WHEN THE Six-Day War broke out. I sent him a two-word telegram — *"Kibbud Av"* — by which I meant that he should return home immediately. He spent the next week in Antwerp, Belgium. At the end of the war, I asked him to return to the States for awhile, since I was

From Quests to Family

very lonely. He did so, resuming his studies at the Mirrer Yeshiva in Brooklyn.

One night, a few months after Akiva's return, I received a call from him at 2:00 a.m. It took me a few moments to recover from the shock of his call and to assure myself that he was fine. He proceeded to tell me that he was bringing home a family of four — father, mother, and two small children. They had just arrived from Morocco via Spain, Paris, and London, with only the clothes on their backs and no place to stay. "We have plenty of room," he announced, "so I'll be right over."

At that hour of the night, I was not able to adjust so rapidly to the idea of sharing my house with four complete strangers, and I told Akiva, "You'll do nothing of the sort. I'll come to the Yeshiva tomorrow, and we can talk about it then."

The next morning, as I walked downstairs on my way to *davening*, I had quite a surprise awaiting me on the stairwell. Standing there were two scantily-clad dark-skinned little boys, who appeared to be about one and two years old respectively. My first question — "Who are you?" — elicited no response. It was quite clear that they didn't understand a word I had said. "Akiva, Akiva," I bellowed, "which room are you in?" (We had four bedrooms upstairs and two more downstairs.)

Akiva called back, "Abba, Abba, please keep it down. The Laniados (the name has been changed) are extremely tired from their travels."

"Akiva," I replied, "I told you I'd talk about it in the morning. Where are they? The kids probably couldn't sleep, and they are running around the living room."

By the time I returned from *davening* that morning, the Laniados had awakened, and we met for the first time. The father, Shlomo, was a young Moroccan rabbi, who had studied in Schneider's Yeshiva in London under Rabbi Zaidel Semiatitcki (Tiktiner), and therefore knew a little English. Shlomo, however, was so scholarly and soft spoken that my primary communication over the year that the Laniados lived together with me was with his wife Zahava. Her fluent Arabic and French were, of course, of somewhat limited utility in terms of communicating with me. I remembered only a smattering of my army French. As a result for the first few months, we had to make do with French, and the handful of Hebrew words we had in common, until Zahava learned English.

Akiva had already decided that the Laniados should move in with me, and proceeded to outline his plan at this first meeting. Zahava would cook and clean and take care of the washing and ironing. Since there was no *kollel* that Shlomo could enter immediately, he would stay in the house and learn all day. When I came home at night, he would be my own private *rebbe-chavrusa.*

The Laniados had fled Morocco because of the anti-Jewish rioting in the wake of the stunning Israeli victory in the Six-Day War, and they had arrived in America with literally nothing but the clothes on their back. That night I went from one home to another in Far Rockaway collecting clothes, cribs, strollers — in short, everything they would need. I recently ran into someone who told me that we had met once before when I came to his house at two o'clock in the morning to pick up a stroller for some newly arrived immigrants.

In any event, Akiva's rosy vision of all the benefits that would befall me as a consequence of having them live with me turned out to be true. The presence of a family, and especially two little boys, lifted much of the gloom that had descended on the nearly empty house. I even got used to eating the spicy Moroccan dishes, which at first were the only thing that Zahava knew how to cook.

Without question, I received much more from the Laniados than they did from me. Within a short while, I felt that they were part of my family. When one of the boys was hit by a car while crossing the street with his mother, I was the first person Zahava called from the hospital, and I immediately dropped everything and rushed down there to make sure that he got the best possible care — something Zahava could not do in her still broken English. To this day, Zahava goes around telling people that I am her brother. Given her dark complexion, this statement occasions no little surprise among those who assume that her maiden name is Birnbaum.

Over time, I began to teach Zahava how to cook Ashkenazi food, while she helped me expand my repertoire to include traditional Moroccan dishes. Her cooking eventually developed into the family's means of *parnassah* (financial support) during their first difficult years in the country. (Today she is considered by many to make the best *kishka* they have ever tasted.) After they had been living with me for a couple of months, I suggested to Zahava that she find a babysitter for the boys, and I arranged for her to work in the Mauzone kitchen where we prepared food for catered functions.

After the Laniados had lived with me for a year, Zahava found a job as the cook for Rabbi Newhouse's Bais Yaakov up in the mountains, and the family moved there. Two days before Pesach that year, Zahava told Rabbi Newhouse that she had to prepare Pesach for her brother in the city, and she came in with Shlomo and the two boys. Staying up two nights in a row, she brought Pesach into my home. I guess that was her way of expressing her *hakaras hatov* (gratitude).

Zahava eventually opened up a successful *glatt kosher* take-out food business in Flatbush and she is justly famous as the cook of a major camp. Today her husband Shlomo is a *rosh kollel* in Flatbush. Their sons are both learning and teaching Torah, and their daughters are all married to *bnei Torah*. I have never missed one of their family *simchos,* and to this day it remains one of my most enduring sources of joy to have been part of their lives.

There is no question in my mind that the Laniados were another of the opportunities that Hashem sent me to earn the *zechusim* (merits) I so desperately needed. Had I turned Akiva down, no one would have been the wiser. Even those who knew would not have blamed a middle-aged man for not wanting to suddenly share his home with four complete strangers. But I suspected that they would prove to be salve for my soul, and so it was.

THE HABIT I DEVELOPED OF LOOKING FOR *MITZVOS* THAT others might have passed by did not end with my marriage.

Sarah During the years in which I was constantly begging Hashem to send me new *mitzvos*, I discovered the truth of what *Chazal* tell us: The *mitzvah* itself is its own greatest reward and each *mitzvah* brings in its wake more *mitzvos*.

A few years after Goldie and I were married, we rented a bungalow up in the country for the summer. For most of the week she was alone with six young children, and I realized that she needed a mother's helper. My friend Ronnie Greenwald ran nearby Camp Sternberg, and I called him to find out whether he could send over a girl who would prefer working in the country to returning to the city at the end of her three weeks at camp.

Ronnie told me that there was a certain public school girl from Queens about whom he was very concerned. He thought she would benefit greatly from being in our home. I didn't reject the idea outright, but told him that our preference was for a girl with a Bais Yaakov background.

That Monday morning my wife called me at work. Ronnie had sent over this girl whom we'll call Sarah. "I don't know what to do with her," my wife said, "she has no clothing, and I wanted a Bais Yaakov girl." I called Ronnie to find out why he had gone ahead and sent over the girl. He told me that he felt that Sarah had tremendous potential and that the experience of living with us would bring a completely different level of *Yiddishkeit* into her life. After discussing the matter again with my wife, we agreed to take Sarah for a trial period.

I arrived back in the mountains on Thursday night and met Sarah for the first time. I was immediately struck by her sweetness and moved by her description of her family background. She had lost her mother as a young girl. Later her father had remarried briefly, but that marriage had failed. As my wife had said, Sarah had almost no suitable clothing, and that Thursday night we drove into nearby Monticello to buy her sneakers and whatever else she needed for the rest of the summer.

Sarah immediately took to our family, and we to her. Soon she was calling my wife and me, Abba and Imma. When the remaining three weeks of the summer were over, she returned with us to Boro Park and helped clean the house I had been living in by myself all summer. She stayed with us our first Shabbos back in the city.

That Shabbos, as I was blessing the other children, Saraleh asked me, "Abba, would you mind giving me a blessing too, just like the other children?" For reasons that I was unaware of at the time that *berachah* caused her to start crying. Only years later did I realize that it was the thought of leaving us that elicited her tears.

After Shabbos, I called her father to tell him that we had returned to the city and to ask whether he objected to her remaining with us a few more days until the start of the school year. He had no objection. When it finally came time for Sarah to return home, all the kids insisted on piling into the family station wagon to accompany her. We made it clear that she was welcome to spend any Shabbos she wanted with us.

Over the course of the summer, I had spoken to Saraleh several times about the possibility of going to Bais Yaakov. I was convinced that she would blossom there. But every time she pushed off the suggestion by telling me that her father did not have money for the tuition. When I met her father for the first time, I broached the subject with him too. As Sarah had predicted, he told me that he could not afford it. In addition, he pointed out that after eight years of public school Sarah would never be able to catch up in her studies. Moreover, she would not know anyone there and would grow depressed. Finally, he refused to send his daughter on any kind of public transportation, and the public school was an easy two-block walk away.

By that time, I was determined to get Saraleh into a Bais Yaakov. Her potential and beautiful *middos* were obvious, but all she knew of *Yiddishkeit* was Shabbos. About *Chumash, Nevi'im, halachah*, she had no clue.

I sat down with her father and answered his objections one by one. "Let us say," I said to him, "that tuition were covered, private tutors were hired, and the school provided its own transportation." I succeeded in securing his agreement to letting her go if all these conditions could be met.

I knew I had to work fast before Sarah's father reconsidered his decision and so I set up an appointment for the next day at the Bais Yaakov of Queens. My trump card was that the director of the school was Rabbi Avraham Schechter, son of my old mentor Joseph Schechter. I had known Reb Avraham since he was a little baby, which made it harder for him to turn down my requests than it would have been had I been a complete stranger.

After I had finished relating Sarah's story, Reb Avraham's initial response was: "We're not a charitable organization. We have to receive tuition." I told him that I would cover the tuition or raise it for him. Next he raised the issue of how Sarah could possibly catch up at the beginning of high school on eight years of Jewish studies she had missed. I suggested that he find girls who would volunteer to help her during their free time, and if that didn't work, he could hire private tutors at my expense. Somewhat reluctantly, he agreed to try it, but only on a trial basis.

With respect to transportation, Reb Avraham dug in his heels. He pointed out that no other girl in the school lived in Sarah's neighborhood, and arranging transportation would be a big expense for the school. "The least she can do is come in by herself," he insisted. But here, too, I ultimately prevailed on him to stretch a point in her favor. And once again, I was told, "But only on a trial basis."

Reb Avraham then asked to meet Sarah, and I drove over to her house and picked her up. Her natural modesty and refinement impressed him, and the first hurdle of getting Sarah in was cleared.

The first year was very difficult for Sarah. She was simultaneously adjusting to a whole new set of friends, completely different standards of behavior, and an entirely new curriculum. Her lack of background left her frequently lost in class, and, as a consequence, she would sometimes drift off. But Saraleh was determined, and in time she overcame all the obstacles and graduated Bais Yaakov high school.

Every summer during high school, she spent with us up in the mountains at Pine View Hill Cottages, and there she made a whole new set of friends from Boro Park, Flatbush, and Queens. She was a full-fledged member of our family, and my wife and I viewed her as another daughter.

After high school, we arranged for Sarah to attend the Bais Yaakov Seminary near us in Boro Park. She lived with the son and daughter-in-law of my old *rebbe* Rabbi Yisroel Perkowski and helped them in the house. Whatever was still missing in her preparation for the seminary, the younger Rebbetzin Perkowski would help her with late at night. *Shabbosim* were invariably spent with us.

After seminary, a *shidduch* was suggested for Sarah with an outstanding *bachur* from a yeshiva outside the New York area. This young man — we'll call him Avraham — came from a non-religious family. His parents were extremely well-to-do and strongly pressured him to take over the family business. But he was interested only in learning, and somehow found the strength to resist all the familial pressure. After the wedding, he became the first member of the *kollel* in his yeshiva.

At the wedding, after the *chassan* (bridegroom) had been escorted to the *chuppah* (wedding canopy) and his friends were singing enthusiastically, all eyes were turned expectantly towards the *kallah* (bride). But no *kallah* appeared. Someone came running out to find me and told me that I should go to the *kallah's* room immediately.

"Abba, how can I go to the *chuppah* without a *berachah* from you?" Saraleh asked me. I had been blessing her every Friday night for nearly six years, and she would not go to her *chuppah* without this last *berachah*. Saraleh's aunt and uncle had come in from Norway for the wedding and were supposed to escort her to the *chuppah*. Her aunt turned to me and said, "Sarah has not stopped talking about you or your wife the entire time, and we think that you should escort her to the *chuppah*." I was in such an emotional state by this time that I doubt I could have navigated my way to the *chuppah* escorting Saraleh and told her aunt, "No, the *kavod* (honor) belongs to you. It would be too much for me." Saraleh wiped away her tears, placed the veil back over her face, and went down to the *chuppah*.

Sarah and Avraham returned after the *sheva berachos* to the out-of-town yeshiva in which he had been learning. Avraham continued in full-time learning for many years, and just recently was appointed director of the yeshiva.

❧   ❧   ❧

Recently, we married off our son Yisrael to Ahuva Sherman in Jerusalem. The day before the wedding, we received a phone call. The next thing I knew my wife was shouting with excitement, "What do you mean you came in?"

On the other end of the line, Saraleh told her, "I wanted to see my Srulie, whom I took care of when he was a little baby. My husband insisted I come and even bought me the ticket himself. 'It's the least you owe them,' he told me."

We hadn't seen Saraleh in nearly ten years and the reunion wasn't until the wedding itself. The first thing I wanted to do at the wedding was find her. When I did, we just stood looking at each other and crying.

After the wedding, Saraleh came back to the house with us, and we took out all the old slides from those long-ago summers in the country. She couldn't stop giggling at the pictures of herself as a young girl of thirteen. Our three youngest children — Eliezer, Aviva, and Bat-Tzion — had no memory of her, but they instinctively knew that she was another member of the family.

Before she left to return to the States, Saraleh told my wife and me, "You have no idea how much I owe you. My life was transformed by meeting you. Until then, I had always wondered what was going to become of me. I was not a happy girl, and felt very disadvantaged because I did not have a mother. You, Imma, became my mother. I will never be able to repay you for what you did for me. If only everyone could have the good fortune to meet people like you, there would be a lot less unhappiness in the world."

As I walked with Saraleh up the steps from our apartment to the cab waiting to take her to the airport, tears of joy started flowing again at the thought of the wonderful opportunity Hashem had given us to help this remarkable young woman.

CHAPTER SIXTEEN
Aliyah

MY WIFE AND I FIRST VISITED *ERETZ YISRAEL* together shortly after our marriage in 1969 and returned frequently after that. In fact, *Eretz Yisrael* was the only place we ever went for a vacation, besides the bungalow colony in the summer.

Our last such vacation was Chanukah of 1980. As usual we stayed with our friends Eliezer and Sarah Moses in Bayit Vegan. Whenever we came, they gave us the key to the house and told us,"Welcome home," and that is exactly how we felt — as if we had come home.

As we boarded the plane to return to the States, after spending two weeks visiting the holy places of *Eretz Yisrael*, we went through a familiar ritual. I gazed out the window trying to take in as much as possible of the country before take-off, and my wife took out a handkerchief, wiped her eyes, and put on sunglasses to hide her tears.

When we were in the air, I turned to my wife and announced, "This is the last time we come to *Eretz Yisrael* as tourists. The next time we return it will be on *aliyah.*"

Goldie was not nearly as impressed with my dramatic pronouncement as I was, and responded somewhat skeptically, "Well, it's a beautiful dream. Maybe one day it'll become a reality."

Seeing that she had not taken me completely seriously, I continued, "No, nothing doing. As soon as I get in, I will call a meeting of my partners and tell them I want out. We'll have to make a settlement according to the partnership agreement."

With that we both sank back into our own thoughts of the past two-and-a-half weeks.

THAT PARTICULAR FLIGHT TURNED OUT TO BE AN exciting one for other reasons as well. As we waited to board the

To the Rescue

plane in Ben Gurion Airport, I had noticed a group of Reb Arele chassidim gathered protectively around their *Rebbe*. I naturally went over to give the *Rebbe* a "*Shalom aleichem*."

We had an hour-long layover in Athens, and the chassidim got off the plane carrying a large package wrapped in paper. As we prepared to reboard the plane, my wife pointed out to me that there was a tumult at the front of the line involving the chassidim and a TWA official. They were gesticulating wildly and speaking in Yiddish, which was obviously not making too much of an impression on him.

I hurried over to where this altercation was taking place and told the TWA official that I spoke their language and could perhaps help resolve the dispute. I found out from the chassidim that they were carrying a *sefer Torah*, which had been commissioned by a wealthy Satmar chassid in Williamsburg and written by a young *sofer* (scribe) in Jerusalem. The *Rebbe* had played an important role in arranging this commission and was thus accompanying the *sofer* to present the *sefer Torah* to the Satmar *shul* in Williamsburg.

The TWA official insisted that the *sefer Torah* was too large to be carried on and would have to be stored in the baggage compartment. The chassidim were equally insistent that they would not part with their treasure.

I explained to the official that they were carrying a holy scroll, which could by no means be thrown into a baggage compartment. "This scroll took a full year or two to write and is worth tens of thousands of dollars," I said. "There is no way they can part with it."

Like most people with a little, but not very much, authority, the TWA official obviously relished this chance to demonstrate his importance and showed no inclination to budge at all on the regulations.

I tried a different tack. "This man," I said, nodding in the direction of the *Rebbe*, "is a revered holy man and these are his followers. Not only are you embarrassing him, you are asking his disciples to violate their religion, which requires them to honor this scroll to the utmost."

The TWA official remained unmoved. "It either goes into the baggage compartment or we send it back to Jerusalem," he said.

By this time I had had enough. "Listen to me," I told him, "I've asked you nicely. Now you're going to do it whether you like it or not." He looked at me as if to say, "Who do you think you are ordering around the manager of TWA's Athens office?"

In those days, Mauzone was a major supplier of products to TWA flights operating out of New York. For that reason I was always able to fly first class for the price of a coach ticket. I carried in my wallet the personal cards of almost every top TWA executive. I now proceeded to take these cards out of my wallet.

I started reading the cards to him: "Pick up the phone and get me this number. It's Danny Kutrandjian. And if Danny is not in, get me Joe Volatti. If he's not in, get me Jimmy Frayle. And if he's not in get me Sam Turezza." We went through another five or so cards of executive vice-presidents before I pulled my trump card — that of John Duggan: "If you can't get any of these people, get me the Transportation Chief of Kennedy Airport, John L. Duggan. If he's not in his office, call him at home in Richmond Hill, New York. Here's the number. Tell him that you're holding up Meyer Birnbaum's flight in Athens. Do it immediately."

The same bureaucrat who had been so happy to lord it over the Reb Arele chassidim a few minutes earlier suddenly did not seem so sure of himself. He considered for a moment whether to call my bluff before deciding against it and asking meekly whether I was on that flight and what section I was sitting in. When I told him first class, he suddenly found a solution to the problem and asked me whether I would be willing to take the *sefer Torah* with me in first class. I explained to the chassidim what had happened, and they happily agreed to entrust me with the *sefer Torah.*

When we arrived in New York, my wife and I went quickly through the line for returning American citizens, while the Reb Arele chassidim and their *Rebbe* had to go through the much slower line for foreign visitors. We exited customs into a sea of black. At least two busloads of chassidim had come to greet the *Rebbe.* I was still holding the *sefer Torah,* and had no choice but to join the throng waiting for the *Rebbe* to pass through customs. When he finally did, he was completely surrounded. There was no way that I could break through the crowd around him to return the *sefer Torah.*

I pulled one of the chassidim aside and told him, "Excuse me, I must see the *Rebbe."*

"All of us want to see the *Rebbe,* not just you," he replied.

I tried again: "I've just come from *Eretz Yisrael,* and I must see the *Rebbe."*

Again he responded, "We all want to see the *Rebbe.* We all want to give him *'Shalom aleichem'."*

"Listen, I'm carrying the *sefer Torah* that this whole celebration is for, and I must hand it to the *Rebbe* myself."

The *sefer Torah* was encased in a rather unprepossessing package wrapped in paper, with a plastic bag thrown over it, and until now, he had not noticed it at all. Apologizing for not having paid me more attention initially, he opened a path, shouting, "Make way, make way." The sea of black parted, and I was suddenly in front of the *Rebbe.* I handed him the *sefer Torah,* and he thanked me profusely.

Like most of my stories, this one also has a sequel. The following Sukkos, after we had made *aliyah,* we went to one of the nightly *Simchos Bais Hashoevah* at the Reb Arele *shul* in Meah Shearim. These are perhaps the most famous of all Jerusalem's

Simchos Bais Hashoevah, and last until two o'clock in the morning throughout *Chol Hamoed Sukkos.* As I was dancing in one of the huge concentric circles with my sons, one of the chassidim approached me and asked, *"Du bist die Amerikaner* — You're the American who brought the *sefer Torah* for the *Rebbe?"* Assured that I was, he insisted that I come over to greet the *Rebbe.*

I expressed skepticism about any human being's ability to pass through the whirl of dancers, but he promised that for me they would part. My sons in tow, we did in fact manage to reach the *Rebbe.* I was introduced, and the *Rebbe* once again gave me a *yasher koach* for having rescued the *sefer Torah* in Athens and blessed each of my sons. Every year since then, there has always been someone who recognizes me, and I always have the honor of wishing the *Rebbe, "Shalom aleichem,"* and receiving his blessing.

I CALLED A MEETING OF MY PARTNERS AS SOON AS I returned to New York. One of the important lessons I had learned

Liquidating over the years is that unless one acts on good intentions immediately, his resolve invariably dissipates with each passing day.

In addition, I realized that if we were going to make the move that it would have to be as soon as possible. My son Avraham Mordechai was almost of an age to start looking for a *shidduch,* and my daughter Leah was due to attend the Bais Yaakov Seminary in Jerusalem the next year, after which she too would be ready for marriage. As far as the younger kids were concerned, the sooner we moved the better off they would be in terms of learning Hebrew quickly and adjusting to a completely new society.

My announcement that I was leaving the business hit my partners like a bombshell. Our lawyer protested that since I had been running the company for almost thirty years, my departure at this point would effectively mean the end of the business. I replied that the cemeteries are full of people who thought they were indispensable and that anyone can be replaced. Apparently my partners sided with our lawyer since the decision was made to liquidate the business.

The major problem confronting us was how to handle our heavy indebtedness. We had been hurt badly four years earlier when many of those whose summer lunch programs we supplied did not pay us and we were stuck with hundreds of thousands of dollars in receivables.

Our lawyer suggested that my partners and I could still emerge as rich men if we went through a Chapter 11 reorganization under the Bankruptcy Act, which would allow us to pay off our creditors for as little as five cents on the dollar. Rabbi Levovitz, my primary partner, however, rejected this advice outright. He pointed out that since the vast majority of our creditors were Jewish, a discharge in bankruptcy would have no effect on our halachic obligation to pay them everything we owed. Together he and I led the fight to ensure that the liquidation be carried out so as to ensure that all our creditors would receive everything that was coming to them.

In the end, we were successful in this regard. The proceeds from the sale of our warehouse and stores (many of them to my partners themselves) proved adequate to cover all our debts and to leave us a little something left over. Nothing gives me greater pride from our twenty-nine years in business than the fact that we closed our books with every creditor paid off in full.

Only one problem was left to prey on my conscience. We had one worker, Phil Itzkowitz, who had been with us since the beginning of Mauzone. To call him hard working and honest would be the grossest of understatements. I trusted him with my money more than I trusted myself, and from his dedication to the business one would have thought that every penny of profit was going straight into his pocket rather than to his employers'. Phil is also one of the most admirable people I have ever met. He was always the first to contribute to any *tzedakah* cause, and in an amount equal to those earning several times as much as he did.

For a number of years I had promised Phil that he would one day become a partner in the business, and now we were liquidating the business and that promise had not been fulfilled.

One day, I received a call from Phil telling me that he was extremely disappointed in me. Our chief competitor, Meal-Mart, had come in to look at the Queens store that Phil managed. When they came in to inspect the store, it dawned on Phil that he was going to be left with nothing to show for all his years of loyalty to the business.

I felt the justice of Phil's complaint and told him, "Just because they're looking doesn't mean I have to sell it to them. How much money have you got saved up?" Phil told me he had nothing besides twelve thousand dollars his wife had accumulated in a pension fund. I said, "Fine, the store is yours for that. And if you throw in another couple thousand, you can have the other Queens store too." Phil borrowed two thousand dollars from his sons, and together they purchased the other store as well. Their business has prospered over the years, as I was sure it would, and Phil's well-deserved success has been a source of great happiness to me.

The Move

BY PESACH 1981 WE HAD COMPLETED THE LIQUIDATION, and I was free to devote myself completely to preparing the lift that would take all our possessions to Israel. July was our target date for the move.

The children were already feeling nervous about leaving behind their friends, and a great deal of my time was spent trying to build up the move to *Eretz Yisrael* in their minds. I told them that they would be the envy of all their friends by virtue of living in the Holy Land.

My mother had also decided that she too would come to live with us in *Eretz Yisrael*, despite being ninety-five at the time. Many years earlier, she had purchased a burial plot on *Har Hazeisim*. That plot meant a great deal to her; she always referred to it as her home. She often said, "My father was a great *tzaddik* and my grandfather was a great *tzaddik,* and they did not have the merit of seeing *Eretz Yisrael* or of being buried there. Why should I have that *zechus?*"

Now she had been presented with an opportunity to live in *Eretz Yisrael,* not just to be buried there, and she was not about to pass it up.

Goldie and I and our eight children arrived in *Eretz Yisrael* the first week in July, as we had planned. We were greeted by my son Aharon from my first marriage. He was already living in *Eretz Yisrael* and was then recovering from a wound sustained in combat. A week later my sister and her husband brought my mother.

The adjustment was not an easy one. All the children — from the oldest to the youngest — missed their friends. Their limited Hebrew was also a barrier to making new friends as quickly as they would have liked, and being in *ulpan* for the first few months, rather than in yeshiva or Bais Yaakov, further impeded their efforts to make new friends. In time, however, all these problems were overcome, and it is impossible today to distinguish any of the younger children from their friends born in *Eretz Yisrael.*

Goldie was expecting at the time of our *aliyah,* and a few months after our arrival she gave birth to a baby girl whom I decided to name Bat-Zion in honor of her birth in Jerusalem. The idea for the name came to me from Rabbi Beinush Finkel, Rosh Yeshiva of the Mirrer Yeshiva. He once told me that his fourth daughter was born while he was in America raising funds for the Yeshiva. When his *Rebbe*tzin called to inform him of the birth, she asked him what they should name the baby. He replied that she should ask her uncle the Chazon Ish to choose a name. The Chazon Ish answered that since the first three girls had been born in Bnei Brak and this one was born in Jerusalem, Bat-Zion would be an appropriate name.

OUR DAUGHTER LEAH MARRIED A WONDERFUL BOY, Yonasan Mayer, shortly after finishing Bais Yaakov of Jerusalem Seminary, and a little more than a year later **Deliverance** her older brother Avraham Mordechai was married to a very fine American girl, Naomi Neuberger of Brooklyn. Avraham's wedding took place in America. We had to leave my mother with a Bubby-sitter while we were in America, and I hurried back in the middle of *sheva berachos* so as to not leave her alone for longer than necessary.

That winter was an unusually cold one in Jerusalem, and the northern exposure of our apartment made it extremely hard to heat. To combat the cold I used three large gas heaters and had all the openings to the outside completely insulated.

My wife returned to Jerusalem from the wedding on a Wednesday night, the day before *Tu B'Shevat*. The weather was still very cold and the heaters were going full blast when she arrived. The next morning was particularly cold. I was forced to don an overcoat for my *vasikin minyan* by the *Kosel*, something I almost never do.

When I returned home from the *minyan*, my wife complained of a headache, which she attributed to jet lag, and asked me whether I would mind preparing Shabbos. Cooking and baking was my livelihood for years, and making Shabbos is no problem for me. As soon as I got the children off for school that morning, I turned on the oven and started with the Shabbos baking and cooking.

When my daughter Aviva returned home from Bais Yaakov, she complained of a headache. I told her to take a nap and not to worry about doing her homework immediately, as she usually did. Next my son Yechezkel came home from *cheder* for lunch. After lunch, he asked me whether he could take a fifteen-minute nap before returning to *cheder* in the afternoon. When I awakened him, he too complained of a severe headache and asked whether he could stay home for the afternoon. He certainly had my sympathy — particularly since the *cheder* had no heat and the boys had to learn with their winter coats on — and I agreed to let him stay home.

During the course of the morning and early afternoon, I went to check on my mother several times. Each time she complained of nausea and a headache and refused whatever I offered her to eat or drink. Sleeping next to my mother in the bed was Bat-Zion, who was about two-and-a-half by this time. Around three in the afternoon, my wife grew concerned that Bat-Zion had been sleeping all day and asked me to take her temperature.

By this time I was not feeling too well myself. My vision was fogged, but I attributed that to a problem with my glasses and to my own tiredness. I must have looked pretty awful, however, because when I went down to a neighbor to borrow a thermometer, she looked at me and asked whether everything was all right.

I took Bat-Zion's temperature, but found that I was too blurry eyed to read the thermometer. At that point, I must have fainted because about fifteen minutes later I woke up and found myself on the bed where Bat-Zion was sleeping. My dizziness was unbearable.

My wife told me to check on Aviva. I found her limp. I slapped her face and there was no reaction. "Aviva, hold your hands up," I begged her, but they dropped like a ton of bricks. It now dawned on me for the first time that there was something terribly wrong in the house.

I picked up Aviva and carried her to the entrance hall to telephone a neighbor. By this time, I could not make out the numbers on the telephone dial, and when I tried to stand up from the chair in which I was sitting I realized I could not do that either. Normally, I am a very strong person, but now I had no strength to do anything more than pray: "*Ribbono Shel Olam*, please help me out. There's something wrong in this house. I must have help. Please, *Ribbono Shel Olam*, help me get out of here."

I made one more attempt to reach the door and somehow managed to get it open. We lived eighteen steps down from street level. How I managed to get up one of those steps, much less all of them, I have no idea. All I remember is seeing Leah Moskovitz, one of our neighbor's youngsters (a year later, to the day, this wonderful girl and my son Shloime were married), before fainting again with Aviva still in my arms.

The next thing I knew I was being examined by an ambulance team. I kept telling the doctor, "*Lematah* (downstairs), *lematah*," but it seemed like an eternity before I could get anyone to understand what I was saying. It was some time before I had recovered sufficiently to make my way back to the apartment. When I got there, the windows had been thrown completely open and the heaters, stove and oven turned off. The doctors were working on my son Yechezkel, who was foaming at the mouth. My wife was sitting motionless, a totally blank look on her face. I was placed on the couch and just lay there watching the action. I learned later that my mother had fallen off her bed onto the floor.

It took nearly two hours until everyone had been fully revived. The emergency doctor told me, "You were very lucky. These cases don't usually end so happily. I cannot understand how the six of you could have been trapped in the apartment with so much carbon monoxide poison and all survived, without even going to the hospital." We soon learned how right he was. The next morning's news brought word of a young couple in Bayit Vegan who had died in their sleep of carbon monoxide poisoning.

The next week, when we had finally recovered from the shock, my wife and I went to Rabbi Cheshin to tell him the story of our deliverance. I still had no explanation of how I had succeeded in climbing up to the entranceway to our building. A few minutes earlier, I had been unable to even stand up. And then suddenly, I had climbed nine steps to the first landing and another nine to the street level, all the while carrying Aviva in my arms.

Rabbi Cheshin just looked at me and smiled. "Do you think that you got to the top of the stairs on your own strength?" he asked me. Without waiting for my answer he continued: "Absolutely not. *Malachim* (angels) carried you up the stairs. I don't know what you've done in your life to merit it, but you had a great *zechus* to be able to save your family."

Two weeks later, we made a large *seudas hodaah* (thanksgiving meal) for about seventy people, and every year since then, we have repeated this *seudah* on the anniversary of our deliverance.

At that meal, Rabbi Cheshin told me to have our *mezuzos* checked. I told him that I had bought very expensive *mezuzos* just two years earlier when we made *aliyah,* but nevertheless did as he suggested. Of the fifteen *mezuzos* in the house, five were *posul* and one was missing altogether. The previous year the house had been painted, and the painters had apparently knocked off one of the *mezuzah* coverings and neglected to replace the parchment.

Rabbi Cheshin also suggested that whatever merits I had to my credit might have been fully depleted by this miracle and that I should get to work replenishing them with acts of *chesed.* I've been trying to follow his advice ever since.

MY MOTHER'S LIFE WAS NOT AN EASY ONE — SHE WAS basically on her own in a strange country from the age of thirteen,

My Mother's Petirah

lived most of her life in abject poverty, and lost a son in combat. But her own intense faith was never diminished by her individual trials. Her last five years with us seemed in many respects a fitting reward for all that she had endured without complaint.

Visitors to our home for Shabbos — whether girls studying in Bais Yaakov or young *yeshiva bachurim* — would almost invariably ask her for a *berachah* at the end of Shabbos. And just as regularly, she would reply, "How can I give a *berachah* to someone who is learning full-time?" When they insisted, however, she complied with their requests. Everyone called her Bubby, and as a result, she used to say, "I wonder how many grandchildren I really have. Everyone is always calling me Bubby."

Particularly gratifying to me was the love and respect every one of my children showed her, whether they were biologically related or not. My second oldest son, Eliyahu, used to drive in to see her once, and sometimes twice, a week from the settlement of Tekoa where he lives, and they would sit and talk for hours. He told me, "I never find Bubby boring. She's always so sweet and full of interesting memories."

My daughter Leah slept in the same room with her and would get up without complaint in the middle of the night to get her a drink or to rub her feet with lotion when she was troubled by dry skin. All the children would take her for walks, sit with her outside in the sun, and tuck her into bed when she was tired. They felt her love and returned it with interest.

My wife waited on her hand and foot. Whatever my mother wanted was provided immediately. Of course, she asked for very little. She had a lifelong ability to be happy with whatever she had. As far as she was concerned, there was always enough, and plenty to share with others.

My mother's mind remained sharp until the very end, and she did not lose her enjoyment in life. Our last conversation was at one o'clock in the morning at the hospital. I had come to check

My mother before her marriage

on her and to inform her that Leah had given birth to a boy that day. Practically her last words were: "I want to be at the *shalom zachor*. I'm going to speak to the doctors, and I think they'll let me come home for Shabbos." The next morning Reb Beinush asked me at the *Kosel* if I had the exact time, and I told him that it was six o'clock. That turned out to be the precise moment of my mother's *petirah*.

Even though she was one hundred years old when she passed away, when it is your own mother it never seems that life is long enough. But at least there was great consolation in knowing that she had fulfilled her major goals in life. She wanted to live in *Eretz Yisrael*, and she did. She wanted to take her last breath from the air of Jerusalem, and she did. She had a special trunk in which she kept the *tachrichin* (burial shrouds) she had sewn for herself and all the receipts from her charitable contributions. She was buried in those *tachrichin*, together with her *tzedakah* receipts, on *Har Hazeisim* in the plot she had purchased so many years earlier.

CHAPTER SEVENTEEN

The Kosel

FIRST SAW THE *KOSEL HAMAARAVI* (THE WESTERN Wall) on our 1969 visit to *Eretz Yisrael*. My son Eliyahu was then learning in yeshiva in *Eretz Yisrael*, and he served as our guide on that first trip to the *Kosel*.

The Early Morning Shuttle

Eli took us through the Jaffa Gate and the adjacent Arab market. Suddenly we found ourselves standing in front of the *Kosel*. I was overwhelmed. Just to confirm to myself what I was seeing, I said aloud, "This the *Kosel HaMaaravi*?" Tears flowed freely from my eyes.

My wife and I walked slowly towards the *Kosel* before separating. As I entered the men's side and approached the Wall, I was overcome with trembling of a kind that I had never before experienced. The thought that I was approaching the *Shechinah* (Divine Presence) left me physically shaken. I could not force my quivering legs all the way up to the Wall itself, and had to content myself with standing about ten feet away while reciting *Tehillim*. I prayed that the *Ribbono Shel Olam* bless our marriage with *Yiddishe nachas*, the only kind that matters. *Baruch Hashem*, He has.

To this day, after thousands of trips to the *Kosel*, the remnant of that original fear still remains.

At the end of his Wednesday night *shiur* in *Zohar*, shortly after our arrival in Jerusalem, Rabbi Cheshin posed the question: "What is the strongest *yetzer hara*?" The answers were almost as varied as the participants in the *shiur*, but no one came up with the answer Rabbi Cheshin was seeking: sleep. "Every morning when you wake up, the first words out of the *yetzer hara's* mouth are: "Forget about *negel vasser* and saying *Modeh Ani*. Turn over for another five minutes of precious sleep."

"That five minutes turns into thirty," Rabbi Cheshin continued. "By the time you get up, the *yetzer hara* is telling you, 'You're already too late for this *minyan*, but you have plenty of time for the next.' You turn over and go back to sleep. By the time you wake up the third time, you jump out of bed in a hurry, but the *yetzer hara* has won. 'You've already missed the last *minyan*,' he says, 'you might as well just walk calmly to *shul* to *daven* by yourself.' "

I didn't agree. "I was a soldier and I can get up at a moment's notice," I told Rabbi Cheshin.

"This isn't my opinion," he replied. "It's what the *Zohar* says." Then he asked me what time I normally *davened*. I told him seven o'clock, and he challenged me to try to make the six o'clock *minyan*. The next morning I set the alarm clock for five o'clock just to be sure I would make it on time. It was still completely dark when I finished *berachos* and *korbanos*, and I thought to myself, "Why not drive down to the *Kosel* for the *vasikin minyan*?" When I got there, I noticed Reb Beinush Finkel, the Mirrer Rosh Yeshiva, who nodded at me to join his *minyan*.

After the next week's *Zohar shiur*, Rabbi Cheshin asked me how my experiment had gone, and I proudly told him that I had been *davening* every morning in the *vasikin minyan* at the *Kosel*. He was obviously pleased, but gave me an additional push.

"*Groisser knocker*, Meyer," he said, "have you forgotten the holy number forty? Let's see if you can keep it up for forty days."

Rabbi Cheshin never asked me again when I was *davening*, but he knew that I was taking a carload of people to the *Kosel* every morning in my little five-passenger Renault station wagon.

Since then, the *vasikin minyan* at the *Kosel* has become one of the focal points of my life, and I have not missed a weekday *minyan* in twelve years, except for brief hospital stays and trips to America. My *davening* has been completely transformed, and I can never thank Rabbi Cheshin enough for giving me that initial impetus.

In our Renault and its successor, a Mitsubishi minivan, I have taken close to twenty thousand riders to the *Kosel*. Almost every morning for five years, we managed to stuff ten people into the Renault — Rabbi Beinush Finkel, *zt"l*, the Mirrer Rosh Yeshiva, and myself in the two front seats, four more in the passenger seat, and another four crammed into the tiny luggage compartment. Reb Beinush got great pleasure from our bringing our own *minyan* to the *Kosel* every morning. When four Mirrer *bachurim* would squeeze into the luggage compartment, he often commented, "Just like sardines. The only thing they're lacking is a little oil."

Five years ago, I replaced the Renault with a Mitsubishi minivan with eight passenger seats. So far our record is twenty-two passengers, and there are always between ten and fifteen. I often receive calls from visitors to *Eretz Yisrael* asking, "Are you the one who *davens* every morning at the *Kosel*? We came to *Eretz Yisrael* specifically to *daven* and would very much like to go to the *vasikin minyan* tomorrow." I have never had to turn down one of those requests. The van always has room for whoever wants to go.

The early morning *Kosel* Express has become something of a public institution. A young man now living in Lakewood stopped me recently on the street to thank me for helping him find a wonderful *shidduch*. The first time he met his wife he was naturally nervous and at a loss for things to talk about. So he started talking about the experience of riding to the *Kosel* in a minivan stuffed to the roof. It turned out that she had heard me lecture while she was learning in *Eretz Yisrael* in seminary, which led to an animated comparison of notes and got the *shidduch* off to a good start.

Needless to say, vehicles as overcrowded as mine have not passed completely unnoticed by the police. Early in my career as a chauffeur, I was stopped by the police. Before I got out of the car, Reb Beinush instructed me not to try to speak in Hebrew. One of the officers tried to convey the law's displeasure in a broken English, but I kept telling her, "I'm sorry, I don't understand your English." After a few minutes, her partner grew frustrated and told her, "A *meshuganeh* American. Let him go." Subsequently, I heard veterans tell new policemen inclined to give me a hefty fine, "Oh, it's the *meshuganeh*. Forget it."

By now, I have become friendly with all of Jerusalem's early morning traffic cops, and especially those assigned to the *Kosel* area. Over the years, they have grown to appreciate my excuse for jamming so many people into the van: I cannot bear to leave Jewish hitchhikers standing there in the middle of the night, especially near the Arab neighborhoods on the way to the *Kosel*. (This has become even more true with the upsurge of attacks on Jews.)

Amazingly, in light of the abuse my cars have taken from the constant overloading, I've never had a single flat tire, a broken spring, or a problem with the shock absorbers. Recently, I ran into the person who purchased my old Renault, and he told me that in his opinion it's the best used car ever sold in Israel. He added that this did not surprise him since he had seen me on many occasions at the *Kosel* with the Mirrer Rosh Yeshiva and had purchased the car for its *zechusim* (merits).

Every *mitzvah* leads to others, and *davening vasikin* at the *Kosel* has been no exception. A neighbor of mine was at the *Kosel* one day for *Minchah*. A group of German tourists heard him speaking Yiddish and approached him. Their neighbor was an elderly Jewish woman. When she heard they were going to *Eretz Yisrael*, she gave them a note and asked them to hand it to someone at the *Kosel*. In that note she had written the names of all those from her hometown who were murdered by the Nazis and had never had anyone to say *Kaddish* for them. She requested that someone say *Kaddish* for them.

Since my neighbor had already *davened Minchah* and knew that I *daven* every morning at the *Kosel*, he passed the list on to me. The next morning, I told the *gabbai* that I had an obligation to lead the *davening*. He knows the *yahrzeits* of all the regulars in the *minyan* and told me that I was mistaken, but when I showed him the letter, he waved me to the *amud* (lecturn). Thus, I had the privilege of saying *Kaddish* for all the Jews on the list.

Arranging to send letters back to America overnight is another *mitzvah* that is a direct outgrowth of being at the *Kosel* every morning. Invariably at least one tourist who is leaving for America that day and wants to *daven* one last time at the *Kosel* is there for the *vasikin minyan*. These tourists are usually happy to be a *shaliach mitzvah* and carry back to the States the large bag of letters that I always bring with me.

ONE MORNING AS I DROVE TO THE *KOSEL*, I SPOTTED REB Beinush Finkel waiting for a ride on Shivtei Yisrael Street

Reb Beinush
alongside Meah Shearim. I stopped and he got into the passenger seat. It was a ritual to be repeated every morning for the next eight and a half years.

I had known Reb Beinush since my son Akiva first came to learn in Mirrer Yeshiva in 1966, but in the eight years of driving him to the *Kosel* every morning, I came to feel like a younger brother to him. Simply put: I loved him. That is not to say, however, that I really ever felt that I knew him well or understood the things that he did. He was a master at self-concealment — a trait he had apparently inherited from his grandfather Rabbi Nosson Tzvi Finkel, the Alter of Slabodka, and his father Rabbi Eliezer Yehuda Finkel, the previous Mirrer Rosh Yeshiva.

His sense of humor was fabled, and there was almost never a time when he was without a joke on his lips. That constant joking was to me the clearest proof of his efforts to conceal himself. A week before his *petirah*, he cheered up one glum-faced visitor to his home. When the young man first came into the room, he just stood there. But after listening to Reb Beinush's usual stream of witticisms, he forgot the depressing nature of his visit. As he was leaving, he went to shake the Rosh Yeshiva's hand, and Reb Beinush teased him, "When you came in you were afraid to shake my hand."

His favorite jokes were ones of which he was the butt. I heard him tell countless times the story of a new *bachur* at the Mir who

Speaking with Mirrer Rosh Yeshiva Rabbi Beinush Finkel

sees a number of the veteran students leaving the *Beis Midrash* before the Rosh Yeshiva's weekly *shiur klali*. The *bachur* asks where everyone is going and is told, "Reb Beinush is giving a *shiur*." The young man rushes into the hall just as Reb Beinush is coming up the stairs. Reb Beinush stops the young man and asks him why he's running so fast. Not recognizing the Rosh Yeshiva, the *bochur* tells him, "*Ihr vaist nist as Reb Beinush zigt dem shiur heint* — Reb Beinush is about to give a *shiur*."

"In that case run faster," Reb Beinush tells him, without identifying himself.

He hid himself from everyone, even from his own family. His sons-in-law relate with amusement his efforts not to be seen learning late at night. If one of them happened to spend a Shabbos in Reb Beinush's home and got up in the middle of the night, he would invariably find Reb Beinush pretending to check the *cholent,* the *sefer* he had been learning quickly hidden away.

Though I don't claim to have really known him, I never

doubted that he was one of the thirty-six hidden righteous men whose merits protect the world.

⚜   ⚜   ⚜

When I dropped off Reb Beinush after we returned from the *Kosel* that first morning, I told him that I would pick him up in front of his home on Rechov Slonim the next morning. But the next morning he was not in front of his apartment. I found him several blocks away waiting as usual on Shivtei Yisrael. Morning after morning I went to his home, and morning after morning he was not there. Fearing that I would get to his building before he left, he even began leaving earlier that usual — more than an hour before sunrise.

When he saw me turning from Meah Shearim Street onto Shivtei Yisrael, he used to ask me where I was coming from, and I would answer that I was coming from his home. And he would say, "Don't go there. I told you I'd be here." But I continued to pass his home every morning in the hope that he would realize that I was being detoured needlessly by his failure to wait for me. I had no idea who would give in first in this battle of wills. Finally one miserable rainy winter morning, I drove past his apartment building and found him waiting.

I leaned over and opened the front door for the Rosh Yeshiva, but he closed the door and opened it again. I may have won the first battle, but the Rosh Yeshiva wanted me to know that he still had no intention of accepting any unnecessary favors.

Not allowing others to serve him was, I soon discovered, one of his strongest principles. Among my passengers every morning were invariably a number of Mirrer *bachurim*. As we walked back to my car, one would always rush ahead to open the door for the Rosh Yeshiva. Then the following scenario — which I must have witnessed a thousand times — would be played out.

"*Vus tust ta* — What are you doing?" the Rosh Yeshiva would ask.

"I'm opening the door for the Rosh Yeshiva," the *bachur* would reply.

"Why did you open the door for the Rosh Yeshiva?"

"It's a *mitzvah* to do something for the Rosh Yeshiva."

"Are you sure it's a *mitzvah?*"

"Yes," the boy would say, smiling sheepishly.

At that point, Reb Beinush would close the door and open it again: *"Ich darf mitzvos oiched* — I also need *mitzvos.* If you say it's a *mitzvah* to open the door for me, then I'll open it for myself."

Although Reb Beinush hated to have others serve him, I have never met anyone who could be so insistent when he wanted to do something for someone else. One morning I had to hurry to the airport after *davening* to pick up my sister. Normally we remained at the *Kosel* for some time after *davening.* People would come up to talk to Reb Beinush, and he always gave them as much time as they needed. But that particular morning, I mentioned to the Rosh Yeshiva that I wanted to leave right after the last *Kaddish* in order to get to the airport. When I pulled up in front of Reb Beinush's home on our way back from the *Kosel,* he insisted that I come up and eat before my journey. I told him that I didn't have time and would grab a cup of coffee when I got to the airport. Before I knew what was happening, however, he had reached over to shut off the engine and remove the key from the ignition.

"Come, I'll make you a coffee. It'll only take a minute," he said. "You're not going to the airport until you eat something, so don't waste any more time arguing about it."

I again protested that I had no time, but I knew from previous experience that when the Rosh Yeshiva played this trick with the key you might as well give up. Before we made *aliyah,* I always went to see the Rosh Yeshiva whenever I was in Israel. One time my wife and I visited him in his apartment on *Erev Shabbos.* In the middle of the conversation, I noticed him go to the door but thought nothing of it. After half an hour, I felt it was time to leave and return to our hosts in Bayit Vegan for Shabbos. We said goodbye to the Rosh Yeshiva and went to the front door. The door was locked and the key nowhere to be found. Reb Beinush informed us that we were locked in and should call our hosts to tell them we had to stay with him and the Rebbetzin for Shabbos. To say that we were unable to leave, Reb Beinush pointed out, was no lie.

With this incident in mind, I realized that my only chance of getting to the airport that morning was to allow Reb Beinush to make me a cup of coffee. We walked upstairs. No matter how many times I was in Reb Beinush's house, I never failed to be struck by its simplicity. Despite the fact that millions of dollars passed through his hands every year, there was not even a cover over the bare light bulbs hanging from the ceiling, and the furniture consisted of nothing more that the plainest table and chairs.

As good as his word, the Rosh Yeshiva quickly made a cup of coffee. To my dismay, he then began looking for some *mezonos* to complete a proper breakfast. A search of the kitchen turned up nothing but frozen *kneidlach* (matzah balls) in the freezer. The Rosh Yeshiva handed me a frozen *kneidel* with the words, "*Dos iz a mezonos* — Here is a *mezonos*. Eat it." I couldn't figure out what to do with the frozen matzah ball, and ended up dunking it in my coffee and eating it half frozen and half soggy.

I have thousands of precious memories from those years together with Reb Beinush which I wouldn't trade for anything. One time a wealthy young friend of mine came from America for a visit. He rented a fancy new car, in which he hoped to have the honor of driving the Rosh Yeshiva home from the *Kosel.* After *davening,* he approached me and said, "I just spoke to the Rosh Yeshiva and he says that you drive him home everyday. So, Meyer, I assume you will give me *reshus* (permission) to drive the Rosh Yeshiva home today."

"Well, I don't give you *reshus,*" I answered to his surprise.

"What do you mean you don't give *reshus?*"

"Just what I said. I won't give up a single ride with the Rosh Yeshiva. Now, if the Rosh Yeshiva wants to go with you, that's all well and good."

My friend went back and reported the conversation to the Rosh Yeshiva, who told him, "*Ich bin nit der baalebus* — I'm not the boss. You have to clear it with Meyer."

One of our regular passengers was Rabbi Abish Zehnwirt, a young man in his thirties who is a walking *sefer Torah.* The Rosh Yeshiva took great delight in Reb Abish's fabulous memory. Almost every morning he would test him by asking where the *Gemara* says such-and-such. Reb Abish would ask whether the

Rosh Yeshiva was referring to the *Bavli* (Babylonian Talmud) or *Yerushalmi* (Jerusalem Talmud) and then proceed to tell him where that piece of information could be found in both. Reb Beinush would chuckle and compliment him, *"Du bist a ganif. Du kenst alles* — You're a thief. You know everything."

Reb Beinush owned an especially precious pair of *tefillin* written by a legendary scribe named Reb Nesanel, who also made the *batim* (phylacteries) himself. The Chofetz Chaim is reputed to have owned a pair of Reb Nesanel's *tefillin,* and only a few pairs are known to still exist today. One morning, after talking to someone for some time after *davening,* Reb Beinush turned to gather his *tallis* and *tefillin.* His *tallis* was in its place, but his *tefillin* had been taken and replaced with someone else's. Reb Beinush turned white at the realization that his *tefillin* were missing.

We combed the *Kosel* for half an hour, but with no luck. The next morning, on the way to the *Kosel,* the Rosh Yeshiva did not say a word about his missing *tefillin,* and none of us dared mention the subject either. As we went inside to *daven,* a *bachur* approached the Rosh Yeshiva and showed him a pair of *tefillin* and asked whether they were his. It is impossible to describe the joy radiating from the Rosh Yeshiva's face as he recognized Reb Nesanel's *tefillin.*

The delighted Rosh Yeshiva handed the *bachur* the pair that had been left in place of his, and said, "These are probably yours." The young man explained that he had left in a hurry the previous morning, without paying attention to the *tefillin* he was taking. Later he realized his mistake, but had no way of identifying whose *tefillin* he had accidentally picked up. He showed the *tefillin* to someone who knew enough about the subject to recognize that they were a very special pair. The man asked which *minyan* the *bachur* had *davened* in. When he replied that he had been at the Ashkenazi *vasikin minyan,* the man figured out that the *tefillin* probably belonged to the Mirrer Rosh Yeshiva, who always *davened* in that *minyan.*

The car ride home was *leibedig,* with everyone talking and telling stories of similar occurrences. It was clear that the Rosh Yeshiva would have given anything for those *tefillin,* which were an inheritance from his father.

MY FONDEST MEMORY OF THE ROSH YESHIVA DOES not directly involve the *Kosel*. Every year I would walk to the

A Special Kiddush *Kosel* with the Rosh Yeshiva on Shavuos morning. On the way back from *davening vasikin*, he always invited me for *Kiddush* and to partake of the Rebbetzin's delicious cheesecakes. In the last year and a half of his life, the disease that was eating away at him made it impossible for the Rosh Yeshiva to walk to the *Kosel*. The first Shavuos I went without him I was walking back to Mattersdorf with a group of young girls whose parents had asked me to keep an eye on them. As we turned into Meah Shearim, who should I see standing there but the Rosh Yeshiva. He was apparently talking in learning to a *bachur*. Excusing himself from the *bachur,* he asked me if I had made *Kiddush* and I replied that I would make it at home. Needless to say that did not go over too well with him: "*Nein, nein, kum mit mir* — No, no, come with me. *Du darfst machen Kiddush bei mir* — You must make *Kiddush* at my house.*"

The next Shavuos I found Reb Beinush standing in exactly the same place as the year before. Once again he was talking to a *bachur*. "*Noch a mahl treftmen sich, Rosh Yeshiva* — Once more we meet again, Rosh Yeshiva," I called out happily, and once again he invited me up for *Kiddush*.

Later that week, I was in the Mirrer Yeshiva and I happened to see the *bachur* to whom Reb Beinush had been speaking when I passed by. I apologized for having interrupted their conversation. The *bachur* told me that no apology was necessary. He had already been standing on the street corner with the Rosh Yeshiva for more that a half an hour when I happened to come along.

"Actually, I was wondering how long I could keep the conversation going," the *bachur* told me. "After *davening vasikin* in the Yeshiva, we walked and walked until the spot where you saw us, and only when he saw you, did the Rosh Yeshiva begin moving again."

I just stood there dumbfounded by the realization that those two meetings with the Rosh Yeshiva were not a coincidence, that he had been waiting to invite me to share his Shavuos *Kiddush* as I had done for so many years.

A few months ago, my daughter Leah called from Lakewood where she and her husband now live. They had made a *bris* that day, and she wanted to tell us the baby's name.

"Abba, what name would you have chosen?" Leah asked.

"Leah, it makes no difference. It's for you and Yoni to choose your son's name," I answered.

"Abba, I'm asking a question. What name would you have wanted. Please answer."

"You've already named the baby, and I don't want you to feel bad if you picked a different name. So I'm not answering."

"Would you approve if we named him Binyomin Beinush?"

I swallowed hard before responding: "Hashem should bless you, Leah, for thinking so much of us even though you are six thousand miles away. Yes, that is definitely the name I would have chosen — Binyomin Beinush."

CHAPTER EIGHTEEN
Epilogue

I T'S LATE IN THE MORNING AS I SIT LOOKING out from my Mattersdorf balcony. The valley below was once no-man's land separating Israel and Jordan, but today it gives way on the other side to the bustling suburb of Ramot. The book is finally done, and I feel exhausted, despite having just awakened from a nap. I wonder if I would ever have undertaken this project if I had realized how draining it would be to remember events so many decades past. There have been moments of searing pain in the process, though thankfully those have been far outweighed by memories that bring only joy.

Perhaps the greatest happiness has been in realizing how that which I once viewed as my greatest failure has given way to my greatest source of satisfaction — having been able to raise a second family of nine children, together with the most wonderful woman in the world. Surely this is a taste of "then our mouths will be filled with laughter" that we will all experience with the coming of *Mashiach,* when all our questions about the Divine plan will vanish like smoke.

My wife and children haven't allowed me the luxury of growing old. Every Shabbos the house is still packed with children, grandchildren, and boys and girls studying in the nearby yeshivos and seminaries.

Looking back on it all, I am struck by how much my life seems to be an ongoing circle. Most of my closest friendships go back over fifty years, and many of them over sixty-five years. The friends of my youth and I have watched each other's children and grandchildren grow up and form one large extended family.

Not a week goes by where some part of the past doesn't become present. Last week, I was driving a young man to the *Kosel*, and he was pressing me for details of the DP camps. He seemed particularly interested in my memories of Rabbi Yechiel Roth, the Sulka Rav. When I was done, he told me he was the Sulka Rav's grandson, and I recalled being at his parents' wedding. A few days earlier, a burly middle-aged man greeted me warmly on the street and asked me whether I remembered him. He had been one of the group of Mirrer *bachurim* with whom I spent a week digging graves during the 1966 New York gravedigger's strike.

Despite being far from a *talmid chacham*, I was privileged to be close to some great men: Rabbi Cheshin, Rabbi Beinush Finkel, Rabbi Hutner, the Klausenberger *Rebbe*, Rabbi Leib Mallin, Mike Tress, and Rabbi Samson Raphael Weiss. They too remain ever present. To this list, I would add one great woman: my mother.

As I continue drifting in my reverie, I hear a key turning in the door. I look up, and standing there with her usual bright smile on her face is my eleven-year-old daughter Bat-Zion.

So much for dreams of the past. Time to get on with the future. There is a lot left to do.

*The following persons and organizations
provided photographs and illustrative materials:*

Agudath Israel Archives pp. 39, 76, 177
Rabbi Amos Bunim p. 183
Dos Yiddish Vort pp. 45, 152, 154, 166
Kaplinsky Family p. 198
U.S. Holocaust Memorial Museum pp. 121, 129,
    131, 139, 153